D1707363

# The Reading
of Proust

# The Reading
# of Proust

DAVID R. ELLISON

Johns Hopkins University Press
Baltimore, Maryland

The Johns Hopkins University Press, Baltimore, Maryland 21218
The Johns Hopkins Press Ltd., London


Library of Congress Cataloging in Publication Data

Ellison, David R.
    The reading of Proust.

    Includes index.
    1. Proust, Marcel, 1871-1922—Criticism and interpretation. 2. Books and reading
in literature. 3. Ruskin, John, 1819-1900—Influence—Proust. I. Title.
PQ2631.R63Z579  1983        843′.912        83-48057
ISBN 0-8018-3048-6

For my parents
and in memory of D.R.B.

# Contents

# Preface

The purpose of the following pages is to elucidate the question of reading in the literary works of Marcel Proust. By literary works I mean essentially the seven volumes of *A la recherche du temps perdu*, but also the writings leading up to the novel, notably *Jean Santeuil, Contre Sainte-Beuve*, and the critical essays contained in *Pastiches et mélanges*. I have avoided any inclusion of the correspondence in my analysis, not because I consider Proust's letters without intrinsic value, but because their relationship to the fictional writings is oblique and difficult to define or categorize. What Proust wrote to others about himself and his artistic striving is of more than anecdotal interest, but the pronouncements on esthetic problems to be found in his correspondence need to be interpreted in the light of the audience for which they were intended and do not compare, in depth or in complexity, to the prolonged meditations on the arts contained in his novel.

When I say I wish to elucidate the question of reading, I imply that the act of reading was both central and problematical for Proust, that the investigation of its significance involves difficulty, and that no easy answer is presupposed. I say this even though Proust theorizes about reading—both in his critical essays and in the *Recherche*—and even though one might be tempted to take his theoretical statements, which are often explicit and unambiguous, as being transparent declarations of truth. Most critics writing primarily or exclusively on reading in Proust have devised admirably coherent and systematic expositions of the various occurrences of the theme, but the apodictic quality of their conclusions rests on two logically fragile assumptions: that one need not doubt the truth value of the narrator's theoretical statements, and that what Marcel says about reading in expository passages expresses the total essence of the act of reading as such. It is my contention that the "truth" of the question of reading is hidden and enclosed within the labyrinthine folds of the Proustian text considered as a rhetorical fabric of truth interwoven with falsehood, and that one cannot get at what Proust means when he writes of reading unless one is attuned to microtextual subtleties. Hence the method I have adopted—of confronting and juxtaposing limited key passages from Proust's writings that mutually illuminate one another. I have avoided thematic generalization in favor of careful reading, and have tried to show, throughout the book, the extent to which shifts of tone and ironic detail undermine the grand claims of the narrator's voice of certainty.

I begin my interpretation with the close analysis of a contextually well-defined episode, "La Soirée chez la marquise de Saint-Euverte," in which the act of reading emerges, not as a process of illumination of understanding, but as the "blind" confrontation of an interpreting consciousness with the irresponsible free play of metaphoricity. Inscribed or embedded within the text, the act of reading in its fictional-poetic disguise in no way resembles what Proust says *about* reading declaratively and theoretically in *Le Temps retrouvé*. It would appear that the principal effect of the "Soirée" is to undo or deconstruct the very notion of clarity on which theoretical insight is predicated. Read as a fiction about reading, the "Soirée" yields a curious and apparently negative message: that it is impossible to penetrate the ultimate meanings of the text, that the text is in an active dialectical relationship with the reader, whom it causes to suffer in an anxious search for final, "invisible" truths. This message lies in the subtext of the episode and is not immediately evident at a first, cursory examination. Proust seems to delight in hiding serious arguments on the nature of literary language underneath a veneer of comic social description, and it is the complexity of the intermingling of surface and depth, mimetic representation and fictional self-representation, that will concern me throughout the forthcoming pages.

My analysis of the "Soirée" has as its principal goal to establish a set of problems and questions on the nature of reading that I then develop in the next four chapters. The first issue needing clarification is the *origin* of Proust's interest in the process of reading. How did Proust arrive at the refined ironies of the "Soirée"? Is it possible to trace the path of his progressive interest in textual interpretation? What we know of Proust's intellectual biography points to the central influence of John Ruskin, and it is my belief that Proust's theory and practice of reading are understandable only in opposition to the ideas of Ruskin on the same subject. However, unlike those *proustiens* who have done traditional "source studies" on the Ruskin-Proust connection, I am less concerned with general thematic parallels than I am with certain not so immediately visible, often involuted textual manipulations. The major thrust of Chapters Two and Three is to demonstrate the way in which Proust *inverted* and strategically transformed Ruskinian critical concepts into novelistic forms. At the heart of my argument is the same essential problem that subtends the "Soirée"— the mutual interdependence of textual theory and *praxis*. I find that many of the most justly celebrated episodes in the *Recherche*—even those as long and "self-contained" as "Un Amour de Swann"—derive from critical/ theoretical arguments in Ruskin.

It is with some trepidation that I write of "Un Amour de Swann" as the fictional inversion of the Ruskinian concept of "idolatry," and that I imply the Swann-Odette and Marcel-Albertine relationships are transpositions of the reader-text paradigm. This trepidation is based upon an obvious fact: that readers of Proust *enjoy* thinking of Swann, Odette, Marcel, and Albertine as "characters" with whom one can identify and empathize through the convention of an accepted fictional *cadre*. It is somehow less enjoyable to recognize that the *Recherche* is also a machine that disguises, in fictional clothing, functions and structures of a conceptual or rhetorical origin. I do not wish to deny any reader pleasure; and I will be the first to confess, without shame or feigned timidity, that my interest in Proust is first and most deeply an enjoyment of Proust. However, since the proximity of enjoyment to self-delusion is nowhere more eloquently analyzed than in Proust's reading of Ruskin, my emphasis here on linguistic and rhetorical models should be taken not as a sign of intellectual antisocial behavior, but as a mere indication of prudence and, I hope, nonidolatrous respect.

The title of my book—*The Reading of Proust*—is consciously ambiguous: it is based upon a confusion of subjective and objective genitives, and can mean both the way in which Proust read other authors (here, Ruskin) and the way in which we as readers might interpret Proust. My principal purpose is to show that Proust's reading of Ruskin in fact contains an implicit theory of reading, and that this theory can be applied to the *Recherche* with positive elucidative results. In the first three chapters, an attempt is made to delineate the diverse ramifications of the problem of reading and to suggest that, in sum, Proust's conception of reading is expressed most powerfully and most consistently as a deconstruction of what Ruskin called "possession-taking." In Chapters Four and Five I apply this conception to two fundamental issues in Proust interpretation: narration (how it is generated and sustained) and autobiography (the modal identity of the *Recherche*). By relating Chapters Four and Five to what precedes I hope to demonstrate convincingly that the question of reading in Proust subtends the issues of narration and autobiography, that only by keeping the semantic core of Proust's theory of reading as a point of reference can we make some progress in our understanding of the literary/theoretical concerns embodied in the *Recherche*.

Just as the *Recherche* would have been a lesser book without the *innu-trition* of the great literary works that preceded it and that make of Proust's novel a vast encyclopedia of literary allusions, in the same way but on a far more modest plane my own work here would be inconceivable without the solid contributions of the teachers and Proust scholars to whom I am indebted. To interpret Proust today is not to face him on the same level of absolute novelty and difficulty as did Albert Feuillerat, Ernst Robert Curtius, and Samuel Beckett. The *Recherche* is by now so satu-rated with critical commentary as to rival, in contemporary literature, the great monumental works of the past by Dante, Shakespeare, Cervantes, and Goethe. For this reason I have attempted to make my intellectual debts as visible as possible and to analyze the *Recherche* not as if I were reading it for the first time, but, more honestly, as I do read it—as a pri-mary text surrounded by a formidably deep sea of secondary material. What I write about Proust is, textually speaking, *en situation:* I recognize the existence of important critical positions taken before my own and develop my ideas often in confrontation with those of other readers. It is my hope that this book will contribute to the critical debate surround-ing the *Recherche* insofar as this debate leads to a further understanding of a novel whose monumentalizing *and* seminal qualities seem equally profound.

My interest in Proust began when I was a graduate student at Yale University. My thanks go first to Paul de Man, who advised me in my dis-sertation, "Proust's Theory of the Novel," and who has been an intel-lectual guide ever since. I also wish to express my appreciation to Georges May, Charles Porter, and Peter Brooks, all of Yale, who have given me en-couragement in recent years as I pursued this and other projects of literary criticism.

As my research on Proust developed, I was fortunate to participate in symposia on modern literature and was able to profit from the vigorous exchange of ideas. I have especially good memories of the MLA in 1978 (New York) and 1980 (Houston), and wish to thank Françoise Dorenlot, who chaired a double section on autobiography (Division on Twentieth-Century French Literature), and Ian Watt, who presided over a discussion on comedy in the modern European novel (Prose Fiction Division), for including me in their respective groups. The paper I delivered in New York in 1978 was later expanded and appeared as "Who is 'Marcel'? Proust and the Question of Autobiographical Identity" in *L'Esprit Créateur,* 20, No. 3 (Fall 1980), 78-86. Permission to reprint this article in the fifth chapter of the present study is gratefully acknowledged.

While in Paris during the winter and spring of 1980 I was privileged to meet and consult with M. Bernard Brun, who directs the Equipe Proust of the Centre National de Recherches Scientifiques, now housed at the

Ecole Normale Supérieure in the rue d'Ulm. M. Brun's polite and gracious help on recent bibliographical material and on the *état présent* of Proustian textual studies in general, is much appreciated.

My research was substantially aided by grants from the National Endowment for the Humanities (summer 1977), the American Council of Learned Societies (summer 1978), and Mount Holyoke College (summer 1978 and academic year 1979-80). The work that appears on the following pages could not have been accomplished as well or as rapidly without this help, for which I am most grateful.

Finally, I wish to thank Mount Holyoke College for its assistance in granting me a sabbatical and leave of absence in 1979-80 and for showing its institutional encouragement of my research in a warm, noninstitutional way. To the Department of French at Mount Holyoke, my thanks for both encouragement and forbearance, and an especial word of appreciation to Professor Margaret Switten, whose genuine interest in my work has been constant.

# The Reading
# of Proust

# 1
# Proustian Metaphor and the Question of Readability

Or, quelles sont les conditions nécessaires de la métaphore? Il faut qu'elle soit vraie et juste, lumineuse, noble, naturelle, et enfin cohérente. . . . Elle sera lumineuse si, tirée d'objets connus et aisés à saisir, elle frappe à l'instant l'esprit par la justesse et la vérité des rapports.
—Pierre Fontanier, *Les Figures du discours*

S'agissant de la métaphore, admettons donc, mais si possible sans sitôt y perdre la vue, une clarté aveuglante: le méthodique recours à cette figure, dans la *Recherche,* selon une perspective stylistique.
—Jean Ricardou, *Nouveaux problèmes du roman*

"Placer sous les yeux" n'est pas alors une fonction accessoire de la métaphore, mais bien le propre de la figure.
—Paul Ricoeur, *La Métaphore vive*

Il est impossible de dominer la métaphorique philosophique, comme telle, *de l'extérieur,* en se servant d'un concept de métaphore qui reste un produit philosophique. Seule la philosophie semblerait détenir quelque autorité sur ses productions métaphoriques. Mais, d'autre part, pour la même raison, la philosophie se prive de ce qu'elle se donne. Ses instruments appartiennent à son champ, elle est impuissante à dominer sa tropologie et sa métaphorique générales. Elle ne la percevrait qu'autour d'une tache aveugle ou d'un foyer de surdité.
—Jacques Derrida, "La Mythologie blanche"

When, in the final pages of *Le Temps retrouvé*, Proust elaborates the retrospective theoretical justification of his novel, he includes an important development on *métaphore*[1] in which he ascribes to the figure the status of cornerstone in the structural totality of his fictional edifice:

> Une heure n'est pas qu'une heure, c'est un vase rempli de parfums, de sons, de projets et de climats. Ce que nous appelons la réalité est un certain rapport entre ces sensations et ces souvenirs qui nous entourent simultanément . . . rapport unique que l'écrivain doit retrouver pour en enchaîner à jamais dans sa phrase les deux termes différents. On peut faire se succéder indéfiniment dans une description les objets qui figuraient dans le lieu décrit, la vérité ne commencera qu'au moment où l'écrivain prendra deux objets différents, posera leur rapport, analogue dans le monde de l'art à celui qu'est le rapport unique de la loi causale dans le monde de la science, et les enfermera dans les anneaux nécessaires d'un beau style; même, ainsi que la vie, quand, en rapprochant une qualité commune à deux sensations, il dégagera leur essence commune en les réunissant l'une et l'autre pour les soustraire aux contingences du temps, dans une métaphore.[2]

For many years this justly celebrated passage was interpreted as the unquestionable proof of Proust's self-consciousness as a writer. Not only did the author of *A la recherche du temps perdu* use metaphor in original and complex ways, but he knew how and why he wrote as he did: Proust had a theory of metaphor that could be said to account for the metaphorical effects of the *Recherche*. More recently, however, a major shift in critical perspective toward the use of linguistic and rhetorical models for literary interpretation has caused readers of Proust to question the value and significance of Proust's theory. Gérard Genette, in his essay "Proust palimpseste" (*Figures* [Paris: Seuil, 1966]), opened the way for a reevaluation of the novel's metaphorical praxis or productivity. Through a detailed interpretation of the *mirages* and *vertiges* of Proustian textuality, Genette observed that the author's vision is "more modern than his theory" (52) and that the *Recherche*, in its structural complexity, is not merely the illustration of the narrator's ideas on esthetics. Thus, although the novel can be read as a retrospective illumination or revelation, a close reading of the text cannot fail to expose what Genette calls "l'expérience négative qui ne devait être qu'un moment du progrès d'ensemble [et qui] . . . entraîne [l'oeuvre] tout entière dans un mouvement inverse de celui qu'elle s'était proposé . . . puisque son point d'arrivée la trouve emportée vers un nouveau parcours, sur lequel il n'est plus en son pouvoir de se fixer un terme" (66). The narrator's explicit declarations on metaphor and the actual metaphorical mobility of the *Recherche* often contradict each other and cannot be reduced to any preconceived theoretical rationale. Such is the conclusion of Genette in this early article that contains, in small, what will be refined and developed later in the essay "Métonymie chez Proust"; such is also the point of departure for many contemporary studies of Proust, which, despite their considerable methodological diversity, all presuppose a fundamental contradiction between a restrictive theory and a liberated metaphorical practice.

When Serge Doubrovsky unravels the skein of metaphorical and metonymical relationships that constitute the totality of the orchid ("catleya") image in "Un Amour de Swann," he admires the "connotative richness" of the narrative fabric "à l'opposé de la mythologie proustienne du 'rapport unique que l'écrivain doit retrouver pour en enchaîner à jamais dans sa phrase les deux termes différents' (III, 889). Bref, ce dont il est question ici, par contraste avec la vétusté et le vague de l'appareil théorique, chez Proust, c'est de l'étonnante modernité de l'écriture."[3] In a similar fashion, in his structural study of autobiography, Jeffrey Mehlman sets out to read Proust against the grain of the declared esthetics of *Le Temps retrouvé* and quotes, to substantiate his own critical method, the assertion of Philippe Sollers: "Lire Proust? Ce serait pratiquer désormais dans la *Recherche* des coupes, des tassements, des blancs, des chocs, des incompatibilités: casser le projet d'ensemble, souligner les points d'aberration mal contrôlés, dégager une logique sous-jacente recouverte par un vernissage de continuité."[4]

If, according to these recent critical assessments, the *Recherche* is a work whose antiquated idealist conception does not do justice to its far more "modern" praxis, the curious reader might well wish to know, Is there a modern theory more adequate than Proust's own, more compatible with the intricacies of the novel's rhetorical displacements? Although no global theory has been proposed that might entirely replace or negate the metaphysical esthetics of *Le Temps retrouvé*, Jean Ricardou's suggestion—that the entire question of metaphoricity in Proust be studied as a problem of representational mode—may be helpful in reformulating the analytic presuppositions underlying the theory of metaphor. According to Ricardou's analyses, there are really two kinds of metaphor in Proust: the first ("ornamental" or "expressive") is metaphor used traditionally, as poetic illustration, where the narrator is constantly in control of the figure he manipulates; the second ("ordinal") is used to "dissoudre, conjointement ou séparément, les catégories du temps ou de l'espace" and is, in fact, "une parfaite machine à subvertir la représentation."[5] Ricardou implies that Proust's novel is the locus of a fundamental figural disjunction and that the *Recherche* occupies a transitional area between representational literature and the more modern novel that thrives on the ironic destruction of its own pretention to mime what is commonly called "reality." Ordinal metaphor dissolves mimesis and functions as self-representation ("auto-représentation" [97]): it points, not to some verifiable "outside," but to itself.

What remains to be discovered by interpreters of Proust is the specific manner in which the *Recherche* enacts the reading of its own textual existence. The analytical method adopted by contemporary critics often consists of the elaboration of a *sous-texte* borrowed freely from the work as a totality. The resulting juxtaposition of passages generally reveals the presence of an "unconscious" thought pattern that contradicts the narrator's commentary and rhetorical intrusions. This method, which Ricardou calls *trans-littérale* (127), involves the classification of those elements that might seem fragmented, heterogeneous, and invisible without the intervention of the perceptive reader. The text is reorganized according to criteria originating outside its defined boundaries, in the consciousness of the interpreter. Inevitably, the context from which each passage is lifted for service in the critic's transliteral commentary is neglected: only a *literal* reading that respects the syntagmatic order of narrated events can "contextualize"—that is, adhere to the complex play of ironies, structural echoes, repeated and modified scenes that make up the visible appearance of the novel's form. For various reasons, both practical and theoretical, the tendency of much recent Proust criticism has been to adopt the transliteral point of view so as to effect, in all freedom, the *coupes, tassements,* and *chocs* suggested by Sollers. One can imagine that the literal reading is no longer fashionable because it is assumed that the context, in its role as controlling mechanism, can be made to serve the questionable ideological interests of the narrator-master. Thus the context would be, on the level of expanded discourse, what the ornamental/expressive metaphor is on the level of the sentence—a method of enclosing or imprisoning meaning. But in this case, is the encounter between the subversion of ordinal metaphor and the limiting effects of context possible, or even imaginable? Or must one conclude a priori that the considerable disruptive potential of the former shields it from all constraint and thus protects it from all contact with the latter? These questions will be at the center of the analysis to follow. I propose to study a passage that is defined by a highly visible contextual frontier but in which metaphorical self-representation is at work. The episode as a unit is called, by the Pléiade editors, "La Soirée chez la marquise de Saint-Euverte" (I, 322–53).

But before interpreting the scene as such, I would like to establish a theoretical frame that will allow us precise access to the complex problems raised by the disconcerting rhetorical movement of the "Soirée." Later we shall see that words such as "frame," "theoretical," and "precision" are problematical in themselves, that our analytical work cannot proceed without an understanding of their conceptual basis; but for the moment it is necessary, for the sake of clarity, to remain within the realm of theoretical distinctions. The two texts that will serve as points of reference for discussion are *La Métaphore vive* of Paul Ricoeur and "La Mythologie blanche" of Jacques Derrida.[6] The intellectual depth of these two studies defies any peremptory résumé of their contents. I will limit myself to an examination of their major themes, and I will use the methodological presuppositions of both Ricoeur and Derrida to elaborate an analysis of Proust's metaphorical strategies.

### HEURISTIC AND DECONSTRUCTION

According to Ricoeur, metaphor is the poet's method of discovery. Thus, the true science of metaphor can be called an *heuristic* ("heuristique"). In the first part of his book, Ricoeur attempts to show that rhetorical classification, whether classical or structuralist in bias, by limiting the definition of metaphor to a distortion of meaning on the level of individual words, does not adequately address the possibility of the figure's predicative use. A rhetoric based on a semiotics of single words tends toward taxonomy and significant stasis, whereas semantics (whose unit is no longer the word, but the sentence) treats metaphor in its movement and its productive force. In Ricoeur's view, semiotics risks reducing the figure to a mere ornament that adds nothing to our knowledge. Indeed, if metaphor is, by virtue of its rhetorical definition, eminently translatable, it is no more than a replaceable element in a substitution chain of which each term is, strictly speaking, indifferent.[7] But if one takes as frame the sentence rather than the word, one can compare metaphor to what Gilbert Ryle calls a "category mistake"—a movement of inventive thought that builds new relationships after destroying the logical basis of the old.

> Ne peut-on pas dire que la stratégie du langage à l'oeuvre dans la métaphore consiste à oblitérer les frontières logiques et établies, en vue de faire apparaître de nouvelles ressemblances que la classification antérieure empêchait d'apercevoir? Autrement dit, le pouvoir de la métaphore serait de briser une catégorisation antérieure, afin d'établir de nouvelles frontières logiques sur les ruines des précédentes. (*La Métaphore vive*, 251)

Thus, metaphor would seem to occupy an important position in the domain of epistemology. Its poetic function does not exclude it from the dialectics of knowledge. In the first chapter of his study, Ricoeur compares a statement from Aristotle's *Rhetoric*—that the metaphor of the poet "instructs us and gives us knowledge through generic classification" (III, 10, 1410*b*13)—to the theory of Max Black according to which metaphor acts as a scientific model (32). The ultimate goal of metaphoric transfer is nothing less than the reordering of reality. After literal relationships have been abolished and revealed as erroneous, metaphorical free play creates another world for the reader to perceive. Hence Ricoeur's assertion that metaphor as movement is an "intermède de déconstruction entre description et redescription" (ibid.).

Viewed as a totality, Ricoeur's project has a double thrust. In a first stage, it is necessary to disengage metaphor from all classification and grant it the subversive potential it might have lost within the confines of rhetorical definitions. But in a second stage, one must see that metaphorical "redescription" is part of semantic innovation, and thus constitutes an initial step toward philosophical knowledge. The negative capacity of metaphor—its tendency to reverse categories or, in Genette's terms, to conjure up *mirages* and *vertiges*—cannot be studied independently of its insertion into the positive elaboration of theoretical understanding. Inevitably, Ricoeur is led to discuss the nature of the logical relationships that link metaphoricity to conceptualization. In the eighth and last chapter of *La Métaphore vive,* the author tries to establish with philosophical rigor the speculative discourse that alone is capable of justifying and explicating metaphor without damaging the very essence of the figure. The stakes are high: one must prove convincingly that an independent language called "philosophy" can describe and master another language (metaphor) that functions as a transgression. This is the nodal point of Ricoeur's argument—the point at which speculation interiorizes and surpasses metaphoricity as such—and it is here that we find a polemical section directed against Jacques Derrida and "La Mythologie blanche" (see *La Métaphore vive,* 362-74).

Ricoeur reminds us that Derrida's reasoning is nearly the opposite of his own, both in its order of presentation and in its conclusions. Indeed, whereas Ricoeur's goal is to give new life to a figure threatened with death by the sterility of rhetorical classification, Derrida sets out to demonstrate that philosophical discourse as such (the very discourse that presumes to justify and delimit metaphor in the sphere of knowledge) articulates itself through loss and forgetfulness on the level of metaphor: each concept is in fact the mask of a poetic figure more or less well disguised by the artifices of speculative thought. According to Derrida, metaphor is pure transgression, irrecuperable, noncontrollable, absolutely indescribable by any so-called *non*metaphorical language. No "métalangage" can master the metaphorical without neutralizing it and reducing it to that which it is not, especially not the language we call "philosophical," which grants itself the right to enclose and com-prehend that which designates the radical impossibility of philosophy *as* theoretical understanding. Philosophy constructs itself and becomes a system by refusing to read its foundation in metaphor: philosophy exists through a forgetfulness of its origins.[8]

The deconstructive enterprise as practiced by Derrida in "La Mythologie blanche" and elsewhere involves an inexorable and repetitious logic: the deconstructor must move against the flow of the current by which each individual metaphor has become so fluidly and "naturally" a concept so that he may arrive at the "veille de la philosophie" ("La Mythologie blanche," 273) where the figure has not yet lost its colors. The difficulty of deconstructive reading results from the recognition that any search for origins contains idealizing temptations, yet this kind of search is the only *necessary* form of reading if we wish to penetrate or illuminate the (metaphorical) presuppositions that subtend all discourse on metaphor. But is it possible to use the expression "illuminate" if metaphorical practice, in its infinite regression, does not allow us to locate the source of all light in a fixed, clearly determined center? Flowers turn toward the sun (and Derrida suggests that this tropism is the paradigm of linguistic tropes), but we must not forget that the sun itself moves and eventually sets in an invisible place: the sun is caught up in its own troping (299). Hence the conclusion of Derrida: it is impossible to make of metaphor a positive instrument of discovery. Heuristic science is thinkable only in a system with an immobile center; and, linguistically, centering is the capacity of discourse to double in on itself and master its transgressions. But if this kind of *dé-doublement* is erroneous in principle, metaphor can only be negative, absolutely, and can only be "thought" or "understood" in its shadowy absence behind the uniform disguise of metaphysical idealization.[9]

The profound difference of opinion between Ricoeur and Derrida on the function of metaphor in philosophical discourse emerges most obviously in the authors' own use of the contrary metaphors of "life" and "death" to express their respective arguments. But these metaphors are also images, not just according to a modern, somewhat vague terminology that designates as "image" all poetic figuration, but also according to an older Western tradition—that of Aristotelian rhetoric. It is by no means surprising to note that Ricoeur follows Aristotle in making an equivalence between metaphor and vision: to see things well is a sign of intellectual distinction and a step in the path of discovery or understanding.[10] In *La Métaphore vive* there is a substantial development, based on the third book of the *Rhetoric* and the discussion therein of the "virtues of *lexis*," which involves an analysis of the most advanced English and American linguistic theories. Whether it be in I. A. Richards (*The Philosophy of Rhetoric*) or Max Black (*Models and Metaphors*), the criterion of clarity is used consistently to judge the poetic effectiveness of metaphor. This clarity is not immediately perceived (since metaphor is first of all transgression, or, to use Richards' term, a *shift*), but it becomes operative later, when scientific rhetoric has dominated the transgression and "commanded the shifts" by contextual insertion (*La Métaphore vive*, 104). Hence the importance of a second major development in Ricoeur's essay, which deals with the contextual value of the sentence in the realm of metaphorical predication. Ricoeur's remarks concerning the book of Stephen Ullmann, *Semantics: An Introduction to the Science of Meaning* (Oxford: Blackwell, 1962), are particularly significant because there is complete agreement between the two authors on the active function of context, which consists of reducing the polysemic meaning produced by metaphorical movement (*La Métaphore vive*, 161–68).

The twin notions of clarity and context do not appear only on the semantic level of the sentence, but also on the "hermeneutic" level of extensive discourse (essay, poem, novel, etc.). Indeed, when Ricoeur speaks of textual interpretation in general, he alludes to Husserlian *elucidation* (*Aufklärung*) on the one hand, and to contextual/conceptual mastery on the other hand (380–83). According to Ricoeur, the natural tendency of the reader is to wish *com-prehension* in the etymological sense: one desires to possess, assimilate, even eliminate what one reads. This is why a rigorous study of the mechanics of metaphor will help balance the act of interpretation, by imposing on the decipherer of signs the necessity of respecting the dynamics of the figure. Interpretation as such becomes the "intersection" of two contrary forces:

> On peut concevoir un style herméneutique dans lequel l'interprétation répond à la fois à la notion du concept et à celle de l'intention constituante de l'expérience qui cherche à se dire sur le mode métaphorique. L'interprétation est alors une modalité de discours qui opère à l'intersection de deux mouvances, celle du métaphorique et celle du spéculatif. C'est donc un discours mixte qui, comme tel, ne peut pas ne pas subir l'attraction de deux exigences rivales. D'un côté elle veut la clarté du concept—de l'autre, elle cherche à préserver le dynamisme de la signification que le concept arrête et fixe. (383)

The metaphorical and the speculative join in the production of what Ricoeur calls an "hermeneutical style," but one should not assume that the two heterogeneous forms of discourse can exchange properties and thereby lose their respective identities. Ricoeur insists on the independent status of the speculative vis-à-vis the metaphorical and grants the former a higher position in the hierarchy of knowledge: the speculative "commence de soi et trouve en lui-même le principe de son articulation. . . . il met en place les notions premières, les principes" (380).

This capacity to found oneself and constitute one's own intellectual space is precisely what Derrida views as the traditional role of philosophy. But unlike Ricoeur, whose interpretive language circulates easily within visible and distinct boundaries, Derrida doubts the validity of *foundations* as such, and thus puts into question the limits that philosophy has established for itself. "La Mythologie blanche" is part of a vast project that exceeds the single volume of *Marges:* here and elsewhere in the philosopher's writings, speculative/conceptual control is demonstrated to be the badly disguised mask of a strictly uncontrollable metaphorical playfulness. In demonstrating his thesis, Derrida inverts all the themes, all the images, all the organizational schemes that underlie and justify Ricoeur's thoughts. We have already seen that Derrida derives much of his argument from a meditation on the decentralized tropic manifestations of the sun, whereas for Ricoeur solar clarity is emblematic of the transparent ease with which metaphoricity can be integrated into a general heuristic. Similarly, when Derrida writes the essay "Signature–Événement–Contexte" (*Marges*, 367-93), he contradicts Ricoeur's postulates by destroying the solidity of contextual domination and by further developing the theme of the *uncontrollable* (*le non-maîtrisable*) that runs throughout "La Mythologie blanche."[11] Finally, it is evident that for Derrida all critical/theoretical discourse is incapable of justifying itself from the outside, and thus cannot be confused with or linked to the speculative mode. The act of interpretation thrusts the reader into the text, dispossesses him of intellectual mastery, and abolishes the neat separation between subject and object of esthetic activity. In the end, only the poem exists—the made object which exists insofar as it is read.

## METAPHOR IN THE TEXT

If one were to examine the theory of Proustian metaphor in abstract isolation, it would be apparent that it resembles an heuristic rather than a deconstruction. Indeed, the essential elements associated with the idea of discovery—clarity, context, reflexive distance, conceptual mastery—can be found in *Le Temps retrouvé* and in the pages of *A l'Ombre des jeunes filles en fleurs* dealing with the esthetics of Elstir. Readers of Proust will remember that style is "une question non de technique mais de vision" (III, 895), and we have seen that metaphor is described as the act of enclosing reality in "anneaux nécessaires" (III, 889). The choice of words here is not a matter of indifference, and Doubrovsky does not exaggerate when he shows the "unconscious" links between the theory of style and the general theme of imprisonment which is, fundamentally, a variation on the sadomasochistic motif.[12] The control exercised by the rigorous logic of metaphor resists even the most radical subversions of Elstir's painted "metamorphoses": the mirages that are so disconcerting on the level of the presentation of phenomenal reality are nevertheless subject to the comprehension and interiorization of the observing consciousness. It is true that Elstir's works produce first a sense of surprise that results from the confusion of natural categories (here, the erasing of those marks that serve to delimit the ocean, the earth, and the sky). But with the intervention of rational intelligence, clarity is restored. In the famous description of imaginary paintings that remind the reader of Turner or of the French Impressionists, Proust plays with the limits of mimesis, but he seems willing to neutralize the *vertiges* he creates by elucidating commentary of the narrator. It may be pleasurable to "regarder une zone bleue et fluide sans savoir si elle appartient à la mer ou au ciel" (I, 835), but this happiness is inseparable from the subsequent reestablishing of distinctions. We are very close to the "category mistake" of Gilbert Ryle that builds new logical frontiers on the ruins of the old: metaphor, through the initial negations of *mirages* and *vertiges,* eventually builds the foundation of a science of perception by teaching us to see beyond deceiving appearances. Metaphorical indirection causes our commonplace vision of the world to vacillate but also sends us back to nature and her laws. Elstir creates according to Turner's formula: "My business is to paint what I see, not what I know."[13] But the talented painter sees reality in its pure visibility, unencumbered by the intellectual abstractions with which we have surrounded it; and this seeing is equivalent to new knowledge. We remain comfortably imprisoned within an heuristic logical scheme.

But does this scheme account for Proustian metaphorical praxis? As I indicated before examining the theories of Ricoeur and Derrida, I would like to elaborate a "literal" (Ricardou) interpretation of a passage from the *Recherche.* I will begin by following the evolution of the episode, by respecting its contextual limits before attempting to conclude on the significance of contextuality in Proust. I have chosen to read the "Soirée chez la marquise de Saint-Euverte" in its function as discrete scene and in its relationship to the totality of "Un Amour de Swann."

We all know the story of "Swann," or rather, we think we know it when we say that the protagonist, at first indifferent to the charms of Odette de Crécy, gradually falls in love with her, then gradually falls out of love, returning to the original state of indifference. Usually the novella is read from a psychological perspective: we admire the way in which the author begins to formulate the "laws" of human motivation that characterize the sections of the *Recherche* devoted to an analysis of fin-de-siècle high society. The formal articulations of the narration are so clear, so "classical," the course of imagined events is so admirably fluid—from the initial encounters, through amorous trysts, evening parties, lies and jealousy—that we tend to concentrate almost exclusively on the human drama of the fictional situation, to the detriment of the rhetorical fabric that provides its poetic underpinnings. A detailed study of this rhetoric allows us to see not only the semantic manipulations that are at the origin of each development in the narrative order, but also the less immediately visible manner in which the text reflects upon itself and designates its own productivity. But how can one speak of self-representation in a text that appears uniquely subject to the rule of mimesis? To answer this question, it is necessary to search out the source of the word "love" as used in the novella and to examine the cause of its central thematic importance.

Psychologically, Swann's love for Odette derives from an inner conflict between desire and esthetic disinterest. It is true that Odette is first "d'un genre de beauté qui lui était indifférent, qui ne lui inspirait aucun désir, lui causait même une sorte de répulsion physique" (I, 195); but later, through association of ideas, Swann eventually falls in love with Odette because she resembles Botticelli's Zephora, because she seems to share certain sensually appealing traits of Vinteuil's musical phrase. Art is the mediating force that intervenes to complete and remedy the protagonist's original lack of passion. The rhetorical movement that makes possible Swann's concentration or focalization on Odette as unique object of desire is the passage from metonymy (here, the pure contiguity of the presence of the two lovers in the same social setting) to a synecdochic *absorption:* Odette is henceforward the center, the point of reference for Swann, the place at which all fantasies and dreams converge: she becomes the part that suffices, by abbreviation, to designate the whole of the protagonist's emotions. As in the experience of the madeleine, it is a chance occurrence that upsets habitual activity or is merely juxtaposed to a "latent" state of mind and redistributes the vectors of reflexive consciousness:

> Et sans doute, en se rappelant ainsi leurs entretiens, en pensant ainsi à elle quand il était seul, il faisait seulement jouer son image entre beaucoup d'autres images de femmes dans des rêveries romanesques; mais si, grâce à une circonstance quelconque (ou même peut-être sans que ce fût grâce à elle, la circonstance qui se présente au moment où un état, latent jusque-là, se déclare, pouvant n'avoir influé en rien sur lui) l'image d'Odette de Crécy venait à absorber toutes ces rêveries, si celles-ci n'étaient plus séparables de son souvenir, alors l'imperfection de son corps ne garderait plus aucune importance, ni qu'il eût été, plus ou moins

qu'un autre corps, selon le goût de Swann, puisque, devenu le corps de celle qu'il aimait, il serait désormais le seul qui fût capable de lui causer des joies et des tourments. (I, 199)

In becoming the organizing center of images for Swann, Odette acquires a magnetic power; she is, so to speak, empty in herself, but she can attract to her own void qualities belonging to other realms of reality or the imagination and neutralize them, dispossess them of their vital force. Thus, the *petite phrase* of Vinteuil loses all intrinsic value, exists no longer as music because it functions, in Swann's mind, as a talisman containing the precipitated essence of his beloved's life. Just as Odette, within her associative network, encompasses all the possibilities of love, in the same way the musical phrase stands for the entirety of the sonata, which, in its unity, is no longer the product of an unknown musician called Vinteuil, but the possession of the lovers: "*notre* morceau" (I, 219).

There is a recurrent structure in "Un Amour de Swann" that resembles closely what Derrida called "metaphysical idealization" in his discussion of Hegel's *Esthetics* (*Marges*, 268). According to the metaphorical genetics of Hegel, a word signifies first something completely sensuous ("etwas ganz Sinnliches") before being translated into the domain of the spiritual ("auf Geistiges übertragen"). After this translative process has taken place, the sensuous content is abandoned and replaced by a spiritual meaning. In a second stage, the metaphoricity of a given word becomes erased through usage ("im Gebrauche," "durch die Gewohnheit") and undergoes a transformation that changes it from improper ("uneigentlichen") to proper expression ("eigentlichen Ausdruck"). In Proust, the structure of love is similar. First there is a sensual encounter that causes problems (Swann's feelings of repulsion toward Odette), but through the mediation of Art there is a transformation from the physical to the spiritual (Odette becomes a mere "écheveau de lignes subtiles et belles" [I, 223] that Swann can admire from a distance). Once the woman's sensual qualities have been forgotten or lost in the mechanism of Proustian habit (in Hegelian usage, *die Gewohnheit*), the loved object can become the possession of the lover, just as the *petite phrase,* by losing its musical content, becomes the proper expression (*expression propre, eigentlicher Ausdruck*) of Swann's sentiments. The associative transformation having been accomplished, the new possession enters (quite literally) into the vocabulary of the protagonist and acquires a quasi magical value: what was once the pure movement of a transfer is now a lexical fixation. Thus, in the case of the analogy between Odette and Botticelli's Zephora, the prestige of the painting allows Swann to forget that "Odette n'était pas plus pour cela une femme selon son désir, puisque précisément son désir avait toujours été orienté dans un sens opposé à ses goûts esthétiques. Le mot d' 'oeuvre florentine' rendit un grand service à Swann. Il lui permit, comme un titre, de faire pénétrer l'image d'Odette dans un monde de rêves où elle n'avait pas eu accès jusqu'ici et où elle s'imprégna de noblesse" (I, 224).

In using the expression "oeuvre florentine," Swann denies the sensual existence of Odette and replaces it by the fetishistic power of a purely esthetic abstraction. This is the kind of logical/linguistic articulation that is at work in the genesis of the "metaphor" *faire catleya*, although the development of the latter figure is much longer and more complex than that of the "oeuvre florentine."[14] At first, when Swann and Odette, reunited after an anguished search in the obscurity of a Paris evening, move gradually closer together as the carriage jostles them, the orchid "orients" Swann's desires by concentrating them on the perfumed body of his beloved. But later the mechanism of habit intervenes (or, in Derrida's terminology, *l'usure métaphorique*), so that the sensuous origin of the flower is forgotten, while the love ritual proceeds according to its own rhythm. Originally a living metaphor (*métaphore vive*), the expression *faire catleya* becomes "un simple vocable qu'ils [Swann et Odette] employaient sans y penser quand ils voulaient signifier l'acte de la possession physique" (I, 234). The acquisition of meaning on the lexical level is not conceivable without an important loss on the level of original metaphoricity: the act of interiorization and conceptual abstraction by which Swann creates for himself a language of mastery isolates him from the essence of metaphor, which is pure movement. The encounter with the unleashed, nonpossessable force of metaphor is the implicit theme of the "Soirée chez la marquise de Saint-Euverte"—to which we turn now for a contextual analysis.

## METAPHOR: APPEARANCE AND APPARITION

In the paragraph that precedes the "Soirée" (I, 321–22), the distinction between live and dead metaphor designates the conflictive state of Swann's mind. A psychological defense mechanism prevents the protagonist from realizing that he is unhappy and that Odette no longer loves him. At this point in the story the lies of Odette have become increasingly prevalent and the clues pointing to her relationship with Forcheville increasingly obvious. But Swann's inner fears, expressed in the mode of detached, disinterested observation ("Il fut un temps où Odette m'aimait davantage" [321]), do not produce real knowledge of his precarious situation. For Swann to understand his predicament, the psychological manifestation of anguish and unhappiness would have to become *visible:* "ce n'est qu'en mettant *en regard* de ce qu'elle [Odette] était aujourd'hui ce qu'elle avait été au début, qu'il aurait pu sonder la profondeur du changement qui s'était accompli" (321; my emphasis). What was previously the transparent expression of true sentiments has degenerated into the fixity of cliché—like the fragmented phrases of Odette's love notes that come back to haunt Swann with the loss of their original passion: "Que n'y avez-vous oublié aussi votre coeur, je ne vous aurais pas laissé le reprendre" and "A quelque heure du jour et de la nuit que vous ayez besoin de moi, faites-moi signe et disposez de ma vie" (321). But the narrator suggests that lost or dead meaning can resuscitate in a living metaphor which, in its turn, will contribute to a clear vision of the world. On the surface, this is precisely what happens during the "Soirée." Whereas before the final triumphant encounter with the petite phrase Swann had to invent "le détour d'un long raisonnement" (322) to avoid its evocative power, to avoid being overwhelmed by the charm of happier days, the return of the music at the end of the scene reawakens all of his past happiness and juxtaposes it, painfully, to his present state—which leads to the logical conclusion of the episode: "A partir de cette soirée, Swann comprit que le sentiment qu'Odette avait eu pour lui ne renaîtrait jamais, que ses espérances de bonheur ne se réaliseraient plus" (353).

The contextual framing of the "Soirée" seems to indicate that the scene involves a dramatic reversal on the level of textual self-representation. If we hypothesize that the mechanism of love with its panoply of realistic psychological detail is, on a deeper plane, the movement of metaphysical idealization by which active metaphor degenerates into abstraction, one can conclude, as a corollary, that the protagonist's comprehension of the metaphorical message represents a revivification of the figure and therefore a reinscription of the text into the heuristic mode. But we must verify how Swann arrives at this final comprehension, how the rhetorical movement of the passage confirms or denies the limitations of contextual clarity.

## Esthetic Distance and Analogical Fancy (Pages 322-27)

From the opening description of the Saint-Euverte residence, it is evident that Proust wishes to play with the boundaries and the laws of mimesis. On the one hand, the narrator emphasizes the "Kantian" atmosphere of perfect detachment in which Swann observes the objects and the characters who come before his eyes: "Swann arriva tranquillisé par la pensée que M. de Charlus passerait la soirée rue La Pérouse, mais dans un état de mélancolique indifférence à toutes les choses qui ne touchaient pas Odette, et en particulier aux choses mondaines, qui leur donnait le charme de ce qui, *n'étant plus un but pour notre volonté, nous apparaît en soi-même*" (323; my emphasis). On the other hand, however, the existence of seen things is rendered problematic, hypothetical, by the vision of Swann, who reorganizes phenomenal reality into a series of esthetic manifestations: "C'est la vie mondaine tout entière, maintenant qu'il en était détaché, qui se présentait à lui comme une suite de tableaux" (323). In the eyes of the protagonist, the domain of the visible becomes an excellent pretext for the creation of hyperbolic analogies whose accumulated "weight" makes of the scene a grand spectacle of Proustian comedy at its best.

Proust places the first pages of the "Soirée" under the aegis of Realism (he calls the grooms of Mme de Saint-Euverte the "inheritors" of Balzac's *tigres* [323]), but one senses immediately that the author's intention is to dismantle all the conventions by which Realism establishes its powers of verisimilitude and "lifelike" appearance. What is it that transforms a description, of which each isolated element could have originated in the nineteenth-century novelistic tradition, into an apotheosis of pure imaginative fantasy? *La métaphore,* in the Proustian sense, or what we call, more precisely, both simile and metaphor—the figures of analogical resemblance. Some examples chosen from a large gallery of striking portraits:

> Swann prit plaisir à voir les héritiers des 'tigres' de Balzac, les grooms, suivants ordinaires de la promenade, qui, chapeautés et bottés, restaient dehors devant l'hôtel sur le sol de l'avenue ou devant les écuries, comme des jardiniers auraient été rangés à l'entrée de leurs parterres. (323)

> il remarqua, réveillée par l'arrivée inopinée d'un invité aussi tardif, la meute éparse, magnifique et désoeuvrée des grands valets de pied qui dormaient çà et là sur des banquettes et des coffres et qui, soulevant leurs nobles profils aigus de lévriers, se dressèrent et, rassemblés, formèrent le cercle autour de lui. (323)

> A quelques pas, un grand gaillard en livrée rêvait, immobile, sculptural, inutile, comme ce guerrier purement décoratif qu'on voit dans les tableaux les plus tumultueux de Mantegna, songer, appuyé sur son bouclier, tandis qu'on se précipite et qu'on s'égorge à côté de lui. (323-24).

The principal effect of these often complex analogies is to disorient the reader, to make him forget exactly where he is: is the true location of the scene in a fin-de-siècle salon, or in the mind of Swann? Proust creates this confusion by exploiting what classical rhetoric calls stylistic *accumulation.* The "grand gaillard" of the third example quoted above, after being compared to a Mantegna warrior, is associated progressively with a wide range of events and works of art—the massacre of the Innocents, the martyrdom of Saint James, the retable of San Zeno, the frescoes of the Eremitani, one of Albrecht Dürer's Saxons, and Greek sculpture. The servant's hair has the appearance "à la fois d'un paquet d'algues, d'une nichée de colombes, d'un bandeau de jacinthes et d'une torsade de serpents" (324). Thus arises a perpetual movement between reality as perceived by Swann and the domain of art, a vacillating, unstable movement that cannot be fixed or limited. Rather than clarify the description of characters, the similes and metaphors superpose separate, disjunct levels that dispute the same place, the same instant of duration.

The comic effect of extreme analogical diversity gives way to a more solemn tone when Swann climbs the monumental staircase separating the vestibule from the room in which Vinteuil's sonata will be played. Encircled by people who resemble saints in their niches, the protagonist receives the progressive consecration of "un énorme suisse, habillé comme à l'église" who signals his arrival by striking the flagstones with a cane, and of servants "assis comme des notaires devant de grands registres" who inscribe his name (325). Two details in the long description point to the level of textual self-representation: it is a doorman "chargé de chaînes" (326) who provides access to the domain of music (esthetic revelation), and this domain is hidden from the vestibule by a curtain of tapestry. Both of these clues designate, by symbolic indirection, the idea *Here begins Art.* The tapestry *is* a work of art; and it is the line that marks the separation between a "before" and an "after"—for Swann, between his nostalgia for the "pestilential stairway" (325) that leads to the apartment of Odette's seamstress friend, and his imminent encounter with the transcendental reality of music. The "chaînes," as we remarked earlier, are the instrument of style (and of torture) by which the writer imprisons reality in metaphor. The text is saturated with figural displacements and emblematic signs which, rather than adding to a preestablished representational meaning, draw attention to themselves. Their very presence in the text is a challenge to all interpretive activity. Self-representational technique is a radical questioning that forces the reader into the paradoxical space where the text enacts its own coming into being.

Beyond the tapestry, the world of Art appears *en abyme* (326–27). Comic tone again predominates, in a passage that ironizes the pseudo-scientific pretensions of the protagonist's analogical vision. The narrator begins by emphasizing Swann's state of esthetic disinterest: when Swann discovers for the first time the "masculine ugliness" of faces he had seen in social settings in the past, it is because their traits, "au lieu d'être pour lui des signes pratiquement utilisables à l'identification de telle personne qui lui avait représenté jusque-là un faisceau de plaisirs à poursuivre, d'ennuis à éviter, ou de politesses à rendre—reposaient, coordonnés seulement par des rapports esthétiques, dans l'autonomie de leurs lignes" (326). The contrast between a practical sign of identification and the autonomy of free esthetic relationships is a Proustian variation on the dichotomy we have seen in the work of Ricoeur and Derrida: that which opposes the two irreconcilable forces of conceptual abstraction and metaphorical "life." Proust's text seems to promise that the attitude of disinterest will lead, quite naturally, to the abolition of old habits of identification and to the elaboration of analogical novelty. It is tempting to see in this passage as a whole the defeat of metaphorical/metaphysical idealization and the victory of a veritable heuristic.

In a combination of "Aristotelian" logic and highly personal humor, Proust now evokes metaphorical *clarity*—by choosing as the object of Swann's observing eyes the monocles of six rather ridiculous gentlemen. It is obvious from the very first of the narrator's fantastic descriptions that the world of Art risks succumbing to pure illusion. Swann's extreme subjectivism is unfettered by any recognizable esthetic criteria that might serve to justify his judgments. The comparisons made in this section of the text are original but disconcerting, in that they arise from the chaotic intermingling of widely divergent categories. Thus, the Général de Froberville has a monocle whose significance derives from the theater of his usual activity (the battlefield) and that resembles both the eye of a mythological giant and the "glorious" wound of a valiant soldier: "Le monocle du géneral, resté entre ses paupières *comme* un éclat d'obus dans sa figure vulgaire, balafrée et triomphale, au milieu du front qu'il éborgnait *comme* l'oeil unique du cyclope, apparut à Swann *comme* une blessure monstrueuse, qu'il pouvait être glorieux d'avoir reçue, mais qu'il était indécent d'exhiber" (326; my emphasis). In a further development, the transparent quality of the monocles motivates complex and extended comparisons. A certain M. de Bréauté possesses "[un monocle qui] ajoutait, en signe de festivité, aux gants gris perle, au 'gibus,' à la cravate blanche et substituait au binocle familier (comme faisait Swann lui-même) pour aller dans le monde, portait, collé à son revers, comme une préparation d'histoire naturelle sous un microscope, un regard infinitésimal et grouillant d'amabilité, qui ne cessait de sourire à la hauteur des plafonds, à la beauté des fêtes, à l'intérêt des programmes et à la qualité des rafraîchissements" (326-27). Here, the monocle, worn not on the nose but on the lapel, becomes a strangely inverted mirror: the glass is the lens of a microscope, and the external world appears as a reduced interiorized reflection. This passage from outside to inside, from reflected reality to the act of reflection itself, emblematizes the text in its movement from representation to self-representation. Proust further accentuates the self-conscious dimension of the text when he describes a "romancier mondain qui venait d'installer au coin de son oeil un monocle, son seul organe d'investigation psychologique et d'impitoyable analyse" (327), who declares emphatically (in order to justify his august presence in such a frivolous gathering):

"J'observe." It is easy to recognize in this portrait Marcel Proust the man—the dandy, the fop, the elegant chronicler of empty social events—as he was judged by those of his contemporaries who were blind to his largely hidden talents.

The last gentleman encountered by Swann in the gallery of monocled figures, M. de Palancy, is compared to a fish. His transformation from earth-creature to sea-creature illustrates the congruence of metaphor and metamorphosis. It is difficult to determine whether Palancy's monocle resembles a fragment of aquarium glass because he possesses a "fat carp's head with round eyes" in the mind of Swann, or if, on the contrary, the presence of a well-placed monocle in a disoriented face causes one to visualize the transparent prison in which dazed animals seem to be seeking an impossible exit. Whatever the logical premise in Swann's reasoning, M. de Palancy becomes a fish, and this first change of appearance is accompanied by a precise rhetorical explanation. The narrator designates "[le] fragment accidentel, et peut-être purement symbolique, du vitrage de son aquarium" as "[la] partie destinée à figurer le tout"—which we recognize as the traditional definition of synecdoche. Now it happens that this figure reminds Swann of Giotto's allegory of Injustice in the Arena Chapel at Padua: "Cet Injuste à côté duquel un rameau feuillu évoque la forêt où se cache son repaire" (327). At first, the comparison between the two analogies seems convincing. In both cases we have a synecdochal relationship, since on the one hand the monocle is like the fragment of an aquarium that suggests a glassed-in totality, and on the other hand the branch shares the same constitutive elements—leaves—as the forest it evokes. But what happens if we try to decipher the way in which the analogy as a unit conveys information and adds to our knowledge of reality? (We have been assuming that we are in the realm of esthetic disinterest, which is that of live metaphor and heuristic science.) In the first part of the phrase, there is already an element that should cause interpretive indecision: the aquarium metaphor vacillates between the *necessity* of synecdoche and the contingency of metonymy, since the fragment is only "accidental," and thus the product of some chance association that the narrator does not mention; the fragment "symbolizes" only if the reader suspends his disbelief and allows himself to be persuaded by the figure. In a similar way, the "necessary" link between the leafy branch and the forest it calls forth by abbreviation is not a given, an evident, or a clear relationship: it results from a reading of Giotto's fresco that makes sense of two juxtaposed (superimposed) fragments. The bottom half of the picture represents "a wood, in a rocky chasm, where . . . robbers are committing their crime. Above this, we see Injustice enthroned, an old man ensconced in his castle, a fabulous image that seems to have been taken from a romance of chivalry."[15] The leafy branch in the top half near

Injustice can suggest the forest in the lower portion only if we understand that the act of robbery depicted below is an *example* of injustice, only if we understand that the cave near the thieves is in fact the lair of Injustice ("son repaire"). The effectiveness of Giotto's fresco hinges on the difference between appearance and reality, between the luxury of a castle surrounded by stylized, decorative trees, and the obscure depth of a cave hidden in the undergrowth of a forest: the quality of Injustice involves, at its source, a hiding. The true home of Injustice is not a castle, but a cave; his residence is, properly speaking, invisible. On the level of textual self-representation, this means that analogical vision contributes to objective knowledge only insofar as one is willing to remain at the surface of a deceiving clarity and unwilling to pursue the movement of transfer to its "blind" origin in darkness. The reader who returns to the source of metaphor must "faire le détour d'un long raisonnement" (322), not to avoid an unpleasant encounter, like Swann, but to enter the universe of metaphoricity itself—the space of twists and turns that challenges our capacity to understand.

### "Mondanité" and Prefigurative Themes (Pages 328-45)

The underlying self-representational message contained in the gallery of monocles seems to be a warning against the temptation of taking at face value the novel but unreliable observations of a mystified protagonist. In the pages that follow, the comparisons used are, once again, more striking and seductively attractive than they are "necessary"; the descriptions are less profound than original and unusual. (Mme de Cambremer has "[une] tête transformée en balancier de métronome" [328]; the "tête rapportée" of Mme de Gallardon makes one think first of a haughty pheasant, then of certain trees which, "nés dans une mauvaise position au bord d'un précipice, sont forcés de croître en arrière pour garder leur équilibre" [379].) Analogical vision contributes to the comic tone of the episode, but there is an important change in perspective. Whereas in the earlier section we saw everything through the eyes (or monocle) of Swann, gradually the narrative point of view is widened, Swann becomes one character among others, and an "omniscient" voice assumes control of the story. The self-representational level of textual reflexiveness disappears, and metaphor is used as simple ornamentation in an analysis of the laws of conduct that define aristocratic society.

In the first part of the passage, elegant ladies react in amusing, individualistic ways to the renditions of Romantic music by a piano virtuoso. The works of Liszt and of Chopin are like insistently posed questions demanding that the audience provide instant indications of its esthetic judgment. Women in the crowd show approbation or varying levels of disapproval in the subtle, ambiguous art of external gesture to which Proust was exceptionally attuned (here, Mme de Cambremer's body oscillates like a metronome; Mme des Laumes's fan beats in counterrhythm). For society, Art is a matter of fashion, necessarily evanescent (Chopin's caressing phrases lose their position of honor as Wagner's new impetuosity casts them aside like leaves in a storm) and without intrinsic merit: it becomes integrated, rather, into the whole of aristocratic language, which is representational and theatrical by nature.

As the text develops, Proust leads the reader closer to the mainspring of society's mechanism, which consists of two intertwined, indissociable elements: its sign-character[16] and its fundamental cruelty. The interdependence of the two is made clear in the conversation between Mme de Gallardon and Mme des Laumes (the future Duchesse de Guermantes). Even before words are exchanged, the narrator allows us an inside view of Mme de Gallardon, whose favorite thought is her family alliance with the prestigious Guermantes (329). She is so wrapped up in social pride, so aware of her own distinction that she wishes people whom she does not know might perceive, in a striking visual image, all her hidden grandeur. The narrator describes this desire for recognition in semiological terms:

> Quand elle [Mme de Gallardon] se trouvait auprès de quelqu'un qu'elle ne connaissait pas, comme en ce moment auprès de Mme de Franquetot, elle souffrait que la conscience qu'elle avait de sa parenté avec les Guermantes ne pût se manifester extérieurement en caractères visibles comme ceux qui, dans les mosaïques des églises byzantines, placés les uns au-dessous des autres, inscrivent en une colonne verticale, à côté d'un saint personnage, les mots qu'il est censé prononcer. (329)

Mme de Gallardon, consumed by the *idée fixe* of her familial unions and relations, reminds one of the vulnerable older women represented in classical comedy:[17] in this context, she is easy prey for the sharp wit of the young Mme des Laumes. It is significant that Mme de Gallardon, despite a certain fragile haughtiness and a penchant for destructive gossip, should have a naïve, regressive desire for the correspondence of sign and meaning. But the first lesson of Proustian society, illustrated in the conversation of the two cousins, is that sign and meaning do not exist in a state of harmony or mutual transparency. The person to whom one speaks may utter apparently understandable words, but if they are "visible," they are often false and misleading.

Thus, in the conversation proper, the correspondence between real sentiments and the exterior manifestation of the sign, unlike the Byzantine mosaic and unlike the metronomical enthusiasm of Mme de Cambremer for Chopin, is entirely lacking. It is evident that Mme des Laumes, made uncomfortable by the arrogant overtures of her cousin, has no desire to attend the latter's musical *fête*. The future duchess does not reply clearly or precisely to the invitation, and instead of stating her true feelings, she finds "plus aimable de lui exposer quelques petits faits d'où dépendraient qu'il lui fût ou non possible de s'y rendre" (334). This, according to the narrator's ironic comment, is an illustration of "sa politesse qui s'efforçait d'être positive, précise, de se rapprocher de l'humble vérité" (ibid.). In fact, we are much closer to lying than to truth: Mme de Gallardon is made to turn through a labyrinth of dissimulation, unaware that she is soon to be "executed."

Temporarily defeated in the verbal jousting, Mme de Gallardon goes on the attack, expressing her dismay that Swann, a Jew, should have been invited to the home of the sister and sister-in-law of two archbishops. Not content to have merely wounded Oriane, however, she goes on to say: "Il y a des gens qui prétendent que ce M. Swann, c'est quelqu'un qu'on ne peut pas recevoir chez soi, est-ce vrai?" (335)—to which her vivacious cousin responds: "Mais . . . tu dois bien savoir que c'est vrai . . . puisque tu l'as invité cinquante fois et qu'il n'est jamais venu" (ibid.). In the social corrida, Mme de Gallardon's wild, brusque charges are easily parried by Mme des Laumes, who has no trouble acting the role of the matador. The "kill" is neat, classically performed, accomplished with flair. The first step of testing, during which the opponents hesitatingly gauge each other's strength, is largely a matter of show, and simply allows the audience to observe the dramatic unfolding of a spectacle. It leads, inevitably, to a second stage, where subtlety gradually turns into violence.

The conversation between the two Guermantes cousins is a comical, seemingly innocuous example of the social cruelty that pervades Proust's novel. Earlier in "Un Amour de Swann" the protagonist is excluded from the Verdurin clan (I, 289) and thus is kept from encountering Odette in the easy intimacy of an established salon: later in the *Recherche* a similar "execution" befalls Saniette (III, 265-66), then Charlus (III, 319-22). The removal of Charlus assumes a special significance, since it is accomplished within the framework of a soirée whose artistic revelations seem, at first, to outweigh all mundane activity. But the juxtaposition of Vinteuil's septet as pure esthetic message to the events surrounding its composition (the actions of the composer's daughter: her lesbianism and staging of profanation scenes) and to the conditions governing its posthumous performance (it is Mlle Vinteuil's friend who deciphers "le grimoire laissé par Vinteuil, en établissant la lecture certaine de ces hiéroglyphes inconnus" [III, 262]) leads one to question the possibility of reading the septet episode without taking into account its contextual ramifications. Not only is the work of art determined by its birth in sadistic ritual, but the integrity of its episodic or scenic representation is threatened by its immediate

textual surroundings. Is the "truth" of the Verdurin evening the septet, or Charlus' execution? Or is it at all legitimate to separate the esthetic
object from its moral envelope? It would be premature to suggest an
answer to this question now: suffice it to say that the problem of contextuality as such is at the heart of Proustian narration, and that the difficulty of choosing between two apparently irreconcilable constellations
of meaning is a primary, unavoidable difficulty in the reading of the
*Recherche.*

After the encounter between the Princesse des Laumes and Mme de
Gallardon begins a series of prefigurative themes (336-41) that form the
crux of the passage's final pages. Oriane's "simplicité de grande dame"
(336) (which, the reader learns later in the novel, consists of the opposite
of simplicity) manifests itself in her lowliest gesture (here, the fact that
she sits down on a small seat without a backrest). Her scintillating and
empty conversation with General Froberville gives evidence of the famous
"esprit des Guermantes" (339) that will be developed in *Le Côté de Guermantes* (see, for example, "la dernière d'Oriane," "Taquin le Superbe"
[II, 478]). The word game, the "double abbreviation" which Swann and
the princess find in Mme de Cambremer's name (341), has the thrust of
parody, especially if one compares it to the serious deconstructive force
of Brichot's etymologies near the end of *Sodome et Gomorrhe* (II, 888-
93, 921-38). One could multiply examples of thematic links that lie hidden in the section's minute detail. One of the most interesting of these is
contained in Oriane's allusion to the "Empire" style furniture in the Iéna
home, furniture which she professes to find in "horrible" taste (339).
She assures her interlocutor: "Moi j'ai aussi des choses comme ça que
Basin a héritées des Montesquiou. Seulement elles sont dans les greniers
de Guermantes où personne ne les voit."[18] But in a subsequent volume,
when the same subject comes up in discussion, the duchess adopts a very
different point of view concerning the esthetic qualities of the furniture's
style: "Je me rappelle qu'à Guermantes je m'étais fait honnir de ma belle-
mère parce que j'avais dit de descendre du grenier tous les splendides
meubles Empire que Basin avait hérités des Montesquiou, et que j'en avais
meublé l'aile que j'habitais" (II, 517). By lying in this second context, she
shows her independence from her mother-in-law and lets the Princesse de
Parme—who, as aristocratic purist, looks down upon the recently acquired
nobility of the Iéna—savor "une des audaces les plus Guermantes de la
duchesse" (II, 518). Here and elsewhere in the *Recherche,* the pursuit of
thematic relationships shows the deceitfulness and deceptiveness that
frame all attempts to "shine" by conversational brilliance, either in society as it is represented in the work, or at an omnipresent symbolic level,
in the frivolous creation of a literature whose descriptive and psychological depth is the result of trompe-l'oeil.

## "Métaphore vive" and Blindness (Pages 345–53)

Swann's attitude of esthetic disinterest, which had allowed him to elaborate a web of fantastic analogical relationships and to participate in the frivolity of mundane conversation, disappears with the return of Vinteuil's *petite phrase*. The protagonist's disinterest had been made possible by the naïve belief that Odette, in the apparently secure company of the Baron de Charlus, would remain entirely absent from the "Soirée." Yet, because of the long process of analogical accumulation that defines the plot development of "Un Amour de Swann," the musical phrase and Odette had become one and the same object of love for Swann. When the violinist begins to play Vinteuil's sonata, Odette *enters* the room: "Mais tout à coup ce fut comme si elle [Odette] était entrée, et cette apparition lui fut une si déchirante souffrance qu'il [Swann] dut porter la main à son coeur" (345). The success of the metaphorical transfer can be measured by the suffering of the protagonist, whose conscious defenses have been penetrated by the subliminal energy of sound. Swann cannot choose to direct his mind's concentration elsewhere; he is no longer free. Live metaphor, the instrument of clarity, destroys metaphysical idealization and the fixed meanings of habitual phrases:

> Au lieu des expressions abstraites "temps où j'étais heureux," "temps où j'étais aimé," qu'il avait souvent prononcées jusque-là et sans trop souffrir, car son intelligence n'y avait enfermé du passé que de prétendus extraits qui n'en conservaient rien, il retrouva tout ce qui de ce bonheur perdu avait fixé à jamais la spécifique et volatile essence; *il revit tout,* les pétales neigeux et frisés du chrysanthème qu'elle lui avait jeté dans sa voiture, qu'il avait gardé contre ses lèvres—l'adresse en relief de la "Maison Dorée" sur la lettre où il avait lu: "Ma main tremble si fort en vous écrivant"—le rapprochement de ses sourcils quand elle lui avait dit d'un air suppliant: "Ce n'est pas dans trop longtemps que vous me ferez signe?"; il sentit l'odeur de fer du coiffeur par lequel il se faisait relever sa "brosse" pendant que Lorédan allait chercher la petite ouvrière, les pluies d'orage qui tombèrent si souvent ce printemps-là, le retour glacial dans sa victoria, au clair de lune, toutes les mailles d'habitude mentales, d'impressions saisonnières, de réactions cutanées, qui avaient étendu sur une suite de semaines un réseau uniforme dans lequel son corps se trouvait repris. (345-46; my emphasis)

According to the logic of this paragraph, it would appear that the narrator sides, philosophically, with Ricoeur against Derrida: live metaphor, in its close link to the phenomenon of involuntary memory (whose prestige is unquestioned on the level of Proustian theoretical discourse), is also an effective method of knowledge, and, more precisely, the dynamic means to the end of self-discovery. The reader will remember that before the unsuspected resurgence of the *petite phrase* Swann was unable to sound the depths of his gradually evolving unhappiness. But now, to borrow again from Aristotelian metaphorical terminology, Swann *sees* the juxtaposition of past happiness and present anguish. He succumbs to the pathetic recognition of his own split self: "Et Swann aperçut, immobile en face de ce bonheur revécu, un malheureux qui lui fit pitié parce qu'il ne le reconnut pas tout de suite, si bien qu'il dut baisser les yeux pour qu'on ne vît pas qu'ils étaient pleins de larmes. C'était lui-même" (347).

The immediate effect of live metaphor is thus to integrate understanding and suffering. The mechanism of metaphorical transfer contains within itself the mainspring of Proustian love as described in *La Prisonnière* and *La Fugitive*. As soon as the simple curiosity at unveiling the secret life of one's beloved has turned into "cette formidable terreur . . . cette immense angoisse de ne pas savoir à tous moments ce qu'elle avait fait, de ne pas la posséder partout et toujours" (346), one can imagine the interminable dialectics of imprisonment and escape that occupies the psychological center of the novel. Without metaphorical life, there can be no resurrection of the true and painful past in its essence, no subjective desire to know the Other, no pursuit of the ungraspable, no novel in the Proustian sense.

But it is precisely when metaphorical self-representation seems to merge most coherently with a general heuristic that the text becomes involuted, tortuous, complex. In a long paragraph (347–50), the narrator tells the story of metaphorical production and tries to demonstrate the central importance of metaphorical transfer in the formation of conceptual and categorical discourse. But the nature of the relationship between metaphor and concept is problematical: the entire passage "turns" on this difficulty. Indeed, if we respect the rhetorical movement of the paragraph, we must recognize that metaphor is blindness—or, more exactly, that energy which blinds the reader. Swann "ne pouvait pas plus la [la petite phrase] voir que si elle avait appartenu à un monde ultra-violet, et . . . goûtait comme le rafraîchissement d'une métamorphose dans la cécité momentanée dont il était frappé en approchant d'elle" (347–48). Swann, who represents the interpreter of texts, immediately personifies the musical phrase and transforms it into "une déesse protectrice et confidente de son amour, et qui pour pouvoir arriver jusqu'à lui devant la foule et l'emmener à l'écart pour lui parler, avait revêtu le déguisement de cette apparence sonore" (348). But this personification, derived from the borrowed "femininity" of the phrase, is the result of a false reading that denies the very essence of metaphorical blindness. In other words, the moments situated before and after the figure on a temporal line allow for an "historical" differentiation that causes us to speak of the metaphor as an understandable object of knowledge. But the moment during which the transfer takes place, because of its nonduration, cannot be conceived: it lends itself to personification and other rhetorical manipulations only if we are willing to ignore the blind spot (Derrida: "tache aveugle") that inhabits its center. On the level of self-representation, the text demonstrates the progressive mystification of Swann, who attempts to possess and control the meaning of a figural displacement that blocks all access to its significant core.

A reading that is sensitive to the self-representational resonance of the passage challenges the truth value of the text's overt persuasiveness and narrative dominance: it is necessarily a deconstruction. Such a reading, in analyzing the origins of Swann's humanism, will see in the "élan de pitié et de tendresse vers ce Vinteuil, vers ce frère inconnu et sublime qui lui aussi avait dû tant souffrir" (348) not the transparent admiration of Marcel Proust for serious artistry, but rather the protagonist's tendency to lose himself in an emotional, inauthentic hero worship while avoiding a more difficult task: his confrontation with the blinding center of the metaphorical process. Similarly, a deconstructive interpretation will discover in the rhetorical twist that confers upon the *petite phrase* a "consistent" and "explicit" meaning (350) the perverse reversal of the original metaphorical *rafraîchissement* (348) whereby Swann lost his ability to *see* (understand) the figure. When the narrator asserts that Vinteuil's phrase has a "latent" existence in the mind of the protagonist, "au même titre que certaines autres notions sans équivalent, comme la notion de lumière, de son, de relief, de volupté physique, qui sont les riches possessions dont se diversifie et se pare notre domaine intérieur" (350), he forgets, or pretends to forget, that metaphor is *dis*possession. When he compares the certainty of knowledge based upon metaphorical clarity to "la lumière de la lampe qu'on allume devant les objets métamorphosés de notre chambre d'où s'est échappé jusqu'au souvenir de l'obscurité" (350), he forgets, or wishes not to recognize, that metaphor *is* metamorphosis, not that which freezes metaphoricity in the uniform appearance of a fixed spectacle. It is only because of this artificial immobility of things (which transgresses the laws and limits of metaphor and destroys the very basis of analogical vision) that one can speak of the phrase as a "sentimental acquisition" which, having "espoused our mortal condition," linked to the future and the "reality of our soul" (350), assures us a place in immortality.

The text presents first the indescribable, evanescent truth of metaphor, then constructs around the central void of the figure an elaborate system of seductive poetic images that deviate the attention of the reader, who, thinking he has followed the logical development of metaphoricity as such, finds himself far from his point of departure, in the domain of "ideas" (Proust) or the "speculative" (Ricoeur). The consequences of this double structure are not without importance in an overall interpretation of the *Recherche*. Indeed, when Swann, in the last paragraph of the "Soirée" (351–53), waits for the return of the petite phrase, he resembles the literary critic who views the work of art as a texture of interwoven themes. But the thematic point of view is possible only when one has removed oneself from the original nothingness of metaphor, only if one stands outside the text, where each detail of the fictional progression seems retrospectively *necessary*. Swann is no longer interested in the musical phrase in itself, but in its subjective associative power, in its sentimental architecture. When substituted for metaphorical truth (blindness), this architecture lends the work not only an appearance of solidity and perennial existence, but also its readability, since it awakens in the interpreter the illusion of knowledge:

> Elle [la petite phrase] avait disparu. Swann savait qu'elle reparaîtrait à la fin du dernier mouvement, après tout un long morceau que le pianiste de Mme Verdurin sautait toujours. Il y avait là d'admirables idées que Swann n'avait pas distinguées à la première audition et qu'il percevait maintenant, comme si elles se fussent, dans le vestiaire de sa mémoire, débarrassées du déguisement uniforme de la nouveauté. Swann écoutait tous les thèmes épars qui entreraient dans la composition de la phrase, comme les prémisses dans la conclusion nécessaire, il assistait à sa genèse. (351)

As the passage progresses, the text turns into itself increasingly and reflects upon its self-generation.[19] Proust recounts the birth of meaning in a "mythological" allegory that represents the dialogue of piano and violin as a struggle for the creation of a transparent, metalinguistic harmony. Divided now into two parts, the *petite phrase* metamorphoses into a multitude of shapes that cannot be reduced to the fixity of semantic determination. At first, "le piano solitaire se plaignit, comme un oiseau abandonné de sa compagne; le violon l'entendit, lui répondit comme d'un arbre voisin" (351). But the transformation of a melody into a bird is only one hypothesis among others: "Est-ce un oiseau, est-ce l'âme incomplète encore de la petite phrase, est-ce une fée, cet être invisible et gémissant dont le piano ensuite redisait tendrement la plainte?" (352). These questions, which can be repeated ad infinitum, are the sign of the protagonist's sense of loss and wonder as he is caught up in the vortex of metaphorical movement. The hypothetical fiction of tropological beginnings derives from the impossibility of remaining within the invisible center of the figure. And if the void is indescribable, if the experience of blindness can be rendered only by metaphorical indirection, then fiction is born of the desire to pursue a fleeing, absent meaning. Thus the violinist wishes to "charm," "tame," and "capture" the phrase/bird, and the account of this effort (which is condemned to failure from the start) provides the text with the element of pathos necessary to its dramatic elaboration. The truth of metaphor emerges in the sentence "Déjà il [l'oiseau] avait passé dans son âme, déjà la petite phrase évoquée agitait comme celui d'un médium le corps vraiment possédé du violoniste" (352). But the Proustian novel is not a text of truths enshrined in metaphor: it is the repetitive process by which the obscure, nonreadable significance of the figure obtains, through a misreading, the lively colors, the deceiving clarity, of full, controllable meaning.

When the musical phrase appears for the last time, it turns into an image that expresses the harmonious perfection of nature and suggests, by self-representational allusion, the promise of formal unity contained in the work of art:

> Elle reparut, mais cette fois pour se suspendre dans l'air et se jouer un instant seulement, comme immobile, et pour expirer après. Aussi Swann ne perdait-il rien du temps si court où elle se prorogeait. Elle était encore là comme une bulle irisée qui se soutient. Tel un arc-en-ciel, dont l'éclat faiblit, s'abaisse, puis se relève, et, avant de s'éteindre, s'exalte un moment comme il n'avait pas encore fait: aux deux couleurs qu'elle avait jusque-là laissé paraître, elle ajouta d'autres cordes diaprées, toutes celles du prisme, et les fit chanter. (352)

But once again, if we wish to respect the complexity of the text, we must distinguish between the empty temporal spacing of pure *différance* (*suspension, prorogation*) that is the metaphorical core in its essence, and the ornamentation (*irisation*) that surrounds it. Jean-Pierre Richard has written that the open, unitary, transparent and multicolored form of the phrase become rainbow "permet de rêver un court instant comme une sorte d'abrégé, ou mieux peut-être de solution, de résolution de l'univers."[20] But this dream can be deployed in its poetic brilliance only when the reader has abandoned the locus of metaphorical production for the enchanting periphery of its stunning effects. Metaphorical energy is magical in that it robs the reader of his rational control and leads him into an invisible domain whose laws are inaccessible to consciousness: the clear vision afforded us by spectral luminosity gives way to a disconcerting groping when we encounter metaphoricity in its own domain.

The real conclusion of the passage is not the apotheosis of light. In an amusing coda, Proust brusquely interrupts the atmosphere of esthetic communion and describes the reactions of the Comtesse de Monteriender to the sublime music of Vinteuil. Unable to resist the temptation of revealing her naïve impressions of the concert to Swann, she makes an apparently stupid remark. But Swann "ne put s'empêcher de sourire, et peut-être de trouver aussi un sens profond qu'elle n'y voyait pas, dans les mots dont elle se servit. Emerveillée par la virtuosité des exécutants, la comtesse s'écria en s'adressant à Swann: 'C'est prodigieux, je n'ai jamais rien vu d'aussi fort . . .' Mais un scrupule d'exactitude lui faisant corriger cette première assertion, elle ajouta cette réserve: 'rien d'aussi fort . . . depuis les tables tournantes'!" (353). This judgment is both stupid and profoundly true: it calls for a double reading. First, on a literal plane, the esthetic experience of the "Soirée" is trivialized; but at a second remove, the irony is much richer, since the expression "table *tournante*" contains the word *trope* (*tropein*, "to turn"). The text designates itself as tropic movement, so that, on the level of self-representation, the "scrupule d'exactitude" of the countess is far from ridiculous. On the contrary, a profoundly ironical *mise en abyme* deconstructs the simple humor of literal meaning and makes of a naïvely comical remark the serious expression of the text's involuted functioning. We have here what one might describe as an "indirect" authorial intrusion. Proust wishes to tell the reader (assuming the latter has not already understood) that the "Soirée chez la marquise de Saint-Euverte" does not merely describe by mimesis the naïveté of countesses, but reveals, by rhetorical deviation, the tricks played by tropes (in French, "les tours que nous jouent les tropes").

The *vertiges* that Genette discovered in the negativity of the Proustian text are the consequence of the fundamental dizziness that inhabits metaphorical play. Live metaphor turns about itself in a circular, unending movement. Proust understood that metaphor can only designate itself: it says what it is and acts out what it says. The explicit theory of the narrator in *Le Temps retrouvé* and the observations of Elstir in the second part of *A l'Ombre des jeunes filles en fleurs* are not merely the expression of an idealistic/transcendental ideology that modern literary studies have put into question: they are, more deeply, the misreading of that "blind" metaphorical truth that Swann tries to avoid at all costs but that Marcel Proust confronts directly in his elaboration of a self-representational subtext. It is necessary to reread the *Recherche* as a pattern of ironies emerging from the juxtaposition of the narrator's mystified discursive declarations to the textual detail that contains, under the mask of visible beauty, the colorless nudity of tropological nothingness. According to Proust, the novel does not exist independently of its reading; and one cannot conceive of a text composed uniquely of truths in assertive form. Proustian writing is both deconstructive and constructive: it represents the impossibility of possessing the inner truth of metaphor as it divests the observing subject of all conscious control; but at the same time it fashions a coherent poetic brilliance, a system of rhetorical ornamentation that is the more persuasive the farther it recedes from its source. And this source is invisible, blinding.

The truth of the "Soirée" consists of little indeed—of a text that designates itself as trope. Yet its erroneous reading produces knowledge ("Swann *comprit* que le sentiment qu'Odette avait eu pour lui ne renaîtrait jamais" [353; my emphasis]) and confers upon the context its limitative value, upon the scene as such its distinct and clear boundaries. Live metaphor cannot be raised/preserved/negated (*aufgehoben, relevée*) by speculative thought, but is that force which deconstructs the pretension of the speculative to imprison by concept/context. A reading that would attempt to erect live metaphor into an esthetic system would betray the inner structure of metaphorical turning. If we reverse the process of metaphysical idealization by which the philosophers tell us that metaphor "loses its colors," we discover that the figure never had colors in the first place, that it is the differential temporal space, the void that the *Recherche* fills with an impressive thematic architecture. To read Proust is no doubt to "casser le projet d'ensemble," to "souligner les points d'aberration mal contrôlés" (Sollers), but one must add that Proust himself had broken his own project before modern critical thought became aware of his novel's constructive/ deconstructive complexity: this is because the total project has its center in a "point d'aberration mal contrôlé"—the twisting, blinding point called *métaphore*.

# 2
# Ruskin and Proust: The Complexity of Influence

On the level of textual self-representation, the "Soirée chez la marquise de Saint-Euverte" tells the story of the origin and function of metaphor. By doubling into itself to produce a figural narration within the wider perspective of Swann's progressive disenchantment, the scene becomes the locus of a semantic disruption, some of whose consequences need to be examined at this point. At first sight, it might seem that the substitution of "metaphor" for "music" merely adds a level of meaning to the text, and that the final pages of the passage on the revelations of the *petite phrase* can be interpreted as the symbolic fiction of tropological play without in any way detracting from the persuasive charm of the musical literality itself. This would imply that the *significant,* although it potentially evokes a multiplicity of *signifiés,* nevertheless can be trusted in itself, as an *analogon:* in the case we are considering, the properties of music as they are described in the scene would resemble the properties of metaphor, thereby orienting the reader toward the discovery that the text is in fact "about" metaphor. The added knowledge we would derive from the passage would not cancel out the literal meaning but rather build upon it and add a certain resonance.

Yet what we encountered in the actual reading of the metaphorical structure tends to complicate and even undermine this semiological scheme. In the analysis of the "Soirée" it became manifest that the clarity of metaphor (its spectral luminosity, its diaphanous coexistence with the elaboration of conceptual truth) was in fact the result of a radical misreading that substituted the understandable seductions of color for the blinding incomprehensibility of an empty, turning void. The relationship of literal (musical) meaning to figural development here is not that of a transparently motivated analogy, but rather the incontrovertible evidence of an insuperable contradiction that divides the text into two mutually exclusive units: the one—representational or mimetic—which allows itself to be integrated and contextualized within a linear narrative sequence; the other, self-representational, free from outside referential bonds, anticontextual, and resistant to any form of semantic control. Given this state of affairs it becomes absurd, in the strictest sense, to speak of the self-representational mode as being included within (i.e., mastered by) the mimetic configuration, since the function of the former is to unveil the false presuppositions of comprehensibility on which the latter is predicated. The contextual inclusion of the metaphorical grants the scene its readability, but it is precisely this readability that the blind structure of metaphor puts into question. In rhetorical terms, the relationship between the sub-passage on metaphor and the surrounding narrative is therefore not that of metaphorical synecdoche, in which the part relates analogously to the whole by a sharing of common properties, but that of a pure metonymical juxtaposition in which the integrity of the whole is revealed to be factitious.

At this juncture it would be premature to assert that the subtext on metaphor is intrinsically more meaningful than the representational frame it deconstructs, and it would be especially dangerous to assume, without further investigation, that the story of metaphor is the truth of the referential error it seems to expose. For the time being it is sufficient to note the existence of two incompatible modes of narration as well as the logical contradictions engendered by their complex interaction. If we wish to continue with a more general analysis of self-representational figuration in the *Recherche,* we must examine the question of reading, or more precisely, of misreading, as it is inscribed within the tropological patterns of the text.

Swann is a reader, and it is only too easy to say that Marcel's principal activity is that of a sign decipherer, but in stating this in the direct manner of objective fact, we do nothing to probe the origin of reading as such. We say that reading takes place, but we do not thereby uncover the conditions of its emergence. If we ask, "How did reading enter into the *Recherche?*" or, phrased differently, "How did the problem of textual interpretation become subsumed within a creative fiction?" we must be careful not to take our own language at face value, since it is not a priori self-understood that the matter of reading can be conceived of as a theme among others that takes its place within the vaster network of signification we call a novel. We do not know at the outset how the act of reading, which is thematized (and thus, pragmatically speaking, located "inside" the text), relates to its outside: the staging of metaphorical movement in the "Soirée" can have done nothing to increase our belief in the inevitability of a synecdochal part-whole structure that would contextualize reading as a mastered and luminous process within the larger fabric of a modern Bildungsroman. What reading in its self-representational inscribed form has to do with the generic problematics of the novel "in" which it is to be found is not immediately obvious: to develop this point we must first isolate the subject of reading and describe its formal properties before following its thematized meanderings through the Proustian textual labyrinth.

The manner in which Proust became preoccupied with the problems of interpretation (literary, artistic, musical) is well documented in what we know of his intellectual biography. Critics generally argue that Proust progressed from an initial naïve stage of fragmentary novelistic composition (*Jean Santeuil*) through a phase of reflection on reading within an artificial novelistic framework (*Contre Sainte-Beuve*) toward the final *apogée* of the *Recherche,* which, according to a teleological synthesis, combines the "better" elements of the earlier developmental process into a successfully elaborated and original form. From the standpoint of common sense, there is much to justify these claims, and the reaction of the reader who is already familiar with the *Recherche* as he examines *Jean Santeuil* or *Contre Sainte-Beuve* may well be that of surprise: how could the same man be responsible for works of such widely divergent quality? What prompted Proust to realize, in his years of artistic maturity, that the imaginary dialogue with his mother concerning the merits and deficiencies of Beuvian literary criticism was in fact the disguised unconscious effort to create a novel now ranked among the masterpieces of modernism? Further study of the manuscripts located at the Bibliothèque Nationale in Paris may shed light on this question, but the question itself may prove to be a false one.[1]

Proust's interest in reading as deciphering of signs and as psychological process of memory association dates from his early analysis and translation of John Ruskin, and it is this period of activity (c. 1899–1907) that needs to be examined thoroughly if one intends to establish the prehistory of the textual convolutions we have called "self-representation," "metaphorical blindness," "misreading," and so on. As will be apparent from subsequent sections of this book, the more obvious, thematically explicit treatments of reading in the *Recherche* are elaborated under the highly visible aegis of John Ruskin. For this reason it is necessary to trace the origins of the Ruskinian intertextual presence in Proust's novel. I propose the following hypothesis, to be developed in four successive stages: that Proust's study of Ruskin involved a profound examination of the act of reading as such, and that the structure of reading according to Ruskin is not (as is generally thought) thematic totalization but an analytic "unravelling" akin to the deconstructive movement we observed in the metaphorical process. In the present chapter, I shall discuss the relation-ship of Ruskin's literary creativity to his theory of artistic production; in the third chapter, the way Proust read and incorporated Ruskin into his writing; in the fourth chapter, the origin and semantic constitution of Proustian narrative; and in the fifth chapter, the problem of selfhood in its relationship to the semiological structure of the *Recherche* as allegorical fiction. Each stage in the elaboration of my argument evolves from an analysis of the act of reading, and behind each independent development of an idea stands the figure of John Ruskin.

## INFLUENCE

Although Ruskin's influence on Proust is now a critical commonplace, the nature of this influence needs to be clarified. The majority of the studies we have on the subject furnish a compendium of generalities in-cluding textual "proofs" of indebtedness: they show beyond any doubt that Proust was not averse to lifting from Ruskin statements concerning the essence of beauty, the deeper meanings of pictorial representation, the spirituality of the artist's mission, and so forth. It has been established that the composite figure of Elstir includes a large dose of Turner as seen through the eyes of Ruskin, and the general tenor and tone of the revela-tions that conclude *Le Temps retrouvé* owe much to the English writer. Jean Autret contends, convincingly, that the themes of painting and religious art in the *Recherche* derive their shape from the mediation of Ruskin, and he reveals the importance for Proustian psychology of the Turnerian-Ruskinian theory of "first impressions."[2] It is significant that Autret's book was written with the encouragement and under the direc-tion of Robert Vigneron, who was the first critic of Proust to make clear the link between an unusual method of novelistic composition (that of temporally "encapsulated" scenes that relate to each other in a quasi-musical series of echo effects) and the thematic structure of the nine-teenth-century *Gesamtkunstwerke* Proust admired so much (the works of Wagner, Dostoevski, Balzac, and also Ruskin).[3] More recently, George Painter and John D. Rosenberg have written on the parallel between Ruskin's use of unconscious memory as an organizational principle in his autobiography *Praeterita* and that of Proust in the *Recherche*.[4]

The major difficulty encountered by all critics who, through intel-lectual honesty, wish to respect the specificity of Proust's talent despite whatever debts their studies uncover, is that Ruskin's Victorian obses-sions with social and moral questions seem far removed from his disciple's more intimate mode of creativity. Autret writes: "Proust ne s'occupe pas ... de ses [de Ruskin] idées de réformes dans le domaine de l'économie ou de la sociologie; quant à sa doctrine morale, il n'en a cure" (*L'Influence de Ruskin,* 27). Maurice Bardèche reiterates this judgment and finds in the "dogmatism" of Ruskin's preaching proof enough that the latter's influence on Proust has been exaggerated:

> L'influence de Ruskin sur l'oeuvre de Proust est évidente si l'on pense à certains détails de la *Recherche,* elle est sensible encore dans certaines préoccupations que Proust a prêtées à ses personnages et encore plus à celui qui le représente et qui est le témoin des vies qu'il décrit. Mais on l'a assurément exagérée, probablement par souci d'intégrer cette période ruskinienne à la biographie intellectuelle de Proust: on a trop oublié que l'importance de la *Recherche du temps perdu* ne vient pas des descriptions d'églises et de cathédrales qu'elle contient, ni même de la conception de l'art qu'elle développe, et, d'autre part, on ne voit pas bien comment on peut accorder la pensée toute dogmatique de Ruskin, dont l'oeuvre est au fond la prédication d'un prophète, avec l'amoralisme fondamental de Proust à la fois en art et dans la vie.[5]

The chapter Bardèche devotes to Ruskin in his *Marcel Proust romancier* is a strange aggregate of contradictory insights whose argumentational concatenation provides an interesting paradigm of the pitfalls inherent in traditional influence studies. As is obvious from the title of his book, Bardèche is concerned with the development of Proust *qua* novelist: everything that precedes the turn toward the novel is nugatory—or rather, Bardèche must make it seem so if his thesis is to be convincing. Ironically, it is in his discussion of a writer for whose preaching he has nothing but impatience that he himself is obliged to preach. The section on Ruskin in *Marcel Proust romancier* is dominated by the critic's will to persuade at all costs. The paragraph just quoted is perfectly clear, but Bardèche comes back to the problem of moralism versus amorality on two other occasions, and ends by characterizing Ruskin as a "vieux fermier des Westerns," as a "prophète barbu du Far West" (142)—descriptive phrases which, as the French say, *détonent dans le contexte.* The reason for such rhetorical bombast is psychological. Bardèche is acutely aware of the power of Ruskin over Proust, while his desire to present Proust as an "original" novelist requires him to minimize the importance of the English theorist. He admits that Ruskin "opened the eyes" of his disciple, teaching him that paintings, cities, and churches were "les reliquaires de précieuses vérités" (134). Here, Bardèche is (for his purposes) dangerously close to critics such as Gilles Deleuze (*Proust et les signes*) and Roland Barthes,[6] who see in the *Recherche* a work in which the act of reading signs (or of *naming* them and experiencing their structure in a series of exemplary interpretive moments) *is* the novelistic process. To defend against the possibility that Ruskin, or the act of reading as theorized by Ruskin, might be an energy with which Proust had to contend, Bardèche then neutralizes the thrust of his own perceptive observations by stating that the insights afforded Proust by Ruskin were in fact simply "le prolongement de vérités confusément perçues quelques années plus tôt" (136-37). The role of Ruskin is thus essentially Socratic: he awakens within the mind of his ephebe what already existed there in a latent state.

According to Bardèche, Proust makes use of certain Ruskinian themes in the elaboration of his novelistic universe, but he immediately transforms them by an act of interiorization. Thus, the obsession with moral contradictions that eventually drove Ruskin from writing about art to speculating about the aberrant social structures of capitalism is no longer a factor for Proust, who is able to understand that "il n'y a pas de morale dans l'art . . . les 'chagrins et les fautes', cela fait partie de l'*humus* dont cette plante [l'oeuvre d'art] se nourrit" (140). Here, Bardèche alludes obliquely to a development in *Le Temps retrouvé* (III, 898-906) in which Marcel attempts to justify his future writing by proposing that it will be capable of effacing the accumulated guilt of his existence, including his ambivalent role in the suffering and death of his grandmother. The rhetorical contortions of the passage are complex and would justify an independent reading: suffice it to say now that the paragraph on guilt and exoneration through art points so obviously to its own persuasiveness as to cause distrust in the reader.[7]

Proust's comparison of the work of art to a plant is an important image that will be analyzed in some detail in the final chapter of this study, but at present we can note already some of its connotations. If guilt is the soil on which the work of art grows, and if the work of art is viewed as a self-sufficient esthetic whole, then whatever existential significance or referential meaning may have been involved in individual guilty actions is overcome or negated (Hegel: *aufgehoben*) as guilt becomes a purified amoral theme. Since Bardèche never questions the essential truth value of the narrator's pronouncements on art and never entertains the idea that narrator and author may relate to each other in a less than transparent way, the plant analogy is a perfect expression of the natural, organic unfolding of the novel from the easily digestible moral "nourishment" that sustains its growth. It is not surprising, then, that the same analogy returns when Bardèche concludes his chapter on Ruskin, although in this context the critic's own rhetorical and logical manipulations attain a certain degree of Proustian complexity. Bardèche's final paragraph (147) is a series of juxtaposed assertions and denegations: one sentence grants to Ruskin's intellectual power what the next sentence takes away. Having read Ruskin, "Proust est prêt à se mettre au travail. Tout est en place en lui." But we know that Ruskin did no more than confirm what Proust already knew. In this sense, the metamorphosis of Proust from 1899 to 1907 was no "miracle" and the English art critic was no "master" of a fledgling author.

This having been stated categorically, Bardèche reintroduces, via metaphor, what he had refused to grant in the mode of direct statement:

> Mais Ruskin a *nourri* sa pensée. Dans les voies indécises que Proust
> avait découvertes l'une après l'autre en lui, Ruskin a *versé un sang*
> *généreux,* vigoureux, grâce auquel elles ont trouvé leur netteté
> et leur force. Et de même, à sa sensibilité vibratile, fureteuse, mais
> réduite aux sensations et aux honneurs de l'intimité, Ruskin a
> donné des horizons, *une sève nouvelle,* il lui a apporté les villes, les
> églises, les peintures. Et à cause de cela, le génie de Proust s'est
> mis à *pousser joyeusement, comme un jeune arbre,* après cette *greffe*
> *étrangère.* Ruskin n'avait rien "sauvé" du tout, contrairement à ce
> qu'affirme George Painter au moyen d'un vocabulaire assez
> étrange. Mais il a aidé Proust à se reconnaître et à voir. (147; my
> emphasis)

This passage is not easy to disentangle because the plant comparison co-exists with the imagery of religious sacrifice. It is true that the two are closely related and share the same property of fluidity (the sap of the young tree relates analogously to the "generous blood" of Ruskin), but they do not merge in their intentional energy, since on the one hand the emphasis is on the self-enclosure of the plant, which merely uses its nutrients (these nutrients possessing no intrinsic value), whereas on the other hand, the "generous blood" of the sacrificial victim has an importance of its own: on it depend the life and salvation of the receiving body. The apparent ease with which these figures exchange attributes is the mask of a fundamental gap which, in the language of literary criticism, separates two contradictory notions of "influence." The conscious purpose of Bardèche was to neutralize the authority of Ruskin by proving that it could be "absorbed" into the prestigious interiority of Proust's novel, but the critic's unconscious use of the sacrifice metaphor introduced into his concluding remarks an unsettling idea: that the disciple not only derives whatever power he has from his master, but that he can disengage himself from the latter's influence only through some form of denial or blasphemy. Yet the simultaneous presence of the traditional model of influence as natural organic growth and the more problematic, psychologically ambivalent notion of a blood-letting is not to be condemned or dismissed out of hand. Bardèche's rhetoric is itself symptomatic of the problems faced by Proust *as* reader of Ruskin, and the rhetorical entanglement that subtends his final paragraph may be a repetition or mimicry of the Proustian text, which, in wishing to "do away" with Ruskin by consciously reusing the Englishman's theories and observations, in fact sinks deeper and deeper into a more twisted and less visible dependency. Far from closing the question of Proust's relationship to Ruskin, Bardèche unintentionally opens it to considerable complication, since it now becomes possible to imagine the *Recherche* as a defense mechanism whose function is to pay tribute while withdrawing praise, or, in the terms of Harold Bloom via Freud, to make antithetical use of the precursor's primal words.[8] It is with this possibility in mind, but without assuming its inevitability, that we need to examine those Ruskinian texts which Proust read and, in effect, rewrote.

Bardèche's caricature of Ruskin as bearded prophet uttering simple, dogmatic statements of principle is itself a caricature of the misunderstanding to which the latter's writings have always been prone. The problem may be that we moderns are now accustomed to the alienated state of man in a technological society and willing to accept as a necessary fact that art's business is no longer that of representing the world but of reflecting upon itself, whereas the constant purpose of Ruskin's work for a half century was to demonstrate the moral imperative of art—its responsibility in the unification of the masses with the creative imagination possessed by the few. What Ruskin always avoided in his criticism was the temptation of enclosing art within purely formal boundaries. In the second volume of *Modern Painters* (1846), he made a terminological distinction that was to remain at the center of his thought for years to come: the "mere sensual perception of the outward qualities and necessary effects of bodies" he called *aesthesis,* whereas to the "exulting, reverent and grateful perception" of beauty he gave the name *theoria* and his full approbation.[9] Although it is true that the reverent appreciation of beauty presupposes a theological scheme in which the elements of nature mirror the attributes of God in a sophisticated typological system,[10] it is not correct to assume that Ruskin always expected works of art to contain a uniform ethical message or forfeit their intrinsic value in the debasement of didacticism. Rather, he was unable to envision his role of critic as essentially separate from the more pragmatic activities of the people for whom he wrote, and was not willing to espouse a theory like that of "art for art's sake" that might isolate him in the domain of *aesthesis.*

Ruskin's career embodied a major conflict of late Romanticism: the problematic existence of artistic aspiration as such in a world characterized by the domination and servitude of bourgeois capitalism. If the referent of representational art had become ugly, one could accept this ugliness and depict it with minimal stylization (naturalism), ignore it and attempt the elaboration of a self-sufficient, esthetic universe that would relate to the outside world ironically (symbolism), or assert the abiding significance of humanistic creative endeavor despite the perils to which industrialization was subjecting it and make of one's work a continuous reconciliation of opposing forces (Ruskin). The underlying coherence of Ruskin's intellectual endeavor becomes apparent when one realizes that his critique of society is implicit in his structural analysis of pictorial composition. John Rosenberg has demonstrated that Ruskin's conception of composition—"the help of everything in the picture by everything else"—foreshadows the ideal of a benevolently patriarchal communistic government that was first formulated in *Unto This Last* (1860, the same year *Modern Painters* was completed).[11] To borrow Rosenberg's concise evaluation: "It is as impossible to abstract the moral tone from Ruskin's esthetic criticism as it is to isolate the esthetic overtone from his social criticism" (*The Darkening Glass*, 43). This merging and confusion of categories often entail a lack of methodological rigor, but also confer upon Ruskin's insights a metaphorical richness that cannot be reduced to the univocal simplicity of a prophetic dogmatism.

Yet even if one can understand Ruskin's broad synthesis of art and life without limiting it to a distinctly non-Proustian moralism, the image of Ruskin as a public figure capable of influencing his readers' taste and political philosophy remains a major stumbling block for critics who seek in him the potential initiator of Proust into the domain of theoretical awareness. What could the cork-lined room of Proust's final creative years possibly have in common with the Englishman's soapbox, or the involuted portrayal of psychological "laws" with the extroverted display of commonsense exhortation? We must examine two separate issues before answering these questions. On the one hand, it is necessary to dispel the myth that Ruskin's rhetoric was only directed outward toward some easily malleable audience, real or imagined; and on the other hand, we must trace the origins of Proust's insistence on the superiority of *innerness* in the creation and appreciation of literature. The first point is best understood if we juxtapose Ruskin's most intimate work, the autobiographical text *Praeterita* (1885–89), to certain aspects of the *Recherche* that it influenced. The second point will involve a lengthier development. We shall begin with an analysis of the logical patterns that characterize the argumentation of Ruskin's esthetic theory, then discuss how the split between artistic form and content expressed in these patterns caused Ruskin to refuse the immanence of fictional significance and turn toward a mode of discourse controlled by referential verifiability. In the case of Proust, the same discovery of a constitutive gap separating the message of art from its ornamental expressiveness led to widely divergent consequences, as we shall see in subsequent chapters.

## AUTOBIOGRAPHY

Ruskin wrote his autobiography in the waning years of his sanity, in an intellectual twilight interspersed by lapses into the madness that was to claim the last decade of his life. *Praeterita* is an account of "things past," but it is also a pathetic effort to ward off the demons of the present against which the book's organizational integrity had to defend itself. Ruskin's final meditations are surprisingly untouched by the anguish of the author's existential predicament. It is as if the act of writing possessed a magic power not only to open the doors of the past, but to close them against the threat of all conflict. In re-creating the strict, austere, orderly childhood paradise of Herne Hill, Ruskin luxuriates in a world of rediscovered sensations and impressions that his prose conveys with a limpid precision. From the patterns in a carpet to the almond blossoms of the meadow, all that is immediately present to the senses becomes matter for reflection, a *gift* for thought according to the French phrase, "tout cela donne à penser."

It is certainly not difficult to imagine why Proust is said to have memorized *Praeterita*.[12] Not only do the general tone and atmosphere of its pages foreshadow the side of Combray that is truly beyond time and removed from the vicissitudes of practical cares and concerns, but a wealth of details seems to have been taken over by Proust and inserted into his novel as an homage to his master. Tante Léonie may well owe a part of her literary existence to Ruskin's aunt, who lived in a strategically located small house on the main street of Croydon. Françoise, whose affection for the family she serves is accompanied by a strain of cruelty, is very close to Ruskin's nurse, Anne, a woman doubling as Angel of Mercy and "diabolic" agent:

> She [Anne] had a natural gift and specialty for doing disagreeable things; above all, the service of a sick room; so that she was never quite in her glory unless some of us were ill. She had also some parallel specialty for saying disagreeable things; and might be relied upon to give the extremely darkest view of any subject before proceeding to ameliorative action upon it. And she had a very creditable and republican aversion to doing immediately, or in set terms, what she was bid; so that when my mother and she got together, and my mother became very imperative and particular about having her teacup set on one side of her little round table, Anne would observantly and punctiliously put it always on the other; which caused my mother to state to me, every morning after breakfast, gravely, that if ever a woman in this world was possessed by the Devil, Anne was that woman.[13]

Other characters in the *Recherche* relate just as obviously to their counterparts in *Praeterita:* Marcel's mother to the mother of Ruskin; Swann to Mr. Telford (the close friend and business associate of Mr. Ruskin); Gilberte Swann to Clotilde Domecq, the daughter of the Europe-based member of the Ruskin sherry firm.[14] In these cases, Proust used the observations and descriptions of Ruskin to create much more complex fictional characters, but the nature of the protagonist's relationship to his mother, Swann, and Gilberte is not without an uncannily precise Ruskinian parallel.

There is no dramatic conflict as such in *Praeterita,* but the text is organized around one central polarity that is also a thematic pillar of the *Recherche:* the contrast between the intimate quietness of private contemplation and the exterior movement and discovery of travel. For Ruskin, to travel is to extend the purely abstract knowledge one possesses into the concreteness of the visible universe, which itself contains in various modes of availability or secretiveness the confirmation of the mind's intuitions. The impetus to leave one's secure dwelling derives from the intellectual curiosity that feeds upon samples of an artistic work whose completeness or essential truth must be found elsewhere. In *Praeterita* Mr. Telford is the mediator who, like Swann in the case of Marcel, provides Ruskin with the book that will challenge his sense of esthetic awareness and determine the course of his future endeavor:[15] Telford gives the young boy the illustrated edition of Rogers' *Italy* that contains examples of Turner's work. Some fifteen years later appeared, in defense of Turner's painting, the first volume of *Modern Painters,* but this occurred after Ruskin had been to Europe in an effort to retrace the footsteps of the man who, in his opinion, had reinvented art.

Ruskin was not content to view the production of Turner as a series of formal experiments; the critic's interest was not exclusively in the interrelationship of discrete elements within a painting considered as a whole, but also in the precise way in which the painting as statement or expression related to the "outside" of nature. It would be improper by Ruskinian standards to speak of the artistic rendition of natural beauty *as* a "whole," since the work of art exists in the mode of a relation and does not have the self-sustaining properties of an entity. *Praeterita* is a travel book in the common sense of the term, but it is also the recapitulation of a sum of ecstatic moments in which Ruskin sensed the perfect interpenetration of mind and nature, self and other, which he believed to be the transcendental condition of Turner's genius. Ruskin's stance as critic was by no means impartially analytic, and his understanding of artists is based as much on a subjective emotional identification as it is on an admirable knowledge of technical detail. *Praeterita* documents the dialectical process whereby Ruskin's search for truth in the correspondence of reality to its Turnerian representation became a communion with nature itself and a means for self-discovery that was simultaneously the confirmation of a vocation.

The initial reading of Rogers' *Italy,* which caused Ruskin to search for the sources of Turner's inspiration and thereby discover his own mission as art critic, is thus in itself an event of exemplary importance: "This book was the first means I had of looking carefully at Turner's work: and I might, not without some appearance of reason, attribute to the gift the entire direction of my life's energies (*Praeterita,* 29). Yet just as Ruskin the critic is not primarily concerned with the intricacies of painting or sculpture studied in abstract isolation, in the same way the autobiographer values the book he read as a child not in itself, but insofar as it leads outward, to the beauty contained in nature and more or less faithfully rendered by the artist. The act of reading is the first step in a process of esthetic initiation: it does not differ fundamentally in its structure or essence from the moment of revelation in nature that it foreshadows transparently. Thus when Ruskin describes his entrance into the Swiss Alps in 1833 and his feelings of awe in such dramatic surroundings, it is with the same emphasis on the fatality of his vocation: "I went down that evening from the garden-terrace of Schaffhausen with my destiny fixed in all of it that was to be sacred and useful. To that terrace, and the shore of the lake of Geneva, my heart and faith return to this day, in every impulse that is yet nobly alive in them, and every thought that has in it help or peace" (116). Two years later, at the Col de la Faucille, the overwhelming grandeur of the scenery "opened to me in distinct vision the Holy Land of my future work and true home in this world. My eyes had been opened, and my heart with them, to see and to possess royally such a kingdom" (167).

The monotonous regularity with which these impressions of euphoria repeat themselves, coupled with the inevitability of the powerful joy accompanying theoretic insight, leave little doubt as to the debt that the narrator of *Le Temps retrouvé* owes Ruskin in the formulation of those memory experiences (the uneven paving-stones, the starched napkin, the tinkling sound of a spoon against a dinner-plate, etc. [III, 866-69]) on which he grounds the future elaboration of his novel. Indeed, just as for Ruskin the encounter with natural phenomena merely confirms the images and words of Rogers' *Italy* and the truth value of Turnerian painting, in a similar manner but in reversed order the narrator of the *Recherche* uses the associative power of certain privileged signs and sensations of the world to prove that the receptive subject, in heeding their message, has in fact within his grasp the solid theoretical basis for his forthcoming writing. In both cases, the relationship between mind and nature, inside and outside, written word and significant landscape, is that of a metaphorical interpenetration and nonproblematic exchange of properties. This leads, in Ruskin and in Proust, to a fetishism of place. Since what the self projects onto reality exists in the mode of a self-confirming echo, it follows that each spot in nature has an identity or "individuality" corresponding to the emotion that awakened its human significance: "My romance was always ratified to me by the seal of locality and every charm of locality spiritualized by the glow and the passion of romance" (*Praeterita*, 94).

The structure of the *Recherche* as novel of self-discovery is a repetition and complication of the Ruskinian "seal of locality." In the beginning, Marcel dreams an imaginary world of names ("Noms de pays: le nom") and assumes that the Balbec or Venice of his thoughts can be found in the world. Then come travel and a series of confrontations between the imaginary and the real ("Noms de pays: le pays" and the Venice episode of *La Fugitive*) in which the *apprentissage* of the hero takes place. What separates Proust from Ruskin, making the *Recherche* a far more challenging and difficult work than the constantly affirmative *Praeterita*, is that the act of naming or dreaming as inner process assumes an independent evocative power (that of the *signifiant* set free from the constraints of the *signifié*), so that the juxtaposition of the imagined place to its real manifestation produces a distinctly non-Ruskinian destructive irony. In Ruskin and in Proust the mental acts of reading or dreaming involve the desire of referential verification, but in Proust this desire is more powerful and more often frustrated. One senses that the admirable unity of tone as well as the poetic coherence of *Praeterita* were achieved by means of a repression or censorship that Proust was unwilling to perform. The easy gratification of the ego's wishes in Ruskin's remembered world without conflict requires some explanation.

Critics of Ruskin have remarked unanimously that *Praeterita* is as noteworthy for what it excludes of the author's life as for what it contains.[16] Death, madness, and sexuality—the three "themes" that are so much in evidence as organizing principles of Ruskin's contradictory and often pathetic existence—are present in the autobiography only as insubstantial shadows. That their elimination from the book is a necessary precondition for the effective functioning of Ruskin's tranquil and somewhat languid prose is especially evident in the last chapter, "Joanna's Care." The penultimate chapter ("L'Esterelle") concludes with a faithfully copied letter addressed to Ruskin by Rose La Touche, the young girl with whom he was infatuated as an older man and who, after a period of religious fanaticism, anticipated the unfortunate end of her would-be lover by herself succumbing to madness; Ruskin then begins "Joanna's Care" as follows:

> The mischances which have delayed the sequence of *Praeterita*
> must modify somewhat also its intended order. I leave Rosie's letter to tell what it can of the beginning of happiest days; but omit,

> for a little while, the further record of them, —of the shadows
> which gathered around them, and increased, in my father's illness;
> and of the lightning which struck him down in death—so sudden,
> that I find it extremely difficult, in looking back, to realise the
> state of mind in which it left either my mother or me. (535)

Here, all is euphemism, omission, and the admission of the problems involved in facing the darker moments of life. The "mischances" which
caused Ruskin to take time from the composition of *Praeterita* were the
increasingly violent attacks of insanity that had drained him of almost all
creative energy. Rose's letter ("L'Esterelle," 529–32) does not so much
"tell of happy days" as it implies the impossibility of returning to the
childlike world in which Ruskin's erotic desires remained imprisoned. His
father's death, which did not entirely liberate Ruskin from a sense of middle-class financial responsibility and forced him into a role of authority
vis-à-vis his mother for which he was unprepared psychologically, stands
as the unstated central event around which the text weaves its poetry
of oblivion. Although this passage is perhaps more explicit and more extreme in its refusal to recognize existential conflict than some others, it is
nevertheless representative of *Praeterita* as a whole: it postulates the separation of unthinkable actions and wishes from the purity of esthetic
revelation that the book attempts to narrate in a series of jubilant subjective triumphs.

The suppression of spontaneity and instinctual satisfaction began early
for Ruskin, during the years of his carefully planned and guarded childhood under the tutelage of his mother. In the second chapter of *Praeterita*
("Herne-Hill Almond Blossoms") the author relates the rigorous early
education he received at home and judges it according to its positive and
negative effects in his subsequent life. Much of his analysis is recopied
from a well-known, highly personal passage of *Fors Clavigera,* the public
letters he addressed to the workingmen of England.[17] Every morning after
breakfast Mrs. Ruskin would isolate herself with her child for the purpose
of teaching him three chapters of the Bible. This regimen was never
allowed to be modified for any reason—interruption by servants or guests
were not tolerated—and as soon as the last dark prophecies of the Apoca-
lypse were reached, mother and son began again with Genesis. It is clear
to the reader of *Modern Painters* and *The Bible of Amiens* that these
morning sessions had a direct bearing on the author's later use of typological or allegorical interpretations of painting and literature. If, as
Harold Bloom says, Ruskin is a forerunner of the modern "myth" or
"archetypal" textual critcism as practiced by Northrop Frye and his disci-
ples,[18] it is amusing to speculate on how much this refined, technically
impressive mode of reading owes to the rather dour figure of Mrs. Ruskin.

But in the passage of *Praeterita* that describes the experience of the young Ruskin under the iron grip of his mother's faith, the emphasis falls not on what was to be gained intellectually from the exercise of interpretation, but on the unpleasantness of "the long hours of toil, as regular as sunrise" during which learning was "forced" upon the child (41).

The discussion of the Bible-reading sessions leads into what is no doubt the most personal, self-consciously lucid pages of the autobiography, in which Ruskin quite literally counts his blessings and examines the "calamities" and "evils" (44) of his upbringing. The three principal gifts he received from his parents he calls Peace, Obedience, and Faith, all of which tended toward a harmonious if formal family bond; the negative effects he recognizes as follows: "I had nothing to love. . . . I had nothing to endure. . . . I was taught no precision nor etiquette of manners. . . . Lastly, and chief of evils. My judgment of right and wrong and powers of independent action were left entirely undeveloped" (45-46). Because his parents were not objects of affection but, as Ruskin says in a striking comparison, "visible powers of nature to me, no more loved than the sun and the moon" (44), the author's inability to function sexually in his disastrous marriage to Effie Gray and his regressive, idealized "passion" for young girls like Rose La Touche become psychologically coherent within the mental logic of his formative years. The other "evils" mentioned by Ruskin, like loss of love, all tend toward some form of paralysis of the self or weakening of the will. An excess of protection produced "the most analytic mind in Europe"[19] and one of the most unhappy of Victorian gentlemen.

Like all authentic autobiographies, *Praeterita* is an attempt to come to terms with the problem of sources and origins. In Ruskin's case, the question that his book sets out to answer could be paraphrased thus: "How did I become an analytic thinker; what caused me to choose criticism as my manner of relating to the world and its representations?" The narrative development that begins with the gift of Rogers' *Italy* and continues with various European travel experiences apparently answers this question, in that it depicts the ecstasies of theoretic understanding in the mode of spiritual revelation. Ruskin discovers the transcendental significance of art in its correspondence to the powerful attractiveness of nature, then decides to devote his intellectual skills to the clarification of such a correspondence. In this sense, the story of *Praeterita* can be said to unfold organically from the kernel awareness of destiny's call, while the exposition of facts and events in Ruskin's life unrelated to the higher plane of artistic vocation are left in the background. But as we have just observed in reading the passage on the Bible and parental influence, the choice of vocation might also be explained negatively, in psychological terms of repression and sublimation—terms whose importance the major flow of the narrative repeatedly denies. The pages on the mother-son bond appear in the text as an unabsorbed residue of family romance which, like a seed falling on rocky ground, is not allowed to attain fruition. *Praeterita* renders antiseptically abstract the double grounding of Ruskin's genius in esthetic aspiration and the madness born of extreme culpability. By separating and isolating the germ of this madness, the autobiography does not remove it, but only emphasizes its persistent presence as the absent center that the text covers in a blanket of deceptively tranquil explanatory prose.

Readers of Proust know the importance of Marcel's struggle to attain the integrity of selfhood in a universe dominated by the protectiveness of maternal figures. Like Mrs. Ruskin educating her son, the grandmother and the mother of the protagonist, well aware of the latter's nervous constitution, attempt to divert and control his emotional excesses. As the narrator says, "Elles m'aimaient assez pour ne pas consentir à m'épargner de la souffrance, elles voulaient m'apprendre à la dominer afin de diminuer ma sensibilité nerveuse et fortifier ma volonté" (I, 37). This description occurs within a highly dramatized scene toward the beginning of "Combray" that associates the mother-son relationship with the act of reading and which, like its parallel passage in *Praeterita,* involves a discussion of the negative consequences resulting from the parental choice of a given disciplinary code. I am referring to the well-known "scène du baiser" in which Marcel manages a bit of sentimental blackmail in coercing his mother to abandon her principles of childrearing for an evening and spend the night in his room. The Proustian scene is an exact reversal of its Ruskinian counterpart, in that both father and mother give in to the wishes of their son; but this subversion of the rules does not produce joy in the mind of the child: "J'aurais dû être heureux; je ne l'étais pas. Il me semblait que ma mère venait de me faire une première concession qui devait lui être douloureuse, que c'était une première abdication de sa part devant l'idéal qu'elle avait conçu pour moi" (I, 38). Whereas Ruskin felt he could criticize, with some justification, the barriers his parents placed between his wishes and their fulfillment, Marcel regrets the ease with which his desires find their target.

The scene of the reluctantly granted kiss is complex and deserves a detailed psychoanalytical interpretation:[20] for our purposes of comparison, some general conclusions will have to suffice. In *Praeterita,* the act of reading was described as taking place in an atmosphere of severity and emotional reserve. The role of the mother was to inculcate in her son certain firm and dogmatic beliefs; his role, to absorb them without discussion. Reading was equivalent to knowledge in the most general sense and completely divorced from the domain of eros. The scene of reading as such had an exemplary significance for Ruskin, who found in it the concentrated essence of the sentimental poverty from which he was to suffer in later years. In "Combray," the order of narrative development is inverted. The "abdication" of parental authority is presented first, as the logical precondition for the representation of reading, which then takes place in an ambiance of freely circulating desires whose goal is the lifting of the taboo on incest. To calm her son's anguish, the mother reads to him from George Sand's *François le Champi* before going to sleep in a bed next to his. That Sand's novel tells the story of an orphan boy, adopted and loved by a woman whose sentiments for him are not merely maternal, only serves to emphasize the strong unconscious resonance of Proust's text.[21] The physical concreteness of the reading experience is conveyed by a lovely description of the mother's soothing voice, in which the narrator stresses the unifying, harmonizing movement of her phrasing: "Elle . . . dirigeait la phrase qui finissait vers celle qui allait commencer, tantôt pressant, tantôt ralentissant la marche des syllabes pour les faire entrer, quoique leurs quantités fussent différentes, dans un rythme uniforme, elle insufflait à cette prose si commune une sorte de vie sentimentale et continue" (I, 43). The unconscious wish of the protagonist is to be reenveloped in the soft firmness of this protective breath, to find again the "uniform rhythm" of life that his mother originally breathed into him.

The final difference between the Proustian meditation on origins and its purified, repressed Ruskinian parallel is that the "scène du baiser" does not remain isolated and undeveloped, but generates a series of repeated, structurally identical passages that all derive from the power of its obsessional core. Thus the emblematic narrow panel separating the grandmother's bed from Marcel's in Balbec, the refusal and subsequent granting of kisses by Albertine, the generalized anxiety that characterizes Proustian love as jealousy—all emanate from the exacerbated desires awakened in nocturnal Combray. *A la recherche du temps perdu,* in elliptical fashion, has two focal points: the madeleine and the kiss. The madeleine articulates all euphoric discoveries of artistic truth, thereby repeating in a specifically Proustian register the privileged moments of Ruskin's Alpine experiences. The kiss organizes a darker but no less important cycle of frustrated desire and probing of elusive signs that Ruskin could not include, for fear of succumbing to madness. *Praeterita* is an artificial uniformity of statement; the *Recherche* is a sinking into duplicity and ambivalence. The *Recherche* overcomes the various forms of *pudeur,* psychological and stylistic, that kept Proust's youthful writings from corresponding to the depth of their author's potential; *Praeterita,* on the other hand, is beautiful only superficially, and is in fact a regression from the theoretical insights of its creator as developed in earlier treatises. Ruskin found ambivalence and entered the contradictions of artistic production not as autobiographer, but as critic. We must examine his method of criticism if we are to understand the precise nature of his influence on Proust.

## CRITICISM AND CREATION

Ruskin's importance as theorist of poetry and painting is universally acknowledged today, and his position within the coherent intellectual context of English Romanticism is easily demonstrable. He was not so much an originator of concepts as a synthesizer of tendencies within the domain of esthetics that might appear contradictory and mutually exclusive at first sight. The best general description of Ruskin's critical stance has been made, quite concisely, by René Wellek: "Ruskin tries to combine naturalism and symbolism: a worship of nature even in its minutest aspects with a supernaturalism which allows a 'typical,' or, as we say, 'emblematic,' 'symbolic' representation of nature."[22] The choice of Turner as embodiment of the ideal artist in *Modern Painters* illuminates this theoretical point of view, in that, according to Ruskin, Turner neither slavishly imitates natural fact nor indulges in artificial stylization. Ruskin often insisted upon the necessity of detailed scientific observation in painting, and the chapters on mineralogy, geology, and atmospherics that swell the volume of *Modern Painters* leave no doubt as to the fundamental place of "naturalism" in his esthetic credo. But technical mastery is always subordinated to the higher purpose of the work's expressive qualities, its ability to convey a moral message. The content of this message was not a matter of indifference to Ruskin, who in the earlier years of his critical activity emphasized the religious thoughts that he found expressed in works of art, and who, in his later, more disenchanted years, concentrated on the humanistic or social value of painting, architecture, and sculpture, sometimes with a peculiar blindness to the specificity of artistic form.

It is not difficult, from our postmodernist perspective, to find fault with Ruskin's critical theories, since they imply a subservience of style to content and on certain occasions prescribe the kind of content that is most suitable for representation. Today, it is more fashionable to say that form *is* content, that any distinction between the two words is itself the expression of a reactionary academic philosophy, and, as a corollary, that the choice of theme or subject is in itself arbitrary, aleatory, contingent.[23] Such notions constitute an attempt to overcome our heritage from Romanticism, to escape from the prison of exalted selfhood in which creative man seems to have confined himself for a century and a half. But it would be wrong to assume that Ruskin merely restated the tenets of Romantic thought and that one could be justified in reducing his criticism to the status of an historically interesting document that we can view now in Olympian detachment since it no longer engages our interest as postmoderns. It is true that Ruskin's theories of art are best understood contextually, as an expression of a certain well-defined intellectual movement, but what emerges from an interpretation of his most perceptive writings is that he was prophetically aware of the potentially self-destructive seeds within the program of "organic" art. Furthermore, he set forth for us, in schematic form, the very real difficulties to be faced in any attempt at bypassing the rhetorical ambiguities on which Romanticism is predicated.

In the first volume of *Modern Painters* Ruskin's emphasis on the primordial function of content as opposed to the outward appearance of artistic phenomena is evident, obvious, and somewhat overstated. Beginning with the supposition that all great art not only communicates various representations of beauty to man, but also influences and, in the best cases, molds the moral dimension of his existence, Ruskin writes: "It appears to me that a rude symbol is oftener more efficient than a refined one in touching the heart, and that as pictures rise in rank as works of art, they are regarded with less devotion and more curiosity" (*Modern Painters I*, 21). Although stated in the form of a questionable and crude generalization, this observation is a foreshadowing of Ruskin's later abandonment of esthetics in favor of social issues. What purpose remains in the study of art if art no longer speaks to the "heart" of man, if it has become excessively (narcissistically) concerned with itself? A later passage in the same volume is just as categorical: "The picture which has the nobler and more numerous ideas, however awkwardly expressed, is a greater and a better picture than that which has the less noble and less numerous ideas, however beautifully expressed" (91). It is necessary to remember these unqualified assertions because they form the unrefined basis from which Ruskin then elaborates the more complex and intellectually convincing theory of esthetics contained in the second volume of *Modern Painters.*

Just as the "rude symbol" was considered by Ruskin superior to the "refined" products of advanced art, just as noble and numerous ideas were given precedence over elegant expressiveness, in the same way the entire theoretical construction of *Modern Painters II* is organized around a series of polar opposites in which the appreciation of the sensual, formal, "outward" qualities of a work is judged intrinsically inferior to the activity of the interpreting consciousness that penetrates beyond the surface of appearance into the very essence of creativity. The distinction we have already encountered, between *aesthesis* ("mere animal consciousness" of beauty) and *theoria* ("exulting, reverent, grateful perception" of the beautiful) (*Modern Painters II,* 47), subtends Ruskin's dialectics of esthetic judgment based upon the active interplay of subject and object. The goal of the observing subject is to intuit the origin of the object's existence *as* artifact and to achieve communication with the Intelligence responsible for the interpretive activity as such: "It is necessary to the existence of an idea of beauty, that the sensual pleasure which may be its basis, should be accompanied first with joy, then with love of the object, then with the perception of kindness in a superior Intelligence, finally with thankfulness towards that Intelligence itself . . . no idea can be at all considered as in any way an idea of beauty, until it be made up of these emotions, any more than we can be said to have an idea of a letter of which we perceive the perfume and the fair writing, without understanding the contents of it, or intent of it" (48-49). Here, the *signifiant* has no value in itself, but receives its teleological justification from the assumed wholeness of a *signifié transcendental.* According to this system, each individual object on the earth must be studied carefully, since its envelope or outer shell relates analogously to an inner core that is itself the sign and proof of God's plan for man. Ruskin's impatience with the mere exteriority of artistic ornamentation arises from his belief that a natural tendency of fallen man is to be deceived, like Eve and Adam, by the seductions of an attractive brilliance. Thus, when Ruskin introduces the most famous and consequential of Romantic theoretical distinctions—between fancy and imagination—he is only repeating the polarity of *theoria* and *aesthesis,* emphasizing once again the inferiority of outwardness as such. Borrowing from Wordsworth and most explicitly from Leigh Hunt,[24] he writes: "The fancy uses the outside, and is able to give a portrait of the outside, clear, brilliant, and full of detail. The imagination sees the heart and inner nature, and makes them felt, but is often obscure, mysterious, and interrupted, in its giving of outer detail" (253).

Ruskin's discussion of fancy and imagination occurs as the consequence of an exegesis: the critic juxtaposes two descriptive passages, the one from Milton, the other from Dante, both of which deal with the image and effect of fire. In a short but well-argued analysis, he contrasts Milton's emphasis on detail and "externals" to Dante's "slight touch," which does not give us "fuel, sublimation, smoke, and singeing . . . the images only of partial combustion" but "pure, white, hurtling, formless flame . . . lambent annihilation" (250).[25] In reaching the heart of things, Dante's poetic power is that of a *penetration,* or, in other terms, a *possession-taking* (251). Imagination is not rational but intuitive, and resembles the work of magic. Only the creative mind is capable of such possession, whereas critical intelligence lags far behind and must be content with a kind of retrospective gleaning: "Every sentence [of imaginative poets], as it has been thought out from the heart, leads us to the centre, and then leaves us to gather what we may; it is the Open Sesame of a huge, obscure, endless cave, with inexhaustible treasures of pure gold scattered in it: the wandering about and gathering the pieces may be left to any of us, all can accomplish that; but the first opening of that invisible door in the rock is of the imagination only" (252). One is reminded of the *Arabian Nights* theme in Proust and of its constant association with artistic creation and discovery.[26] A subsequent observation in the same chapter—that the "play and power of imagination" depend on "our being able to forget ourselves and enter like possessing spirits into the bodies of things about us" (287)—foreshadows the madeleine episode of the *Recherche,* in which the narrator finds plausible the "Celtic belief" in the transmigration of souls.[27] In the fifth chapter of this book the problem of Proustian selfhood will emerge from an examination of the Romantic imagination as it relates to the psychologically significant desires of penetration and magical possession. For the time being it is sufficient to note that what was for Ruskin an issue of critical theory became for Proust a matter of conviction from which the "superstitious" tone of his novel's esthetic revelations derives.

The central purpose of the second volume of *Modern Painters* is to define the beautiful and describe its relationship to man. Since the esthetic object has an intentional energy—the capacity to signal its meaning and lead man to the act of interpretation (which, as we have seen, involves the discovery of a divine plan imprinted in natural phenomena)—the temptation might be to postulate a necessary link between the realm of the beautiful and the psychology of the observing subject. Indeed, the moments of beatitude Ruskin experienced in Europe in his "imitation" of Turner were not the accessory effects of a beautiful landscape, but the proof of beauty's power, its realization and humanization. Yet the theoretically rigorous fourth chapter of *Modern Painters II,* "Of False Opinions Held Concerning Beauty," attempts to distinguish the beautiful from the true, the useful, custom, and association. In so doing Ruskin is faithful to the Kantian paradigm of critical practice, which consists of isolating and defining the areas of human mental capabilities before analyzing them into constituent parts. The result of this method in its Ruskinian guise is to objectify beauty and remove it from any interference with subjective impressions. George Landow has written cogently on the contradictory theoretical positions taken by Ruskin at various points in his career, and has hypothesized that the objectification of beauty was performed in order to lend coherence to an esthetic system, whereas in later writings, when Ruskin was truer to his personal feelings, an undeniable emotional subjectivism reemerged.[28] That is, the true, the useful, custom, and association were banished from an interaction with the beautiful in *Modern Painters II* largely for the sake of argument, but later tended to surface and mix in an impure, anti-Kantian amalgamation of categories as Ruskin turned from theory to more intimate and rhetorically complex forms of discourse.

This turn or shift may not simply be an indication of one critic's idio-syncracies; it may be that criticism itself, as theoretical activity, necessarily remains on the far side of penetrative imagination insofar as it functions by "discrimination"[29] and logical dismemberment. Creation, on the other hand, the opening of unforseen doors, takes place within and through the confusion of categories, and owes its quasi-magical powers to a suspension or "prorogation" (Proust) of the very possibility of categorization/classifi-cation. Without sharing the questionable value judgment implicit in Ro-mantic theory that creation is of itself superior to criticism, we shall pursue the idea that the former is the inversion or reversal of the latter, a troubling mirror image of rational thought whose relationship to its logical source is hidden under the mask of "originality." A case in point is the manipulation of "custom" and "association" in Proust's novel: dis-carded by Ruskin as inimical to theoretical coherence, these two forces function with the inevitable regularity of recurrent themes in the *Re-cherche*. Because they have the potential of theoretical obfuscation, they produce textual complexity and cause the novel to thrive upon its own self-generating contradictions.

According to Ruskin, custom "has a twofold operation: the one to deaden the frequency and force of repeated impressions, the other to en-dear the familiar object to the affections" (68). In the fictional universe of the *Recherche* the "twofold operation" of custom (*habitude*) helps define the essentially defensive way in which the protagonist relates to an outside world perceived as threatening in its initial appearance. Thus, when Marcel arrives at the Grand Hôtel in Balbec for the first time (*A l'Ombre des jeunes filles en fleurs,* "Noms de pays: le pays"), he must adjust to the un-familiar objects in his room; or as Proust puts it more dramatically, the protagonist must "make room for himself" in a space filled with things that do not "know" him: "C'est notre attention qui met des objets dans une chambre, et l'habitude qui les y retire et nous y fait de la place. De la place, il n'y en avait pas pour moi dans ma chambre de Balbec (mienne de nom seulement), elle était pleine de choses qui ne me connaissaient pas, me rendirent le coup d'oeil méfiant que je leur jetai et, sans tenir aucun compte de mon existence, témoignèrent que je dérangeais le train-train de la leur" (I, 666). If Marcel feels such a sense of alienation in his new quarters at Balbec, it is because the first step of the double process of habit—the deadening of impressions—has not yet had time to take place here. He still senses the presence of objects *as* objects; they have not yet become an extension of his subjectivity. His anguish is rendered more acute by the remembrance of his former room in Combray, where the second step of the process had been accomplished long since: familiar objects had been "endeared to the affections" and had taken on an anesthetizing quality.

The theme of habit is linked closely to the problematic constitution of the self within a reality that tends to be full of unpleasant surprises: logically, it is at work whenever Marcel travels, since travel implies an encounter with the unknown. But habit is also intimately bound up with the functioning of Proustian love, which itself depends upon the complex interaction of memory and forgetfulness. To "love" someone in the Proustian manner is not to lose oneself in that person, but to attain a state of tranquillity equivalent to the narcotic force of habit by reducing the beloved's essence to a series of completely known elements. If one lives long enough with someone who remains predictable, then the deadening of impressions can lead, smoothly enough, to a kind of endearment or affection. But if this precarious affection becomes dull through disuse, the rational mind of the loving subject can conclude that his mistress in indifferent to him. He falls out of love by forgetting the very process that made him fall in love in the first place. He does not remember that his present psychological calm depends upon the web of habit that he has woven around his beloved; once she is gone, the web collapses and the subject recognizes his solitude, which is absolute. This is what happens at the beginning of *La Fugitive,* after Françoise announces that Albertine has fled her elegant prison:

> Oui, tout à l'heure, avant l'arrivée de Françoise, j'avais cru que je n'aimais plus Albertine, j'avais cru ne rien laisser de côté, en exact analyste; j'avais cru bien connaître le fond de mon coeur. . . . Je m'étais trompé en croyant voir clair dans mon coeur. Mais cette connaissance, que ne m'auraient pas donnée les plus fines perceptions de l'esprit, venait de m'être apportée, dure, éclatante, étrange, comme un sel cristallisé, par la brusque réaction de la douleur. J'avais une telle *habitude* d'avoir Albertine auprès de moi, et je voyais soudain un nouveau visage de *l'Habitude.* Jusqu'ici je l'avais considérée surtout comme un pouvoir annihilateur qui supprime l'originalité et jusqu'à la conscience des perceptions; maintenant je la voyais comme une divinité redoutable, si rivée à nous, son visage insignifiant si incrusté dans notre coeur, que si elle se détache, si elle se détourne de nous, cette déité que nous ne distinguions presque pas, nous inflige des souffrances plus terribles qu'aucune et qu'alors elle est aussi cruelle que la mort. (III, 420; my emphasis)

Habit is treated allegorically in this passage, as a personified abstraction that appears in different, apparently contradictory forms. Hence the distinction between "une telle habitude d'avoir Albertine auprès de moi" (an illustration of habit's anesthetizing quality) and the capitalized "nouveau visage de *l'Habitude*" which subsumes all of habit's powers within one denomination. The same distinction is made in a vertiginously playful way at the beginning of "Noms de pays: le pays" when the narrator foreshadows the importance of the Balbec episode as the shifting of place necessary to his "convalescence" from a now faded love for Gilberte:

> Mais cette souffrance et ce regain d'amour pour Gilberte ne furent pas plus longs que ceux qu'on a en rêve, et cette fois, au contraire, parce qu'à Balbec l'Habitude ancienne n'était plus là pour les faire durer. Et si ces effets de l'Habitude semblent contradictoires, c'est qu'elle obéit à des lois multiples. A Paris j'étais devenu de plus en plus indifférent à Gilberte, grâce à l'Habitude. Le changement d'habitude, c'est-à-dire la cessation momentanée de l'Habitude, paracheva l'oeuvre de l'Habitude quand je partis pour Balbec. Elle affaiblit mais stabilise, elle amène la désagrégation mais la fait durer indéfiniment. Chaque jour depuis des années je calquais tant bient que mal mon état d'âme sur celui de la veille. A Balbec un lit nouveau à côté duquel on m'apportait le matin un petit déjeuner différent de celui de Paris, ne devait plus soutenir les pensées dont s'était nourri mon amour pour Gilberte: il y a des cas (assez rares, il est vrai) où, la sédentarité immobilisant les jours, le meilleur moyen de gagner du temps, c'est de changer de place. Mon voyage à Balbec fut comme la première sortie d'un convalescent qui n'attendait plus qu'elle pour s'apercevoir qu'il est guéri. (I, 643-44)

A change of habit (or momentary suspension of Habit's laws) causes a transformation in the protagonist's sentiments, or rather, confirms that his feelings for Gilberte have run their course. This is accomplished by the sudden elimination of all memory associations that had kept the young girl's image artificially alive in the Parisian context. The two-page passage leading up to the paragraph on Habit just quoted is a complicated Proustian variation on the theme of accidental idea association that Ruskin defines thus: "The accidental connection of ideas and memories with material things, owing to which those material things are regarded as agreeable or otherwise, according to the nature of the feelings or recollections they summon: the association being commonly involuntary and often times so vague that no distinct image is suggested by the object, but we feel a painfulness in it or pleasure from it, without knowing wherefore" (71-72). If we substitute for the words "material things" the expression "love-object," we have a definition of Proustian love. If we make no substitution but interpret Ruskin's ideas literally, we have a textual echo of Marcel's predilection for involuntary memory—the associative process that grounds the *Recherche* in the instant of a self-discovery.

For a critic whose explicit purpose, in *Modern Painters II*, was the delineation of beauty in isolation from the vicissitudes of subjective involvement, Ruskin was extraordinarily aware of the subject's capacity to project powerful emotions onto objects which, later, through memory, would *seem* beautiful or ugly, according to their original mental or visual context:

> Let the eye but rest on a rough piece of branch of curious form during a conversation with a friend, rest, however unconsciously, and though the conversation be forgotten, though every circumstance connected with it be as utterly lost to memory as though it had not been, yet the eye will, through the whole life after take a certain pleasure in such boughs which it had not before, a pleasure so slight, a trace of feeling so delicate as to leave us utterly unconscious of its peculiar power, but undestroyable by any reasoning, a part, thenceforward, of our constitution, destroyable only by the same arbitrary process of association by which it was created. Reason has no effect on it whatsoever. (72–73)

According to Ruskin's precise formula, the process of accidental idea association is entirely arbitrary. The presence of a friend and a curiously formed branch in the same place confers upon the branch an emotional aura it would not have otherwise; the rhetorical figure played out here is metonymy, or contingent juxtaposition. But as Proust was to demonstrate in numerous sections of his novel, the subject *feels* this relationship not in its factual contingency, but in the mode of necessity—that is, within the totalizing and unifying scheme of metaphor. What Proust calls "love" is the subjective mystification that consists of changing a metonymy into a metaphor through a series of figural transfers whose deceptive transitional fluidity takes on a properly narrative form. The disillusionment that follows upon and concludes the original infatuation involves an analytic moment in which the subject discovers the error he had made in falsely assuming the necessity of what was a chance association. This is the case for Swann, who, after loving Odette because of her resemblance to Botticelli's depiction of Jethro's daughter, ultimately finds that has wasted his time chasing a phantom.

Critical awareness of the rhetorical fallacy whereby idea association constructs a syntagmatic fictional chain called "love" leads to a radical questioning of love's existence as identifiable totality. Since emotions can be attached arbitrarily to any charming fact, then evolve away from their object, how can one affirm the "reality" of what is in fact a constantly metamorphosing sentimental flux? In the opening pages of "Noms de pays: le pays" Proust writes:

J'étais arrivé à une presque indifférence à l'égard de Gilberte,
quand deux ans plus tard je partis avec ma grand'mère pour Balbec.
Quand je subissais le charme d'un visage nouveau, quand c'était à
l'aide d'une autre jeune fille que j'espérais connaître les cathédrales
gothiques, les palais et les jardins de l'Italie, je me disais triste-
ment que notre amour, en tant qu'il est l'amour d'une certaine créature, n'est peut-être pas bien réel, puisque, si des associations
de rêveries agréables ou douloureuses peuvent le lier pendant quelque temps à une femme jusqu'à nous faire penser qu'il a été in-
spiré par elle d'une façon nécessaire, en revanche si nous nous
dégageons volontairement ou à notre insu de ces associations, cet
amour, comme s'il était au contraire spontané et venait de nous
seul, renaît pour se donner à une autre femme. (I, 642)

For Proust, custom (*habitude*) and association provide the narrating subject with ways of neutralizing the hostilities of reality and imprisoning
objects of beauty in the circuitous logic of his discourse; yet both of these
processes, when revealed in their internal structure, prove threatening to
the stability of a unified and self-contained consciousness. The suspension
of Habit means pain and solitude. To understand the workings of association is to be confronted with the total gratuitousness and unreality of love
as well as the fragmentation of the mind into separate individual "selves"
corresponding to the potentially endless procession of easily substitutable
love objects. These mental mechanisms, in producing pathos, also produce
narrative. Because Proust does not believe in the disinterested contemplation of beauty, because he sees beauty as the metaphorical illusion of a
highly *interested* subject, the fiction of the *Recherche* can tell the story of
the construction/deconstruction of that illusion, repeating it as long as its
arbitrarily necessary episodic organization will allow. Proust's novel then
becomes a plunge into the rhetorical embarrassment (entanglement,
*enchevêtrement*) that Ruskin's critical theory explicitly avoided and condemned.[30]

Ruskin's critique of the emotional projective powers that falsify reality
was not confined to his elimination of custom and association from the
domain of beauty in his early theoretical work. After *Modern Painters II*
the same critique appears in varying guises, but always with the apparent
purpose of safeguarding the esthetic object from overinterpretation or
protecting the expressivity of poetic language from excessive authorial
self-indulgence. The duty of the painter should be to respect the formal
integrity of natural phenomena without "reading into them"; the role of
the poet should be to restrict his metaphorical discourse to a decorous
minimum. No doubt the most coherent and analytically convincing

exposition of these ideas occurs in the well-known twelfth chapter of *Modern Painters III* (1856), entitled "Of the Pathetic Fallacy." Ruskin begins by differentiating between "the ordinary, proper, and true appearances of things to us, and the extraordinary, or false appearances, when we are under the influence of emotion, or contemplative fancy; false appearances, I say, as being entirely unconnected with any real power or character in the object, and only imputed to it by us" (*Modern Painters III*, 204). The first example of the pathetic fallacy given by Ruskin is a classical case of mental projection in which a subject's violent emotions are transferred to nature: "They rowed her in across the rolling foam—/The cruel, crawling foam." In these lines from Kingsley's *Alton Locke*, the foam is humanized. Ruskin comments: "The foam is not cruel, neither does it crawl. The state of mind which attributes to it these characters of a living creature is one in which the reason is unhinged by grief" (205). Ruskin later postulates that the greatest poets generally do not give in to such outbursts of overruling passion, whereas the "second order of poets" is most generously prone to such excess. To illustrate this point, he contrasts a passage from Dante to a description by Coleridge, both of which use leaves in an evocative or emblematic way:

> When Dante describes the spirits falling from the bank of Acheron "as dead leaves flutter from a bough," he gives the most perfect image possible of their utter lightness, feebleness, passiveness, and scattering agony of despair, without, however, for an instant losing his own clear perception that *these* are souls and *those* are leaves: he makes no confusion of one with the other. But when Coleridge speaks of
>
> > "The one red leaf, the last of its clan,
> > That dances as often as dance it can,"
>
> he has a morbid, that is to say, a so far false, idea about the leaf: he fancies a life in it, and will, which there are not; confuses its powerlessness with choice, its fading death with merriment, and the wind that shakes it with music. (206-7)

In explicitly stating his preference for simile over metaphor, Ruskin opts for the mode of *illustration,* in which the clarity of distinction is preserved. We know that Dante conceived of the leaves as a poetic device to exemplify the characteristics of homeless souls: through his comparison, the author of *The Divine Comedy* adds to the reader's understanding of the plight that awaits the unsaved. Poetry contributes to knowledge precisely insofar as it separates tenor from vehicle, subordinating imagistic function to the fullness of meaning. The "confusion" that Ruskin finds in Coleridge results from the semantic constitution of metaphor. Tenor and vehicle merge to form a combined unit of meaning: from this melted significant totality the reader must then derive each constituent *sème* in an act of analysis. Coleridge does not provide us with two elements, leaves and souls, where the former is merely illustrative of the latter. He gives us a "red leaf" whose symbolic potential is apparent from the beginning, but whose precise significance can be determined only through examination of a wider context. What truly disturbs Ruskin is that the leaf of Coleridge, in attracting attention to itself, suspends the act of understanding: we live with the poetic image for a long time and enjoy this cohabitation, deriving from a confusion of categories the kind of pleasure that Ruskin finds suspect. As we shall see in the fourth chapter of this study, the confusions of the pathetic fallacy, like those of idea association, belong to the ravelling/unravelling movement of Proustian narrative; for the present, we will limit ourselves to an examination of the semiological implications, within Ruskin's esthetic system, of subjective immersion in the surface beauty of artistic forms.

Although Ruskin's expression "second order of poets" generally designates the Romantics—Wordsworth, Coleridge, and other exponents of the pathetic fallacy—it would be wrong to limit the inherent anthropomorphism of metaphorical discourse to the nineteenth century and consider it an aberrant, essentially "modern" deviation from the truths expressed in Dante, Milton, and Shakespeare. For Ruskin, the fall into figural confusion has a coherent history whose source lies far removed from modernity, and this history is itself the temporal component of a linguistic sign structure. It is in *The Stones of Venice* (1851-53), Ruskin's most powerfully rhetorical work, that we find a sustained allegorical narrative telling of an original semantic integrity and its gradual degradation.[31] In the beginning, before the printed word could be circulated widely by the press, cathedrals like St. Mark's in Venice were quite literally a "Book of Common Prayer," a "poor man's Bible" (*The Stones of Venice II*, 129). Statues and inscriptions and windows functioned in the manner of Dante's simile: they illustrated a transcendental message that had the power and evidence of revealed truth. The relative lack of technical refinement in the cathedral ornamentation of the Middle Ages in fact enhances the communicative ability of what Ruskin called elsewhere "rude symbols."

When the Christian of the Middle Ages "read" his church, his solidly grounded beliefs encountered their representation in the transparency of an immediately understandable artistic form. According to this scheme, the *signifiant* effaces itself in favor of the *signifié*, which is the true center of the believer's concentrated attention. But with the beginning of the Renaissance (the historical period which, for Ruskin, is synonymous with

a decline in artistic values) the interrelationship of sign and meaning is
exactly reversed. Loss of faith entails an interest in the seduction of
colors and forms for their own sake, and a consequent disinterest in the
universal theological guarantees of significance. This turn toward the
*signifiant,* which, as we saw in the "leaves" of Coleridge, generates a
poetically (metaphorically) productive confusion of categories, is given
the religious name of *idolatry* in *The Stones of Venice II.* [32] Idolatry is a
diversion of the mind of the beholder from the represented object's meaning to the artist's compositional skill, where admiration takes the place of
devotion. In this sense, St. Mark's is the cathedral of idolatry, or more precisely, a place of entangled images that envelops the spectator in a web of
beauty beyond which it is difficult to see the unifying purpose of God.
After describing the dramatic character of the cathedral's chiaroscuro
lighting, Ruskin evokes the actual experience of walking through the edifice's maze of representations:

> Under foot and over head, a continual succession of crowded
> imagery, one picture passing into another, as in a dream; forms
> beautiful and terrible mixing together; dragons and serpents,
> and ravening beasts of prey, and graceful birds that in the midst of
> them drink from running fountains and feed from vases of crys-
> tal; the passions and pleasures of human life symbolized together,
> and the mystery of its redemption; for the mazes of interwoven
> lines and changeful pictures lead always at last to the Cross, lifted
> and carved in every place and upon every stone; sometimes with
> the serpent of eternity wrapt round it, sometimes with doves be-
> neath its arms, and sweet herbiage growing forth from its feet; but
> conspicuous most of all the great rood that crosses the church
> before the altar, raised in bright blazonry against the shadow of the
> apse. (88-89)

The admirable evocative quality of Ruskin's description derives from an
"idolatrous" intermingling of forms. Although the conscious purpose of
the passage is to show that the Cross is everywhere present and visible as
the totalizing, subsuming power of the redeeming divinity, in fact the passage owes its considerable poetic persuasiveness to the very process of
"mixing" and "interweaving" it explicitly condemns. Such a text thrives
upon the error it denounces: it is, on the level of self-representation, a
struggle between significant unity and rhetorical complexity, between the
dominance of a *signifié transcendental* and the deconstruction of this
dominance through the irresponsible play of the liberated sign. Here,
Ruskin becomes a fiction-maker, an image producer despite himself. In
wrapping the serpent of eternity around the symbol of Christ, in placing

doves and sweet herbiage in the midst of its glory, his words, like the edifice they imitate, combine a critical knowledge of the "falseness" of poetic effects with the creative exploitation of this falseness in the guise of ornamental beauty.

The depth of Proust's intellectual indebtedness to Ruskin cannot be measured by a list, however exhaustive, of parallel themes, or by an analysis, however precise, of stylistic parody. Theme and style are surface effects that divert critical attention from the semiological core of both writers' preoccupations. In Ruskin's case, the original wholeness of meaning that he found in the artistic universe of the Middle Ages and that presupposed a theocentric, transcendentally grounded system of analogies, gradually gave way to a splitting of the sign into two noncommunicating parts, or, in Saussurian terminology, to a differentiation between *signifiant* and *signifié* in which excessive attention to the former was given the negatively valued terms of "pathetic fallacy" and "idolatry." Ruskin, in preferring the clarity and explicitness of simile to the melted significant unity of metaphor, was expressing the ideal of a zero-degree language as free as humanly possible from the entanglements of tropological free play. That this ideal is unattainable is made obvious by Ruskin's own use of idolatrous rhetoric; that it never ceased to entice Ruskin as moralist and arbiter of poetic license is equally clear in the critic's persistent condemnation of ornamental language and of the seductions of form in general.

The double nature of the linguistic sign and the duplicities inherent in all rhetorical discourse were well understood by Ruskin, but were felt as frustrating obstacles to the transparent communication and peaceful social interaction of men that later became the express utopian goals of his work. If *Unto This Last* and *Fors Clavigera* analyzed modern man's alienation in industrialized society and elaborated the theoretical model for a return to the kind of immediacy experienced by the artisans of the Middle Ages in their handmade products, *Praeterita* is the attempt within language to accomplish a similar movement backward, toward a self-sufficient world in which sign and meaning would relate fraternally, as "helpers" in the establishing of an earthly paradise. The fact that Ruskin needed to eliminate much of his past experience in order to safeguard the integrity of this artificially pure atmosphere underlines the major frustration of his career: his inability, except in unusual circumstances, to combine his extraordinary analytic gift (i.e., his capacity to unmask the false underpinnings of apparently coherent systems of thought and representation) with the creative, "imaginative" urge, whose potential was diverted into nostalgic, regressive dream worlds.

*A la recherche du temps perdu* is a reading of Ruskinian semiology that both maximizes the theory postulating a transparently analogous link of sign to meaning and also deconstructs the naïve but poetically productive fallacy on which such a theory is predicated. The creative or imaginative Proust conceived a self-enclosed domain of names in which the resonances of the *signifiant* engendered a privately coherent set of subjective meaning. These meanings constitute the beliefs according to which the protagonist of the novel "understands" the world before encountering it as such. The childhood paradise of Combray is appealing, like all well-made utopias, because the arbitrary relationship of dreamed names to supposed reality is suspended and transformed, in the mind of the young Marcel, into the necessary link of a metaphorical fusion. But when Marcel travels and tries to locate his imaginings in the outside world of the referent, his experiences, as we shall see later, differ radically from the ecstasies described in *Praeterita:* here, the analytic Proust intervenes to demonstrate the arbitrariness of the sign in a series of repeated subjective disillusionments. Before the unity of meaning can be recovered (albeit by rhetorically devious means) in *Le Temps retrouvé,* a long section of sobering narrative must unfold—a space in which the initial beliefs of the protagonist are shattered, a space whose existence derives from the impossibility of closing the sign's constitutive split. Whereas Ruskin, upon discovering the fall from transcendental significance and the consequent idolatrous proliferation of forms, turned toward the referent to ground his social and political criticism, Proust, in making the same discovery, descended within the sign to elaborate a convoluted inner world, a world where the Ruskinian conception of history as decline and fall becomes allegorized as the archaic mythology of Sodom and Gomorrah.[33] The role of reading in the Proustian inward-turning process and the relationship of reading to properly novelistic structures will emerge from an examination of the lucid manner in which Proust translated and interpreted the works of Ruskin.

# 3
# Proust
# Reads Ruskin

In psychological terms, literary influence can be conceived as a struggle by a son to overcome the genius of a father figure, where the son, by the very fact of his chronological lateness, feels separated from the creative center his father had successfully discovered, exploited, exhausted. To write, the younger author must find a space of his own, a place belonging to him and no other; this he accomplishes by various strategies of confrontation and evasion whereby he attempts to render harmless the writings of his predecessor. Referring to the cultural context of Romanticism, Harold Bloom evokes the successor's "loss of reciprocity with the world, as compared to the precursor's sense of being a man to whom all things spoke."[1] Although Bloom, like Ruskin, leaves room for Dante, Milton, and Shakespeare as exceptional figures whose creative energies seemed relatively untouched by the anxiety of influence, he sees in the Romantic agony and its modern inheritance an inward-turning movement that has affected all "strong poets," determining the path of their increasingly strained and conflictive relationship with what can be called "reality"—the immediate givens of sensual experience that provide metaphorical discourse with its objective correlative, its solidly fixed anchor in nature.

The same structure of increased innerness taken to the point of extreme solipsism characterizes the evolution of the contemporary novel. Loss of reciprocity with the world can be considered the major factor responsible for the transformations undergone by the fictional protagonist, whose increasing inability to control the social conditions of his existence leads, inexorably, to a defensive withdrawal. The path from Balzac through Flaubert and Huysmans to Proust, from the naïvely energetic hero to the burlesque antihero to the isolated ambivalence of a nonpersonal "I" (with its apparently logical end point in the disembodied shadow voices of Beckett's universe), has the convincing (historical) rigor of a geometrical curve. Each successive step in the process challenges the individual writer to reinvent a language capable of moving farther away from the threats of the outside.

As Richard Terdiman has demonstrated in the best recent interpretation of Proust from the standpoint of historical determinism,[2] Proust's creative response involves a turn away from the traditional temporality of successive actions oriented toward a dramatic finality (embodied, in nineteenth-century narrative, by the alternation of past definite and imperfect-descriptive tenses). With the elaboration of a fluid, indeterminate, imperfect modality that Genette has called the "iterative,"[3] the laws of memory re-create and re-form temporal progression, subordinating it to the inner mechanism of subjectivity. According to Terdiman, the final result of this historical/technical development is a radical change in the subject matter of the novel: "An entire literature about the creation of literature will follow from the failures of life outside" (*The Dialectics of Isolation*, 82). Whereas Balzac's novels, in their adherence to the mimetic mode of representation, could be said to rivalize with nature, Proust concludes that art's only justification is its ability to justify itself *as* art. The *Recherche* uses the external trappings of the available social facts of its period, but bends them and subjects them to the overriding coherence of a highly personal vision.

At first sight, the intertextual relationship between Ruskin and Proust as described in the preceding chapter would seem to fit this pattern perfectly. Whereas Ruskin subordinates his considerable talent as decipherer of iconographic and poetic symbols to an established, referentially grounded moral code, Proust plays with the ambiguities of this code in order to deepen a subjective meditation on the motivations of the linguistic sign. In Bardèche's view, such a reversal of priorities implies that Proust is able to overcome or neutralize the moral energy of his predecessor by an act of formal reconversion. What Ruskin considered meaningful only through an appeal to experience and referential validity becomes, for his disciple, thematic material that can be voided of its concrete reality: thus guilt as existential pathos becomes the soil from which the *Recherche* can grow. But the question must be asked, Is the transition from realism to formalism made smoothly and unproblematically, according to the inevitable process that we call literary history, whose *telos* in the absolute of silence is now the hypothetical subject of postmodern fictional creation and criticism? Or, in the passage from moral force to novelistic form, is there some residue left behind that makes it difficult for the later author to master his master? Is the movement inward an easy shedding of superfluous and now outmoded representational *préjugés,* or can it be demonstrated that this movement itself has a rhetorical structure requiring independent analysis? Ultimately, we must leave open the possibility that literary history, far from being the abstract line of an inevitable geometric involution, may in fact arise from a misreading of its own logical premises. For our purposes, this would mean that in Proust's reconversion of Ruskin's imprisonment in common experience and morality we need to observe how referential *evidence* as such is made to function thematically, how it is enveloped by a fictional frame, so that a literary-historical interpretation of Proust's work can enjoy the rigor of a visible and understandable progression.

With these questions in mind we can examine now in greater detail and more systematically than in the previous chapter Proust's actual reading of Ruskin. I use the word "actual" here in contradistinction to the analytically demonstrable but somewhat hidden "reading" that was performed by Proust in his complication of Ruskinian "custom" and "association." We are fortunate to possess Proust's thoughts on Ruskin as they evolve from admiration to critical distance in the justifiably acclaimed translations of *The Bible of Amiens* and *Sesame and Lilies.* To see Proust read Ruskin is to study the series of repetitions, exchanges, contradictions, and strategic reworkings of ideas that link four stages of reflection in a complex unity: (1) the original Ruskinian opus and its translation; (2) Proust's notes, showing varying degrees of approbation and disagreement with the original text; (3) Proust's critical articles based upon *The Bible of Amiens* and *Sesame and Lilies;* and (4) the *Recherche* itself, insofar as its fictional forms and episodes elaborate the problems raised by Ruskin. In my analysis of Proust's three major articles on Ruskin—"Journées de pèlerinage," "John Ruskin," and "Journées de lecture"[4]—I will examine the question of contextuality that was at stake in the first two chapters of this study: namely, in what way does the novel *A la recherche du temps perdu* relate to the "theme" of reading, or, in other words, how does the novel "swallow," "digest," or otherwise incorporate reading as one theme among others? The innerness of modern fiction consists of its capacity to speak about itself, or to place itself within itself and make of itself an object of (self-) understanding. How this occurs in the process of reading and how the act of reading relates rhetorically to the critical moment of self-understanding will be the focus of the present interpretations.

## THE BIBLE OF AMIENS AND "JOURNÉES DE PÈLERINAGE"

*The Bible of Amiens* was written in spurts from 1880 to 1885. Characteristic of Ruskin's later style, it is a hodgepodge of digressions and idiosyncratic pronouncements on many tenuously related subjects. Its ostensible main theme is, however, never quite fully lost from view. After giving a short history of the Amiens cathedral, including the legends of Saints Martin, Geneviève, and Firmin, and after a fairly lengthy develop-ment on the passionate, warlike instincts of the Franks, Ruskin discusses the problems of scriptural interpretation, the career of Saint Jerome, and finally, elaborates his own allegorical reading of the Bible as repre-sented in the stones of Amiens. We may assume that Proust's interest in *The Bible of Amiens* arose from his desire to penetrate the world of symbols that the Middle Ages had created to house its beliefs, and to examine, through Ruskin, the manner in which the literal appearance of the statuary related to the figurative meanings that we moderns, without a first-hand knowledge of the Bible, might not grasp immediately. But Ruskin's solid erudition is accompanied by a sense of humor, a playful-ness, that also must have appealed to Proust. This lightness of touch is especially evident in Ruskin's interpretation of the personified abstractions Obedience, Rebellion, and Charity,[5] and in the original, quasi-Heideg-gerian probing and stretching of etymological laws that Proust did not hesitate to qualify as a *"manie étymologique"* in his notes, but that sur-faced in the *Recherche* as the private obsessions of Combray's curé and the demystifying scientific accuracy of Brichot.[6]

As is well-established in the critical literature, Proust's knowledge of English was limited, though by no means as threadbare as his modesty compelled him to confess. His method of translation (which heralded the patchwork construction of his novel in a *palimpseste* of "paperoles") involved a double collaboration—with his mother for a literal rendition of the original, and with Marie Nordlinger for stylistic subtleties—thereby insuring a high degree of accuracy from which Proust could work to at-tain a smooth and elegant French version. Jean Autret has analyzed the two translations in painstaking detail, and has revealed a minimal tally of significant errors, concluding that the final result is faithful to and respect-ful of the Ruskinian text.[7] Of primary interest to us is that the process of translation, among the most minute forms of word study, led Proust to meditate on the possibilities and limits of literary criticism as intellectual activity. Faithfulness to the translated author—that is, the perhaps impos-sible goal of avoiding the stigma *"traduttore, traditore"*—is the first obligation of the critic, who, in restating and clarifying the ideas of the author he studies, must take care lest he swerve from the letter of the text, lest he simplify or otherwise distort the original corpus of writings in an attempt at systematization.

The ideal of adherence to the set of intended meanings that constitutes *The Bible of Amiens* is thus the entire task of the translator and the first step in the commentator's work. But Proust was not satisfied to remain at this level, since the relatively short, late book of Ruskin is merely a part of a much larger whole within which it awakens, in the mind of the reader, textual correspondences or "echoes" of ideas he may have seen previously in other books of the same author. In his *Avant-propos* to *La Bible d'Amiens,* Proust justifies his extensive use of notes with an appeal to the reader's intuitive understanding of the thematic integrity that characterizes Ruskin's literary production as a whole. At the beginning of his introductory paragraph, the critic writes:

> Je donne ici une traduction de la *Bible d'Amiens,* de John Ruskin. Mais il m'a semblé que ce n'était pas assez pour le lecteur. Ne lire qu'un livre d'un auteur, c'est voir cet auteur une fois. Or, en causant une fois avec une personne, on peut discerner en elle des traits singuliers. Mais c'est seulement par leur répétition, dans des circonstances variées, qu'on peut les reconnaître pour caractéristiques et essentiels. Pour un écrivain, pour un musicien ou pour un peintre, cette variation des circonstances qui permet de discerner, par une sorte d'expérimentation, les traits permanents du caractère, c'est la variété des oeuvres. Nous retrouvons, dans un second livre, dans un autre tableau, les particularités dont la première fois nous aurions pu croire qu'elles appartenaient au sujet traité autant qu'à l'écrivain ou au peintre. Et du rapprochement des oeuvres différentes nous dégageons des traits communs dont l'assemblage compose la physionomie morale de l'artiste.

And later on in the same passage:

> Ainsi j'ai essayé de pourvoir le lecteur comme d'une mémoire improvisée où j'ai disposé des souvenirs des autres livres de Ruskin— sorte de caisse de résonance, où les paroles de la *Bible d'Amiens* pourront prendre plus de retentissement en y éveillant des échos fraternels. (*La Bible d'Amiens,* 9-10)[8]

The *mémoire improvisée* that founds thematic criticism and, through Proust's critical intervention, contributes to a better understanding of the "symphonic" structure of Ruskin's works, is, of course, closely related to the specifically Proustian method of novelistic composition. But the difference between improvised (retrospectively schematized) memory and involuntary remembrance is that the latter is a lived process in which the mind measures the inner distances it traverses in thought and feels fully "la résistante douceur de cette atmosphère imposée qui a l'étendue même de notre vie" (*La Bible d'Amiens,* 10). The act of writing can recreate what Proust calls the "poetry of memory"—the movement of remembrance in its essence—whereas reading can only reproduce by degrees the abstract form of this movement as it appears to the rational mind after the fact. Nevertheless, Proust does not insist upon the separateness or mutual exclusion of creation and criticism at this juncture; rather, he prefers to delineate their structural similarity and make of his own critical study the closest possible reflection of Ruskin's interpretive insights.

Proust's admiration for Ruskinian esthetics is especially evident in the first of the two essay-length developments of the translator's preface to *La Bible d'Amiens:* the article originally titled "Journées de pèlerinage." In it, Proust attempts to convince the reader to visit Amiens in "a kind of Ruskinian pilgrimage" ("Journées de pèlerinage," 69). In following Ruskin's text with a scrupulous attention to detail, in quoting long passages from its pages, in adding explanatory commentary, Proust abides by his program of interpretive faithfulness, to such an extent that it might appear he is renouncing his own personality in an act of total self-effacement. This is not quite true, as we shall see, but certainly the reader's first impression is that of a relative lack of critical intrusion. In allowing Ruskin to speak through him, however, Proust in no way refrains from what might be called a participatory enthusiasm. Indeed, "Journées de pèlerinage" is characterized by pleasure—physical, intellectual, esthetic—for it reproduces the joyful atmosphere of discovery through travel that permeates *The Bible of Amiens.* The exhilarating quality of Ruskin's writing derives, in part, from his theory of reading, which, as was evident in the ecstatic experiences of *Praeterita,* involves the interpenetration of observing subject and esthetic object in an act of transcendental revelation. The voyage to Amiens is already colored by the jubilant tone of the later interpretive experience; and conversely, the act of reading takes place in the open air, the beautiful natural context in which the voyage unfolds. Reading is the unveiling of truth in nature. The desire for knowledge is fulfilled as the previously enigmatic cathedral stones reveal their secrets at the call of Ruskin's voice.

At the beginning of his essay, Proust makes a distinction that subtends the entire logic of his further argumentation. He differentiates between the kind of pilgrimage that seeks in the referent the imprint of an author's intellectual presence (we visit Amiens in order to find, incorporated in the statues of its cathedral, the essence of Ruskin's thought) and the false adoration, or *fétichisme* (70), which consists of visiting the writer's tomb, where nothing remains of his thinking power. If this distinction is to hold and possess an unquestionable validity, it is necessary that the statuary of Amiens reveal with perfect clarity the message that Ruskin attached to its signifying surface: that is, between the book brought by the disciple in his mission of adoration and the building's meaning there can be no esthetic distance, no possibility of interpretive misunderstanding. In other words, if the stones became too interesting in themselves, there would be a danger of fetishistic contemplation inherent in the structure of the reading experience itself. Proust uses several rhetorical strategies to avoid just such a danger, and evokes, in the process, a conception of artistic creation and reception based upon transparency and unmediated communication. He begins by hypothesizing that intellectually sincere work, accomplished without the goal of pleasing others in a superficial way, will necessarily reach a wide group of readers, for we as individuals are part of a "trame universelle" that surpasses our egotistically limited perspectives. Readers of Ruskin can understand *The Bible of Amiens* because the physical/mental unit called "Ruskin" is composed of certain universal elements that all men have in common. Thus, the act of reading becomes contextualized within the higher enjoyments of the spirit:

> Quand on travaille pour plaire aux autres on peut ne pas réussir, mais les choses qu'on a faites pour se contenter soi-même ont toujours chance d'intéresser quelqu'un. Il est impossible qu'il n'existe pas de gens qui prennent quelque plaisir à ce qui m'en a tant donné. Car personne n'est original et fort heureusement pour la sympathie et la compréhension qui sont de si grands plaisirs dans la vie, c'est dans une trame universelle que nos individualités sont taillées. Si l'on savait analyser l'âme comme la matière, on verrait que, sous l'apparente diversité des esprits aussi bien que sous celle des choses, il n'y a que peu de corps simples et d'éléments irréductibles et qu'il entre dans la composition de ce que nous croyons être notre personnalité, des substances fort communes et qui se retrouvent un peu partout dans l'Univers. (71–72)

If Ruskin is not perceived as a threat at this point or as an energy to be overcome through the catharsis of an anxiety-ridden creative consciousness, it is because he has lost his identity and become abstracted in the general Laws of personality. This decomposition/dissemination of "Ruskin" into analyzable components allows "Journées de pèlerinage" to function as text of pleasure while giving us as readers the opportunity to participate in what Barthes has called the "pleasure of the text."[9]

The ease with which Ruskin's thoughts penetrate and illuminate the referent derives from his literary creativity, which, Proust insists, does not involve conscious labor, but rather flows from the natural revelations of memory. Ruskin did not *write* his book, if the act of writing is conceived as taking place within the necessary separation of the author from the reality he seeks to transform. Ruskin merely opened his memory to us, and this process occurs without the interference of mediating steps, and even without the desire of the critic to influence his reader in any way. In absolute terms, then, *The Bible of Amiens* would not be a book. It is, instead, the chance recording of a disinterested remembrance that was not so much deliberately published as simply not prohibited from circulation. Proust would like us to believe that Ruskin's work is free from the rhetoric of persuasion, that it is simply a footnote, an afterthought of a great mind. These interesting but debatable conceptions are introduced in a discussion of the Vierge Dorée, one of the statues of the Amiens cathedral that Ruskin had mentioned casually in *The Two Paths* (1858) before analyzing its symbolical significance in 1885. As esthetic object, the statue had always interested Ruskin, so that when it becomes the center of a lengthy analysis, the critic is not engaged in an innovative interpretation, but in the kind of *resuscitation* that attains to the poetic dimension of Time. Proust explains:

> J'ai pensé que vous aimeriez mieux *La Bible d'Amiens,* de sentir qu'en la feuilletant ainsi, c'étaient des choses sur lesquelles Ruskin a, de tout temps, médité, celles qui expriment par là le plus profondément sa pensée, que vous preniez connaissance; que le présent qu'il vous faisait était de ceux qui sont le plus précieux à ceux qui aiment, et qui consistent dans les objets dont on s'est longtemps servi soi-même sans intention de les donner un jour, rien que pour soi. En écrivant son livre, Ruskin n'a pas eu à travailler pour vous, il n'a fait que publier sa mémoire et vous ouvrir son coeur. J'ai pensé que la Vierge Dorée prendrait quelque importance à vos yeux, quand vous verriez que, près de trente ans avant *La Bible d'Amiens,* elle avait, dans la mémoire de Ruskin, sa place où, quand il avait besoin de donner à ses auditeurs un exemple, il savait la trouver, pleine de grâce et chargée de ces pensées graves à qui il donnait souvent rendez-vous devant elle. (83)

In these sentences and in the subsequent paragraphs devoted to the Vierge Dorée, Proust is inaugurating the kind of meditation on the temporal modality of artistic works that will be so prevalent in the *Recherche.* The dialectic struggle between time as destructive force and the resurrecting power of involuntary memory that structures the conclusion of *Le Temps retrouvé* is already to be found in "Journées de pèlerinage," where the interpretive-vivifying efforts of Ruskin must fight against the wind and rain, whose repeated blasts will gradually render the features of the statue unrecognizable (85). The meanings that Ruskin wrests from the cathedral's biblical text are more than successfully deciphered signs relating to an artifact; they convey the transcendental purpose of the creative act, and as such, provide the metaphysical justification for the artistic process.

Ultimately, it turns out that there are two mutually conflicting ways to read "Journées de pèlerinage." On the one hand, if we adhere as closely to Proust as he did to Ruskin, if we enter into the atmosphere of enthusiasm, discovery, pleasure, and transparency that characterizes both *The Bible of Amiens* and its Proustian commentary, the result is that we will share the two writers' sentiments, we will be persuaded by the apparently disinterested tone of their prose, we will be made to believe in the poetry of Time and the capacity of art to rise above and conquer its finite limits. In fact, it is impossible to avoid performing this reading unless we are completely insensitive to the pathos of temporal loss and recuperation. The question which arises, however, and which leads to a second (deconstructive) reading, is, How does the logic of disinterest succeed in convincing us and moving us to adopt given authorially intended beliefs—or, What is the rhetoric of a "nonrhetoric"? We can gain some help in answering this question if we remember that the origin of memory as poetry of time is in a nonwriting that presumably results in a nonreading: Ruskin did not write, but "opened" his remembrances to Proust, who, in turn, insists that *The Bible of Amiens* is not a work of art, that the Vierge Dorée is not a symbol to be interpreted but a *person* with an individuality whose true significance resides in her ability to awaken in us "la mélancholie d'un souvenir" (86). Ironically, the moments in "Journées de pèlerinage" that remind us most of the *Recherche* and foreshadow major themes of the novel are the consequence of a delusion or misreading. It is precisely because we do not read, because we, in superficial adherence to an author's thought, no longer examine the works he discussed *as* works, that the following poetry, the Proustian charm of persons and places, is made possible:

> Un jour sans doute aussi le sourire de la Vierge Dorée (qui a déjà pourtant duré plus que notre foi) cessera, par l'effritement des pierres qu'il écarte gracieusement, de répandre, pour nos enfants, de la beauté, comme à nos pères croyants, il a versé du courage. Je sens que j'avais tort de l'appeler une oeuvre d'art: une statue qui fait ainsi à tout jamais partie de tel lieu de la terre, d'une certaine ville, c'est-à-dire d'une chose qui porte un nom comme une personne, qui est un individu, dont on ne peut jamais trouver la toute pareille sur la face des continents, dont les employés de chemins de fer, en nous criant son nom, à l'endroit où il a fallu inévitablement venir pour la trouver, semblent nous dire, sans le savoir: "Aimez ce que jamais on ne verra deux fois," —une telle statue a peut-être quelque chose de moins universel qu'une oeuvre d'art; elle nous retient, en tous cas, par un lien plus fort que celui de l'oeuvre d'art elle-même, un de ces liens comme en ont, pour nous garder, les personnes et les pays. (85)

As the Vierge Dorée is transformed, in the mind of the observing subject, from a work of art to the equivalent of a person, there is both a loss of universality and a gain in affectivity. The rhetoric of Proust's argument sets out to convince us that the gain eliminates the loss, that our heightened awareness of the emotional aura surrounding the statue will compensate for whatever purely denotational value our interpretive efforts might have uncovered. In fact, the basis of Proust's logic here is that of Ruskinian *association:* we are interested in the esthetic object not for intrinsic reasons but because it is linked, in our minds, to a given city, to a given place with a specific name. The "personality" of the Vierge Dorée derives from the individuality of the city of Amiens, which, by the process of naming (railroad employees cry out the word "Amiens" as we arrive at the station, thus magically creating the place linguistically symbolized), assumes shape and the power of a sensual attraction. Indeed, the traveller, having shed all pretense at disinterested esthetic contemplation, relates to the city of Amiens and to the Vierge Dorée much as a lover relates to his mistress.

The Proustian motivation for travel can be described, in Ruskinian terms, as a *possession-taking.* Psychologically, the purpose of the voyage is to realize an initial desire, to seize and penetrate in the real world, what had been merely imagined at an earlier moment. Thus, in the lyrical conclusion of his article, Proust describes the effect of Ruskin's knowledge upon the faithful disciple in the erotic imagery of the Song of Solomon, with emphasis on the metaphors of opening and penetration:

> Comprenant mal jusque-là la portée de l'art religieux au moyen
> âge, je m'étais dit, dans ma ferveur pour Ruskin: Il m'apprendra,
> car lui aussi, en quelques parcelles du moins, n'est-il pas la vérité?
> Il fera entrer mon esprit là où il n'avait pas accès, car il est la
> porte. Il me purifiera, car son inspiration est comme le lys de la
> vallée. Il m'enivrera et me vivifiera, car il est la vigne et la vie. Et
> j'ai senti en effet que le parfum mystique des rosiers de Saron
> n'était pas à tout jamais évanoui puisqu'on le respire encore, au
> moins dans ses paroles. (104)

Initially, the follower, recognizing his own intellectual and spiritual limitations, must abandon himself, open himself to the truths of the master, thereby assuming the classical female role of a vessel waiting to be filled. But in a second phase, through the success of an initiation ritual, the disciple can enter with the master into the promised land, thereby obtaining by proxy the masculine attributes of domination and possession. "Journées de pèlerinage" terminates on a note of triumph, combining and intertwining in the best Ruskinian/thematic fashion the feminine beauty of lilies and the masculine promise of an Open Sesame. It seems as if the future author of the *Recherche*, in submitting first to the force of Ruskin, can then exercise his own creative energies and enter the sacred domain of art. Thus the passionate hope of Proust as formulated in 1904 would appear to express allegorically the transition from the secondary, weak position of critical work to the primary activity of authorial control that was later to be achieved in his novel. In this sense, the conclusion of "Journées de pèlerinage" is a prophetic statement, the unconsciously traced path of a career.

If we now ask the question, To what extent does Proust's novel realize or actualize this dream of authorial domination as possession of the personified esthetic object? we should keep in mind that the answer cannot be abstract or a mere matter of our critical conviction. Rather, we can assume that the *Recherche,* in emulating the Ruskinian voyage to Truth, will explicitly stage the dream of possession-taking in a fictional guise and will provide us with the clues necessary to locate its contextual development. It is not difficult to see that "Journées de pèlerinage" is the most evident textual origin of the young Marcel's reveries on names and that the voyage to Amiens commented on in the critical article is the early equivalent of the train ride to Balbec in the second part of *A l'Ombre des jeunes filles en fleurs.* In both cases, the hope of attaining new knowledge orients the physical movement of travel; but in the novel there is a long separation between the Protean metamorphoses of subjective desire and the process of referential testing, which corresponds, in the book, to the three hundred pages that lie between "Noms de pays: le nom" and "Noms de pays: le pays."

Like Proust's adoration of the Vierge Dorée, Marcel's love of Balbec is impure, "mixed"; it is based upon an association of the cathedral with its town and with its supposed location on a precipice overlooking the fierce ocean of the Normandy coast. As a child the protagonist perceives the whistling of the wind in Combray as the harbinger of a project later to be carried out: "Alors, par les soirs orageux et doux de février, le vent— soufflant dans mon coeur, qu'il ne faisait pas trembler moins fort que la cheminée de ma chambre, le projet d'un voyage à Balbec—mêlait en moi le désir de l'architecture gothique avec celui d'une tempête sur la mer" (I, 385). Gradually, by a process of metaphorical fusion, the vague desire of Balbec with its panoply of erotic fantasies becomes subsumed within the monolithic power of its pronounced syllables. The word "Balbec" not only replaces the geographic place it represents, but, according to the rhetorical manipulation of the narrator, *encloses* and *absorbs* the city, and in so doing, grants it the attribute of particularity or individuality. (This was also the case for the Vierge Dorée, enclosed within the personified limits of "Amiens.") But the process whereby *contenant* and *contenu* exchange functions is accomplished in an act of subjective defiance of reality, thus raising the possibility, as Proust here foreshadows, of a later disillusionment:

> Mais si ces noms absorbèrent à tout jamais l'image que j'avais de ces villes, ce ne fut qu'en la transformant, qu'en soumettant sa réapparition en moi à leurs lois propres; ils eurent ainsi pour conséquence de la rendre plus belle, mais aussi plus différente de ce que les villes de Normandie . . . peuvent être en réalité, et, en accroissant les joies arbitraires de mon imagination, d'aggraver la déception future de mes voyages. (I, 387)

Using a technique that has been called, quite aptly, a "devaluation of suspense,"[10] Proust resumes in one sentence the future result of the protagonist's visit to Balbec. We know in advance, five pages after the beginning of the section on names, that the freely circulating *signifiant* owes its charm to its irresponsibility, that it is already inscribed in a movement of error that will be explained in "Noms de pays: le pays." Indeed, when Marcel arrives at Balbec, he finds that the presumed global unity of the dreamed word hides two radically different realities: Balbec-en-terre (or Balbec-le-vieux) and Balbec-plage (I, 658).

The two elements previously associated in the protagonist's mind—the cathedral and the ocean—are now revealed to exist in separate contexts. This means that the passage describing the progressive disillusionment that results from the encounter with reality will unfold from a disentanglement of the falsely constructed rhetorical associations in "Noms de pays: le nom." In a first step, the capacity of names to contain or enclose the "idea" of a city is shown to be impossible, since the one designation "Balbec" is not monosemic. Consequently, the individuality or personality conferred upon the imagined city by the evocative power of the name no longer exists: what remains for the observer to see is not a system of subjectively postulated, necessarily related elements, but an amalgam of pure contingency, a group of arbitrarily juxtaposed objects whose chief attribute is resistance to synthetic understanding. Rather than rise above the waves of a storm-battered coast, the cathedral's belltower "se dressait sur une place où était l'embranchement de deux lignes de tramway, en face d'un Café qui portait, écrit en lettres d'or, le mot 'Billard';" and the church itself, "entrant dans mon attention avec le Café, avec le passant à qui il avait fallu demander mon chemin, avec la gare où j'allais retourner—faisait un tout avec le reste, semblait un accident, un produit de cette fin d'après-midi, dans laquelle la coupole moelleuse ou gonflée sur le ciel était comme un fruit dont la même lumière qui baignait les cheminées des maisons, mûrissait la peau rose, dorée et fondante" (I, 659).

It is significant that the accidental quality of the cathedral's presence on the town square, which indicates the unfounded nature of Marcel's dreams, is immediately negated and recuperated in the unified golden harmony of the afternoon. The deconstruction of a fragile metaphorical system of resemblances is superseded, in the brusque transition from "accident" to "*produit* de cette fin d'après-midi," by a metonymic system of juxtaposed illuminated objects, whose beauty is the result of a spatial or contextual totalization. It is as if, for Proust, even in a moment of heightened critical lucidity, the tendency of the mind were to continue constructing associative frameworks as a defense against the devastating threat of an absolute significant void.

The ironical relationship between these pages on Balbec-en-terre and the article "Journées de pèlerinage" becomes most obvious in the final paragraph of the passage (I, 659-61). Here, the Vierge du Porche of Balbec can be read as the negative, inverted image of the Vierge Dorée at Amiens. Unlike its Ruskinian model, which possessed the resilient charm of a defined personality, the Vierge du Porche, as it stands in a cruelly dissonant city environment, "[est]... réduite maintenant à sa propre apparence de pierre, occupant par rapport à la portée de mon bras une place où elle avait pour rivales une affiche électorale et la pointe de ma canne, enchaînée à la Place, inséparable du débouché de la grand'rue, ... soumise à la tyrannie du Particulier" (I, 659-60). Later in the same context, Proust contrasts the poetically imagined "oeuvre d'art immortelle et si longtemps désirée" to its real manifestation as "une petite vieille de pierre dont je pouvais mesurer la hauteur et compter les rides" (I, 660).[11]

The degradation of universality to the tyranny of the Particular, the use of the travel experience as a vehicle for subjective demystification, the evident allusions to *The Bible of Amiens* in the inverted form of parody— all point to a conception of artistic creation radically opposed to Ruskinian *possession-taking* and imply, as well, that the transition from criticism to creation, from the contemplation of artistic forms to the self-composed energy of authorial force may be more difficult than the lyricism of "Journées de pèlerinage" seems to indicate. In the latter work, it was assumed that the "female" critical role of openness to the strength of the master would change to a "masculine" power once the act of mediation had been accomplished; then, the disciple turned new master could open his own doors with the magical commands of his will. But this smooth procedure can occur only if the mediator can be trusted, only if he incorporates the Truth. Significantly, in the ironical Proustian development of this Ruskinian scheme of transitions, the mediator, Swann, who had told the young Marcel that Balbec was "délicieux ... aussi *beau* que Sienne" (I, 660; my emphasis), cannot lay claim to any form of trust, since the episode as a whole renders problematic the very idea of beauty. It is logical, then, that the image of *opening* that structured Ruskin's ideas should now be reversed and complicated in the concluding sentence of Proust's description, where the play between *contenant* and *contenu* is evoked in a physically precise and witty manner:

> Pour Balbec, dès que j'y étais entré, ç'avait été comme si j'avais entr'ouvert un nom qu'il eût fallu tenir hermétiquement clos et où, profitant de l'issue que je leur avais imprudemment offerte, en chassant toutes les images qui y vivaient jusque-là, un tramway, un café, les gens qui passaient sur la place, la succursale du Comptoir d'Escompte, irrésistiblement poussés par une pression externe et une force pneumatique, s'étaient engouffrés à l'intérieur des syllabes qui, refermées sur eux, les laissaient maintenant encadrer le porche de l'église persane et ne cesseraient plus de les contenir. (I, 660–61)

Like Pandora's box, the name "Balbec" is the receptacle of illusory virtues and beliefs which, when released, can never be reappropriated; and yet the hope of a return to original harmony remains. The protagonist of the *Recherche* will continue to think that there are "d'autres villes encore intactes pour moi, que je pourrais prochainement peut-être pénétrer, comme au milieu d'une pluie de perles, dans le frais gazouillis des égouttements de Quimperlé" (I, 660); but the inexorable negativity of the novel will continue to demonstrate the arbitrariness of the relationship between sign and referent, between the poetically evocative "perle" of Quim*perlé*" and the actual appearance of the city in the particularity of its geographic prison. According to the semiology of Marcel Proust, there is no such thing as an "empty" sign that could exist in and for itself, detached from impure commerce with associated, interested desires. As soon as the name "Balbec" is emptied of its oceanic mythology, the referential pressure of metonymic relations (the cathedral in its immediate surroundings, suffused with the all-enveloping light of the sun) exerts itself upon the available nothingness of the sign and fills it with new meanings: *signum abhorret vacuum*. If, on an allegorical level, the protagonist of the *Recherche* is emblematic of the interpreter in general, then we see now that the process whereby he "reads" the world is not to be confused with an act of understanding and certainly not to be confused with the idea of authorial *possession*. Reading is based upon a potentially infinite series of erroneous, subjectively motivated transfers and substitutions. We can open the sign, but we will be condemned to do so with "imprudence," and we can only stand by as it closes itself immediately upon new illusions, which are our own creations.

The results of the Balbec-en-terre episode are paradoxical. If we understand that the text tells the story of the sign's arbitrariness and embeddedness in asociative rhetoric, we can then conclude that the text is "about" the sign, that it manages to be the positive vehicle which assumes the responsibility of narrating a negative message. But if we respect the integrity of microtextual detail, we are compelled to see that this understanding of ours is the consequence of a delusion that the deconstruction of "naming" has forced into the open. One can say that the *Recherche* is "about" the inner structure of the linguistic sign, but in so doing we need to question the spatial metaphor of *aboutness* and its claims of comprehensiveness, control, mastery, and so forth. Such a questioning is precisely what the *entr'ouverture* of "Balbec" performs, its allegorical significance being that although the envelopment and imprisonment of reality in the sign is aberrant and illusory, it is also necessary and productive of the misreading without which what we call literature could not exist. The juxtaposition of microtext to macrotext, of episodic detail to thematic systematics, places the drama of Proustian textuality within the split of the sign, in the ambivalent, immediately closed opening of a promised meaning that our desire seeks to grasp.

## "JOHN RUSKIN"

The second of Proust's critical articles based upon *The Bible of Amiens* is included in *Pastiches et mélanges* under the general title "John Ruskin." It consists of parts III and IV of the translator's preface to *La Bible d'Amiens,* the latter section being a "postscript" whose separateness from the main body of Proust's analyses is no longer visible in the version of *Pastiches et mélanges.* We must keep this in mind, because part IV is in many respects a refutation of part III:[12] it shows with a high degree of explicitness specific areas of disagreement between Proust and Ruskin and serves as an interesting self-criticism of the French disciple, who accuses himself of an excessive "respect" for the ideas of his master. The final pages of "John Ruskin" can be read as a Proustian declaration of artistic independence, while the essay as a whole emphasizes the same close relationship of criticism to creativity that we observed in the intertextual links of "Journées de pèlerinage" to the Balbec-en-terre episode of the *Recherche.* But "John Ruskin" cannot be reduced to a series of themes or ideas: although the essay appears straightforward and logical (analytically rational), it has a rhetorical mechanism worth examining and an undercurrent of unresolved psychological tensions that combine to make of it a complex meditation on the nature and limits of literary influence. In the following analysis, I will be less concerned with restating or reformulating Proust's opinions of Ruskin's esthetics (these opinions are, in fact, wellargued and constitute a real contribution to Ruskin studies) than with an illumination of the more secret obsessive thoughts that cause the essay to repeat itself and hover around a central knot of preoccupations.

Proust begins "John Ruskin" with a long catalogue of those contradictions in Ruskin's thought which had caused readers of the nineteenth century to object that the theorist of Beauty and prophet of industrial times was in truth disorganized and incoherent. The first part of Proust's article is, in general terms, a refutation of this view. Following the lead of Robert de la Sizeranne, France's most intelligent disciple and critic of Ruskin,[13] Proust demonstrates that all of Ruskin's writings were the manifestation of his "religion of beauty," but he immediately refines upon La Sizeranne's terminology, in an effort to eliminate from it all connotations of *dilettantisme* or *esthétisme*. Indeed, in a period of artistic hypersensitivity and excessive devotion to the self, it might appear that "un adorateur de la Beauté, c'est un homme qui, ne pratiquant d'autre culte que le sien et ne reconnaissant pas d'autre dieu qu'elle, passerait sa vie dans la jouissance que donne la contemplation voluptueuse des oeuvres d'art" ("John Ruskin," 100). Proust contends that "la principale religion de Ruskin fut la religion tout court" and that if Ruskin searched for truth in the varied guises of Beauty, one needs to understand that "cette Beauté à laquelle il se trouva ainsi consacrer sa vie ne fut pas conçue par lui comme un objet de jouissance fait pour la charmer, mais comme une réalité infiniment plus importante, pour laquelle il aurait donné la sienne" (111).

The first few pages of Proust's *défense et illustration* of Ruskinian esthetic theory have a familiar ring to the reader of the *Recherche*. In demonstrating the superiority of his master's ideas over those professed by the adherents of *l'art pour l'art*, Proust is already suggesting certain key notions of his own theory as later expressed in *Le Temps retrouvé:* the importance of instinct and inspiration in art; the emphasis on reading as deciphering of signs; and the central focus on involuntary memory in the process of literary creation. But the undeniable parallels that exist between the two authors on the level of explicit statement should not cause us to see in "John Ruskin" a mere rewriting of "Journées de pèlerinage" on a more sophisticated analytical plane, where once again the disciple is willing to pay tribute without question or critical confrontation. Throughout the initial laudatory section of his essay, Proust continually returns to the problematic coexistence with Ruskin's writings of the moral or religious impulse and its esthetic object. Proust postulates that religious thoughts *determined* esthetic sentiments for Ruskin ("C'est ansi que son sentiment religieux a dirigé son sentiment esthétique" [113]), but in stating this so dogmatically, he must defend against the possibility that Ruskin's religion may have interfered with and falsified his esthetics. Rhetorically, this defense is accomplished by a subtle twist of reasoning whereby Proust equates religious beliefs with the "force" of genius. Since we are students of Ruskin's genius, since we as readers stand beneath the shadow of its energy, it matters little whether any given belief is true or demonstrably false, as long as the Ruskinian process of interpretation is productive of new meanings:

> Tous ceux qui ont quelque notion des lois de développement du génie savent que sa force se mesure plus à la force de ses croyances qu'à ce que l'objet de ces croyances peut avoir de satisfaisant pour le sens commun. Mais, puisque le christianisme de Ruskin tenait à l'essence même de sa nature intellectuelle, ses préférences artistiques, aussi profondes, devaient avoir avec lui quelque parenté. (113)

In expressing his unqualified admiration for the properly creative power of Ruskin, Proust makes it possible to "excuse" his predecessor for whatever interpretive errors he may have perpetrated, thus *de facto* liberating Ruskin's work from the purview of critical scrutiny. Indeed, if we find in Ruskin's argumentation traces of logical fallacies or in the detail of his highly imagistic prose a tendency to enchant the reader and influence him to adopt given opinions, Proust is saying that we should not therefore find fault with the writer, but rather, consider these factors as a part of the force of genius, which is beyond analysis or dissection.

According to the first section of "John Ruskin," the analytical act, which consists of uncovering and exploiting contradictions in an author's work, is condemned as a sign of unproductive disrespect, while the process of reading is equated with original creativity. Whether Ruskin was correct in stating that Le Beau Dieu, Amiens' Christ-figure, "dépassait en tendresse sculptée ce qui avait été atteint jusqu'alors" or whether Huysmans was right in mocking it as a "bellâtre à figure ovine" (128), the important fact is that the same statue fascinated two minds and engendered two interpretations. Proust's conclusion is, therefore, that reading is a cycle of errors, but that these errors are the unessential by-product of a higher power called *enthusiasm:*

> Les grandes beautés littéraires correspondent à quelque chose, et c'est peut-être l'enthousiasme en art qui est le critérium de la vérité. A supposer que Ruskin se soit quelquefois trompé, comme critique, dans l'exacte appréciation de la valeur d'une oeuvre, la beauté de son jugement erroné est souvent plus intéressante que celle de l'oeuvre jugée et correspond à quelque chose qui, pour être autre qu'elle, n'est pas moins précieux. (128)

The question that inevitably arises is whether Proust's critical practice truly corresponds with this theory, whether his reservations concerning Ruskinian style and esthetics are easily subsumed within the transcendence of an "enthusiastic" discipleship. Does Proust seem willing to become an initiator of "beautiful" erroneous judgments like his precursors, thus integrating himself into the cycle of creative reading as the equal of Ruskin and Huysmans? Or is there a level of his critical discourse which resists assimiliation to the creative impulse, which remains independent, analytical, detached, disapproving, which, embedded in the complexity of forms, remains separated from the primacy of force and genius? To answer these questions, we will examine those elements of "John Ruskin" that might have gone undeveloped if Proust had not reread himself in an admirably lucid "postscript."

From a psychological point of view, the last twelve pages of "John Ruskin" represent a successful overcoming of the repression that had caused Proust to adopt an attitude of pure admiration toward the author of *The Bible of Amiens*. The major reservation that had been cautiously expressed in the earlier development becomes the center of Proust's reflections: namely, Ruskin's tendency to "adore" the surface of signs, to worship the external trappings of stylistic effect at the expense of logical coherence and intellectual sincerity. In the first stages of his article, Proust had qualified his criticism with the kind of elegant politeness characteristic of his social self. Describing the intellectual affinities between Gustave Moreau and Ruskin, Proust had observed that both men condemned the depiction of violence in art, especially insofar as this violence could arise from a superficial formal virtuosity appealing excessively to the senses. But this having been observed, Ruskin and Moreau are said to be immune from such "fetishism" themselves ("fétichisme peu dangereux d'ailleurs pour des esprits si attachés au fond au sentiment symbolique qu'ils pouvaient passer d'un symbole à l'autre, sans être arrêtés par les diversités de pure surface" [117]). When we arrive at the second part of the essay, we discover what Proust had wished to elaborate all along: that Ruskin was constantly guilty of this sin of idolatry, that his prose is an impure mixture of rhetorically devious statements and counterstatements, that he often forced his thoughts to fit the mold of his ornamental style. Here, Proust sheds the mantle of respect and assumes the more difficult, for him more painful, function of demystifying critic.

Since all of Proust's argument derives from the central accusation of *idolatry*, we need to define the term, or, more modestly, reconstruct its semantic field. The denotative meaning of the word is, of course, religious. In Pascalian terms, idolatry is a *divertissement* of the mind from the true object of worship (in the Christian context, the risen Christ) to a false substitute, whereby the energies of our spiritual nature are misdirected and misapplied. It is in this religious sense that Proust introduces "idolatry" into his analysis. He quotes from Ruskin's *Lectures on Art:*

> Ç'a été, je crois, non sans mélange de bien, sans doute, car les plus grands maux apportent quelques biens dans leur reflux, ç'a été, je crois, le rôle vraiment néfaste de l'art, d'aider à ce qui, chez les païens comme chez les chrétiens—qu'il s'agisse du mirage des mots, des couleurs ou des belles formes, —doit vraiment, dans le sens profond du mot, s'appeler idolâtrie, c'est-à-dire le fait de servir avec le meilleur de nos coeurs et de nos esprits quelque chère ou triste image que nous nous sommes créée, pendant que nous désobéissons à l'appel présent du Maître, qui n'est pas mort, qui ne défaille pas en ce moment sous sa croix, mais nous ordonne de porter la nôtre. (129)

As Proust indicates in a footnote to his translation,[14] this passage is the conclusion of a development on "realistic" religious art in Europe, where Ruskin takes exception to the "morbid" representations of the suffering and death of Jesus that are so prevalent in the cathedrals of the Southern countries. To worship the dying Christ is to misunderstand the very reason for his death, which is not death for the believer, but eternal life. The artists who concentrate their creative powers on the symbolization of such violence themselves commit idolatry and are to be held responsible for the fallaciously constituted faith of the semiologically unsophisticated multitudes.

When Proust applies the word "idolatry" to Ruskin's writing, he does not adhere to the strict denotational sense of the definition, but refers to a stylistic manipulation in which unconsciously chosen esthetic preferences undermine the integrity of consciously stated moral ideas. In a nutshell: "Les doctrines qu'il [Ruskin] professait étaient des doctrines morales et non des doctrines esthétiques, et pourtant il les choisissait pour leur beauté. Et comme il ne voulait pas les présenter pour belles, mais comme vraies, il était obligé de se mentir à lui-même sur la nature des raisons qui les lui faisaient adopter" (130). To illustrate his criticism, Proust quotes from a passage of *The Stones of Venice* that describes the reasons for the great city's fall. Ruskin's logic of condemnation can be resumed as follows: Venice was privileged over other places because it had, in the cathedral of St. Mark, an illuminated Bible of stone; its decadence is the less excusable since it took place within proximity of God's concretely depicted message:

> Pour les nations du Nord, une rude et sombre sculpture remplissait leurs temples d'images confuses, à peine lisibles; mais pour elle

[Venise], l'art et les trésors de l'Orient avaient doré chaque lettre, illuminé chaque page, jusqu'à ce que le Temple-Livre brillât au loin comme l'étoile des Mages. Dans d'autres villes, souvent les assemblées du peuple se tenaient dans des lieux éloignés de toute association religieuse, théâtre de la violence et des bouleversements; sur l'herbe du dangereux rempart, dans la poussière de la rue troublée, il y eut des actes accomplis, des conseils tenus à qui nous ne pouvons pas trouver de justification, mais à qui nous pouvons quelquefois donner notre pardon. Mais les péchés de Venise, commis dans son palais ou sur sa piazza, furent accomplis en présence de la Bible qui était à sa droite. (131-32)

Here, Proust protests that the Ruskinian confusion of *forme* and *fond*, of attention to artistic detail and elaboration of prophetic discourse, causes the reader to be falsely persuaded that the Venetians were *more* guilty of their faithlessness than other corrupted Christians. In other words, the difference between a multicolored marble cathedral inlaid with golden mosaics and a more soberly decorated Northern church should have nothing to do with our judgment of the worshippers themselves. In rhetorical terms, Ruskin has manipulated what is in fact a strict metonymical relationship (spatial copresence of people and a cathedral) into the fluid appearance of a metaphorical synecdoche (the people are part of a whole represented by, incarnated in, the cathedral). Seventy years before "Métonymie chez Proust," the author of the *Recherche*, in laying bare the mechanism of Ruskin's rhetoric, has anticipated the deconstructive rigor of modern textual analyses.

But Proust is not content to separate himself from Ruskin in the Olympian detachment of the lucid interpreter: he is just as interested in the complex reasons for the charm and persuasion of this passage as he is in the demonstrable deviousness of its tropological play. In a description reminiscent of Ruskin's evocative prose, Proust relates the "mixed joy" (*joie mêlée* [133]) he felt while reading the paragraph about Venice's decline and fall and emphasizes the contagious magic of the text and the cathedral, the strange power of mutual attraction that made of his idolatrous pilgrimage a moment of unexplainable beauty:

A quel ordre de vérité peut correspondre le plaisir esthétique très vif que l'on prend à lire une telle page, c'est ce qu'il est assez difficile de dire. Elle est elle-même mystérieuse, pleine d'images à la fois de beauté et de religion comme cette même église de Saint-Marc où toutes les figures de l'*Ancien* et du *Nouveau Testament* apparaissent sur le fond d'une sort d'obscurité splendide et d'éclat changeant. Je me souviens de l'avoir lue pour la première fois dans Saint-Marc même, pendant une heure d'orage et d'obscurité où les mosaïques ne brillaient plus que de leur propre et matérielle lumière et d'un or interne, terrestre et ancien, auquel le soleil vénitien, qui enflamme jusqu'aux anges des campaniles, ne mêlait plus rien de lui; l'émotion que j'éprouvais à lire là cette page, parmi tous ces anges qui s'illuminaient des ténèbres environnantes, était très grande et n'était pourtant peut-être pas très pure. Comme la joie de voir les belles figures mystérieuses s'augmentait, mais s'altérait du plaisir en quelque sorte d'érudition que j'éprouvais à comprendre les textes apparus en lettres byzantines à côté de leurs fronts nimbés, de même la beauté des images de Ruskin était avivée et corrompue par l'orgueil de se référer au texte sacré. Une sorte de retour égoïste sur soi-même est inévitable dans ces joies mêlées d'érudition et d'art où le plaisir esthétique peut devenir plus aigu, mais non rester aussi pur. Et peut-être cette pages des *Stones of Venice* était-elle belle surtout de me donner précisément ces joies mêlées que j'éprouvais dans Saint-Marc, elle qui, comme l'église byzantine, avait aussi dans la mosaïque de son style éblouissant dans l'ombre, à côté de ses images sa citation biblique inscrite auprès. (132–33)

Underlying Proust's analysis of Ruskinian imagery is the hypothesis that some form of truth must reside in the experience of esthetic pleasure: otherwise we would not be motivated to read Ruskin in the first place. Yet the farther one penetrates the mixed mode of poetic discourse, the more difficult it becomes to distinguish what is presumed to be artistically revealed truth from the rhetorical lie in which it is enveloped. When Proust opens *The Stones of Venice* and reads its descriptions of St. Mark's while he stands in the darkly illuminated cathedral, the knowledge he gains from a comparison of literary text and iconic representations is not a pure knowledge, but the "proud" understanding of an egotistical *retour sur soi-même,* where the pleasure of an erudite mastery substitutes itself for rigorous, unprejudiced contemplation. The depth, complexity, and originality of Proust's paragraph derive from the fact that this substitution of narcissistic gratification for analytic sobriety is not condemned or otherwise neutralized: it is viewed as a constitutive part of the process of reading, as a logically necessary step in the temporal deployment of the text's interpretation. Ultimately, although his conscious purpose was not so formulated, Proust questions the theoretical possibility of a pure or unmixed method of writing which would, in fact, "tell the truth." If we say that we search for the manifestation of truth in the form of an esthetic object, we tend to forget that this search is really a desire, that this desire is the effort to possess, incorporate, interiorize the object in an act of anxious imprisonment. This pattern holds not only for the reader but for the writer before him, who is principally a reader and reinterpreter of earlier texts, and for the writer before him, *en abyme*. Hence the parallel mirror-sequence of referential idolatry that opens the Proustian description, causing it to trail outward from the impossible truth it seeks to unveil. In attempting to understand the hieroglyphics of St. Mark's, Ruskin imitates the cathedral's surface and falls prey to a formal fetishism; in attempting to probe the origins of the esthetic pleasure he feels in reading Ruskin, Proust reproduces the impure beauty of Ruskinian rhetoric which, in turn, charms us as readers, causing us to remain within the infinitely repeatable cycle of desire.

At its deepest textual level, "John Ruskin" is a reflection on the relationship of criticism to creation, reading to writing. In his conclusion, Proust emphasizes the unbridgeable distance separating us as readers from the originality of the text we seek to decipher by comparing the translator or critic to the restorer of a tomb: like Antigone, we cannot hope to conquer death, but we can assume the task of preserving the remnants of what once lived and breathed. In a foreshadowing of the vocabulary of *Contre Sainte-Beuve,* Proust associates creation with involuntary memory, and criticism with its purely voluntary, rational counterpart:

> Ne pouvant réveiller les flammes du passé, nous voulons du moins recueillir sa cendre. A défaut d'une résurrection dont nous n'avons plus le pouvoir, avec la mémoire glacée que nous avons gardée de ces choses, —la mémoire des faits qui nous dit: "tu étais tel" sans nous permettre de le redevenir, qui nous affirme la réalité d'un paradis perdu au lieu de nous le rendre dans le souvenir, nous voulons du moins le décrire et en constituer la science. C'est quand Ruskin est bien loin de nous que nous traduisons ses livres et tâchons de fixer dans une image ressemblante les traits de sa pensée. Aussi ne connaîtrez-vous pas les accents de notre foi ou de notre amour, et c'est notre piété seule que vous apercevrez çà et là, froide et furtive, occupée, comme la Vierge Thébaine, à restaurer un tombeau.
> (141)

According to this categorical description, criticism and creation relate to each other as polar opposites. Criticism is a "cold" act of the fancy: it can only restate facts abstractly; it remains separate from its object; it adheres to the surface of things and is forever "too late" with respect to the creative source it cannot reach. Creation takes place through the "warm" imaginative process of a memory that descends into the inner essence of phenomena and reveals them in their atemporal, universal significance. By formulating this distinction, Proust announces his desire to cease working at the outside of Ruskin's domain and to begin elaborating the remembered world of Combray from the inside, from the storehouse of his guarded impressions. If we take this argument seriously, we then conclude that the novel *A la recherche du temps perdu* becomes possible once the critical act as such is negated and overcome definitively. But as was apparent in the convoluted cycle of idolatry, the Proustian praxis of reading combines the two intellectual elements that the end of "John Ruskin" separates: the moment in which we recognize the fetishistic rhetoric of the creator, thereby affirming our own critical distance, is followed by our *engagement* into this rhetoric as we also succumb to the persuasive seductiveness of forms.

Reading, then, is neither properly critical nor creative: it is that which renders the discriminatory rigor of analysis incapable of accounting for textual complexity, that which deconstructs the pretensions of a precisely limited genre, such as what we call the "novel," to develop on the far side of rhetoric, in the supposedly self-sufficient isolation of memory's re-created paradise. We need to leave open the possibility that what we call a novel is able to inaugurate itself only by forgetting its dependency on the texts it refuses to read. But this means that the *Recherche,* as texture of memory and forgetfulness, will alternately weave and unweave the reading of its writing,[15] thus reproducing in fictional shape the alternations of lucidity and blindness that constitute literary idolatry.

When Proust tells the story of his successive reactions to Ruskin's work, the mechanism of passion and indifference sounds familiar to the reader of the *Recherche.* This is because what we have been calling "reading" is given the name of "love" in "Un Amour de Swann," where the purely rhetorical substitutions and exchanges of an argument are clothed in the color of fiction. I quote now from "John Ruskin" a passage in which Swann and Odette appear as disincarnated shadows of a plot résumé:

> Cette idolâtrie et ce qu'elle mêle parfois d'un peu factice aux plaisirs littéraires les plus vifs qu'il nous donne, il me faut descendre jusqu'au fond de moi-même pour en saisir la trace, pour en étudier le caractère, tant je suis aujourd'hui "habitué" à Ruskin. Mais elle a dû me choquer souvent quand j'ai commencé à aimer ses livres, avant de fermer peu à peu les yeux sur leurs défauts, *comme il arrive dans tout amour. Les amours pour les créatures vivantes ont quelquefois une origine vile qu'ils épurent ensuite. Un homme fait la connaissance d'une femme parce qu'elle peut l'aider à atteindre un but étranger à elle-même. Puis une fois qu'il la connaît il l'aime pour elle-même, et lui sacrifie sans hésiter ce but qu'elle devait seulement l'aider à atteindre.* A mon amour pour les livres de Ruskin se mêla ainsi à l'origine quelque chose d'intéressé, la

joie du bénéfice intellectuel que j'allais en retirer. (137–38; my emphasis)

Here, a series of rhetorical transfers foreshadows the organization of a novella. The stages of Swann's love for Odette are rigorously parallel to the dialectics of "idolatrous" reading in which interest and disinterest contend for mastery in the mind of the subject. Reading is "like" love (*"comme* il arrive dans tout amour") and love is "like" reading, insofar as they both evolve in the mixed mode of fetishism and intellectual sincerity. "Un Amour de Swann" is thus a rewriting of "John Ruskin" and a repetition, in fictional terms, of a critical argument. But how is it that the *mise en scène* of an analytical act—be it called "love" or "reading"—generates a narrative structure? To develop this question, we must turn to Proust's later study of Ruskin.

## SESAME AND LILIES AND "JOURNÉES DE LECTURE"

In 1906, two years after the publication of *La Bible d'Amiens,* Proust's translation of *Sesame and Lilies* was completed. Soon afterward Proust was to abandon his interpretation of Ruskin and begin the project of *Contre Sainte-Beuve* that led to the first drafts of the *Recherche.* From the standpoint of intellectual biography, *Sésame et les lys* represents a transition and a change in attitude: Proust's impatience with the ideas of Ruskin is evident in the footnotes of his translation, which, unlike those of *La Bible d'Amiens,* are no longer basically informational but openly critical; these notes, in turn, reflect the preoccupations that are developed with admirable coherence in the prefatory essay "Journées de lecture."

*Sesame and Lilies* (1865) is composed of three essays, each of which is a transcription of an oral address. The thematic unity of the volume is questionable, especially the relationship of the final talk, "The Mystery of Life and Its Arts," to the first two, "Sesame" and "Lilies," both of which deal with the subject of reading. For understandable logical reasons, Proust did not translate the third article. This editorial decision has the interesting result of rendering Ruskin's translated work more rationally appealing than it was in 1865. Yet even the reduction of the text to a diptych does not eliminate one central problem: that Ruskin's essay merely begins to treat its theme and soon digresses to include a catalogue of concerns that have little to do with reading itself. One can restate the fundamental line of argumentation in "Sesame" as follows: unlike the laws of social life, which are based upon "advancement" and competition, the essence of reading is nobler, in that it engages the best part of a person and makes it possible for him to enjoy the higher "friendship" of books. Unlike human beings, who are fickle and often unavailable for communication, books are our constant companions, the pure colleagues of the philosophical life. But reading is not to be confused with solipsistic enjoyment: on the contrary, our duty as faithful interpreters is to adhere painstakingly to the text, thereby "annihilating our own personality."[16]

Immediately after these remarks directly concerned with books and their human significance, Ruskin becomes involved in a somewhat tedious discussion of the vulgarity of modern English life, then passionately condemns capitalist exploitation and the violence inherent in the hierarchies of social nobility. Ruskin's conclusion: "I do not know why any of us should talk about reading when our lives need mending" (*Sesame and Lilies*, 83). After this point, the author heeds his own advice and does very little talking about reading. During this period of his career, Ruskin's consciousness of economic inequalities and social injustice caused him to adopt the attitude of "first things first"; intellectual pursuits such as reading had to wait until the primary necessities of life were achieved for all citizens. Although he returns briefly to his theme in an association of reading with the "Open Sesame" of magical possession-taking, most of "Sesame"'s second section is about "money-making mobs" and the excesses of so-called free trade.

In "Lilies" books are discussed in their relationship to the education of women: the emphasis is not on the act of reading as psychological or intellectual process but rather on its beneficial or nefarious moral effects. The sudden diminution of translator's footnotes is an obvious indication that Proust has little interest in or sympathy for Ruskin's overly protective and delicate paternalism.[17] "Journées de lecture" will criticize, complicate, and invert Ruskin's "Sesame" and virtually ignore "Lilies."

Proust's ambivalently admiring and critical attitude toward Ruskin's theory of reading is evident not only in his prefatory essay but also in the running commentary furnished by his copious notes, which, when combined in sequence, form a second essay worth examining in itself. Indeed, the printed page of *Sésame et les lys* is a double text, with Ruskin and Proust alternately speaking and exchanging opinions: commentary and original work merge in what might be called a "conversational" unity. The extent of Proust's ambivalence is immediately clear from the first note,[18] in which he both praises Ruskin for the latter's polysemic variations on the word "Sesame" and also warns against the tendency toward fetishistic adoration that resides in such a love of words in themselves. In literary terms, the praise amounts to an eloquent defense of thematic structure and, by anticipation, a justification of the thematic/symphonic harmonies of the *Recherche*.

Within the word "Sesame" Proust finds three principal meanings: the literal sense of the sesame seed, the metaphorical sense of a magical opening (*Arabian Nights*), and the allegorical level that derives from the metaphorical: "La parole magique qui ouvre la porte de la caverne des voleurs . . . étant *l'allégorie de la lecture* qui nous ouvre la porte de ces trésors où est enfermée la plus précieuse sagesse des hommes: les livres" (*Sésame et les lys*, 61; my emphasis). Later variations split the three themes apart and add connotative nuances, so that in the end Proust thinks he can recognize as many as seven themes inextricably mixed, illuminating each other in a mutually reflective radiance.[19] Yet this apparent total identification of critic and author in shared esthetic beliefs is accompanied by the warning against idolatry which, throughout the notes of *Sésame et les lys*, becomes a veritable obsession for Proust. On the one hand, the author of the *Recherche* excuses the disorderly appearance of Ruskin's argument by postulating that the thematic richness of the word "Sesame" imposes retrospectively on the essay a "logique supérieure" (62); yet at the same time the reiterated accusation of idolatry constitutes an analytical dissection of Ruskin's logical/rhetorical fallacies. As in "John Ruskin," the notes to *Sésame et les lys* expresses a certain theoretical discomfort, because the critic finds it impossible to choose definitively between the attitudes of polite respect and negative judgment.

On the whole, the scale is tipped toward criticism and judgment, and the general mechanism of fetishism or idolatry allows Proust to unveil contradictions at every step of his master's path. When Ruskin equates reading with a higher form of friendship, he distinguishes between the fortuitousness of human encounters and the "necessary" relationship that links a reader to his books. Our friends in life are simply there, present, whether we like it or not: books are the instruments of conscious choice, they come to us only on command and leave us when we tire of their momentary charm. According to Proust, this line of argument is based upon a "raisonnement spécieux" (70). The true difference between what Montaigne called two forms of *commerce* is, in Proust's words, "la manière dont nous communiquons avec eux [les amis et les livres]" (62). By revealing the logical fallacy on which Ruskin's thought is constructed (i.e., it is not really true that we cannot choose our friends; and furthermore, even if we can choose them freely, they are really not comparable to books, being of a different "essence"), Proust then can introduce his own theory: reading is to friendship what reflective solitude is to conversation—that is, a superior form of communication in which we reach the inner heart of things:

> Notre mode de communication avec les personnes implique une déperdition des forces actives de l'âme que concentrent et exaltent au contraire ce merveilleux miracle de la lecture qui est la communication au sein de la solitude . . . on peut dire qu'en général la

conversation nous met sur le chemin des expressions brillantes ou
de purs raisonnements, presque jamais d'une impression profonde.
Donc la gracieuse raison donnée par Ruskin (l'impossibilité de
choisir ses amis, la possibilité de choisir ses livres) n'est pas la vraie
. . . une conversation avec Platon serait encore une conversation,
c'est-à-dire un exercice infiniment plus superficiel que la lecture, la
valeur des choses écoutées ou lues étant de moindre importance
que l'état spirituel qu'elles peuvent créer en nous et qui ne peut être
profond que dans la solitude ou dans cette solitude peuplée qu'est
la lecture. (70–71)

Proust's conception of reading as an exercise of innerness can be linked to
the penetrative power of the Romantic imagination, whereas Ruskin's
conversational bias is a product of the fancy, a worship of formal decoration, of brilliance for the sake of brilliance, an idolatry.

In examining the deviousness of Ruskin's rhetoric, Proust isolates one
constantly recurring feature: the presence, on a metaphorical level, of the
themes of "advancement" and "noble superiority" that had been condemned in the literal explicitness of declarative statement. In "Sesame,"
books were said to be incompatible with the competitiveness of capitalism
on the one hand and with the superficial concerns of aristocratic snobbery
on the other. Yet when Ruskin attempts to persuade his audience that
reading is inherently more worthwhile and more ethically admirable than
all necessarily impure social motivations, he resorts to such comparisons as:
"Will you go and gossip with your housemaid, or your stable-boy, when
you may talk with queens and kings?" (*Sesame and Lilies,* 62; here, the
queens and kings stand for the "noble" company of books). And later,
describing the "kingdom" of books, he comments: "By your aristocracy
of companionship there, your own inherent aristocracy will be assuredly
tested, and the motives with which you strive to take high place in the
society of the living, measured, as to all the truth and sincerity that are in
them, by the place you desire to take in this company of the Dead" (ibid.).
Referring to the first of these passages, Proust writes: "Quelle vanité que
la métaphore quand elle donne de la dignité à l'idée précisément à l'aide
des fausses grandeurs dont nous nions la dignité" (*Sésame et les lys,* 79).
And in the second case, his demolition of Ruskinian logic foreshadows the
social criticism of the *Recherche.* In the following paragraph we see how
*snobisme* relates to *sophisme:*

En réalité la place que nous désirons occuper dans la société des
morts ne nous donne nullement le droit de désirer en occuper une
dans la société des vivants. La vertu de ceci devrait nous détacher
de cela. Et si la lecture et l'admiration ne nous détachent pas de

l'ambition . . . c'est un sophisme de dire que nous nous sommes
acquis par les premières le droit de sacrifier à la seconde. Un
homme n'a pas plus de titres à être "reçu dans la bonne société"
ou du moins à désirer de l'être, parce qu'il est plus intelligent et plus
cultivé. C'est là un de ces sophismes que la vanité des gens intel-
ligents va chercher dans l'arsenal de leur intelligence pour justifier
leurs penchants les plus vils. Cela reviendrait à dire que d'être
devenu plus intelligent, crée des droits à l'être moins. Tout simplement diverses personnes se côtoient au sein de chacun de nous,
et la vie de plus d'un homme supérieur n'est souvent que la coexistence d'un philosophe et d'un snob. (82)

An examination of the notes to *Sésame et les lys* reveals the semiological
coherence of Proust's theoretical reflections and tends to confirm that the
*Recherche* is, at its deepest level, a fictional working-out of the deconstruction of idolatry. As we have seen in the juxtaposition of "Journées de
pèlerinage" to the Balbec-en-terre episode, the central Proustian experience
is the discovery of the constitutive cleavage that splits the sign into a
liberated, irresponsible *signifiant* and a referentially determined meaning
(the *signifié* cannot remain "pure," but is imprisoned in the referent,
caught up in an incestuous metonymical bond with the constraints of
reality). The error demonstrated in the passage from "Noms de pays: le
nom" to "Noms de pays: le pays" is that of an excessive adherence to the
surface of the *signifiant*. This is precisely the mistake of the idolater or
snob, who attaches too much value to the outside of forms, at the expense
of the significant core that these forms hide. The intellectual insincerity
that Proust discovers in the metaphorical fabric of Ruskin's writing is the
purely intellectual equivalent of the narrator's naïve admiration of the
name and symbolic attributes of the Guermantes family, the only difference being that of a structural reversal: whereas Ruskin believes he speaks
in the mode of truth, he in fact lies to himself and undermines his credi-
bility; the narrator of the *Recherche,* beginning in a state of idolatrous
adoration of the nobility, must learn to recognize his self-deception in
order to achieve the gift of revealed truth from which his future work will
emanate. This ideal pattern composes the outward narrative progression
of the novel, but the extent to which a language of truth is possible is
made questionable by the ironical presence of idolatry within all discourse, especially within that discourse which presumes to tell the truth.
As we turn now to "Journées de lecture," we will proceed further in an
analysis of the interaction between reading as semiological process (discovery and understanding of the truth embedded in signs) and reading as
rhetorical articulation (exploitation of "idolatrous" poetic effects).

To read "Journées de lecture" analytically is to enter a magic world of *correspondances* and break its charm: one hesitates at the threshold, as might any perpetrator of sacrilege aware of the destruction he is about to cause. Doubtless, Proust's preface to *Sésame et les lys* is one of the most beautiful, sensually appealing, and intellectually rigorous accounts of "l'acte psychologique original appelé *Lecture*" ("Journées de lecture," 172) in French literature. It is divided into two parts, the first being essentially an evocation of the protective atmosphere enveloping a young reader whose resemblance to the "Marcel" of Combray is obvious, the second being an elaboration of Proust's theory of reading as compared and contrasted to that of Ruskin, with special emphasis on the values of reflection, innerness, and solitude. The problem which the present interpretation addresses is that of the logical relationship between the first twelve pages (160–72) and the last twenty-two (172–94). How is it that the prefigurative sketch of Combray's charms, in which the act of reading is depicted not for itself, but in a labyrinth of metaphorical associations, coexists with a far more rational discourse of theoretical distinction and discrimination? On the level of direct declaration, Proust provides an answer to this question himself at the close of the first section, when he says: "Avant d'essayer de montrer au seuil des 'Trésors des Rois' pourquoi à mon avis la lecture ne doit pas jouer dans la vie le rôle prépondérant que lui assigne Ruskin dans ce petit ouvrage, je devais mettre hors de cause les charmantes lectures de l'enfance dont le souvenir doit rester pour chacun de nous une bénédiction" (171–72). Proust's initial appeal to what, in Ruskinian terms, might be called the "common treasury" of all readers— those never-to-be-forgotten days in which we entered the pages of a book and lost contact with the vicissitudes of reality—is a necessary catharsis which, once accomplished, allows us to speak seriously of reading in the purer context of theoretical discernment. Proust admits, in the succeeding sentences, that the very length and tone of the first part indicate his own vulnerability to the "sortilège" (172) of which he must rid himself before assuming a properly critical stance; but the assumption remains that we can walk the straight path of analytical clarity and systematic theoretical exposition only when the "chemins fleuris et détournés" (1972) of childhood sensations in the re-created paradise of memory have been interiorized and subordinated to the higher purpose of rational understanding.

If, by an act of critical incursion, we penetrate the flowery and devious web of Proust's rhetoric at the beginning of "Journées de lecture," we find that the unquestionably seductive beauty of the passage derives from the "association of ideas" that Ruskin condemned in *Modern Painters II*. More precisely, we see that the reason for the passage's powerful psychological effect upon us is that it does not limit itself to a discussion of books as such, but, in developing a network of physical impressions that "surround" the process of reading in the mind of the young writer/narrator, it entices us to abandon our own posture of theoretical vigilance and allow ourselves to be bathed in the sunlight of a spring afternoon in the country. Proust begins his essay with the sentence: "Il n'y a pas de jours de notre enfance que nous ayons si pleinement vécus que ceux que nous avons cru laisser sans les vivre, ceux que nous avons passés avec un livre préféré" (160). The remainder of the first paragraph and, in a sense, the entirety of the first twelve pages constitute a sophisticated persuasive argument which demonstrates that the time we thought to have wasted in reading is in fact recuperable on the level of deep inner experience. In other words, although the mature Marcel Proust may no longer be enchanted by the content of the books he read as a child, his remembrance of "le jeu pour lequel un ami venait nous chercher au passage le plus intéressant, l'abeille ou le rayon de soleil gênants qui nous forçaient à lever les yeux de la page ou à changer de place, les provisions de goûter qu'on nous avait fait emporter et que nous laissions à côté de nous sur le banc" (160) is closely (metonymically) linked to the printed page. It is this remembrance—of what for the young boy was mere contingent distraction—that now becomes the necessary chain of associative phenomena granting access to the essence of past time: "S'il nous arrive encore aujourd'hui de feuilleter ces livres d'autrefois, ce n'est plus que comme les seuls calendriers que nous ayons gardés des jours enfuis, et avec l'espoir de voir reflétés sur leurs pages les demeures et les étangs qui n'existent plus" (ibid.). The resurrection of involuntary memory on which Proust's novel will be based has its origin here, in the reflected, recoverable beauty of youth. But we must not lose sight of the paragraph's rhetorical *glissements,* which ground the poetry of remembrance in a nonreading. We "live" and relive our former existence only because the actual act of reading as enjoyed by the child has been forgotten and is now replaced by the pleasurable fabric of a unified fictional world.

But what is the essence of reading as concrete intellectual activity? Although it is only in the second part of "Journées de lecture" that Proust attempts to answer this question explicitly and in theoretical terms, one can find in the initial pages of the essay a coherent series of remarks pointing to a psychological solution. If we accept that the term "essence" here implies an inner constitutive core without which the process of reading cannot come into being, then we can define the essence of reading as the desire of the self to possess the other while remaining protected from the other's actual embrace. The theme of protectiveness, everywhere present in "Journées de lecture," is tied closely to the idea of hiding and to the delightful possibility of an unobservable observation point or inviolable sanctuary. Some examples:

Qui ne se souvient comme moi de ces lectures faites au temps des vacances, qu'on allait *cacher* successivement dans toutes celles des heures du jour qui étaient assez paisibles et assez *inviolables* pour pouvoir leur *donner asile.*

Je montais en courant *dans le labyrinthe* jusqu'à telle charmille, où je m'asseyais, *introuvable.* . . . Dans cette charmille, le silence était profond, *le risque d'être découvert presque nul,* la *sécurité* rendue plus douce par les cris éloignés qui, d'en bas, *m'appelaient en vain.*

Et quelquefois à la maison, *dans mon lit,* longtemps après le diner, les dernières heures de la soirée *abritaient* aussi ma lecture. . . . Alors, *risquant d'être puni si j'étais découvert* et l'insomnie qui, le livre fini, se prolongerait peut-être toute la nuit, dès que mes parents étaient couchés je rallumais ma bougie. (161, 168, 169; my emphasis)

The scene of reading has a constant structure which is infinitely repeatable. Whether the writer imagines his mental adventures as being hidden within the "hours of the day" or, more concretely, as taking place inside the refuge of a thicket or the dark silence of a room, in each case the experience of reading is a threat to the stable bourgeois virtues of the family context and is also itself threatened by the constraints of real life. The protective cocoon in which the young Proust is sheltered is an artistic representation of the womb. The proliferation of rooms that the narrator of the *Recherche* evokes at the beginning of the novel derives from the impossible, exasperated desire to recover the fragile isolation of the original matrix. Proust's novel is thus the progression of a regression: the changes of location and evolution of characters, the protagonist's obstinate search for artistic truth and his successful discovery of a vocation, serve to mask the fact that with each positive step "forward," there is an increasingly violent effort to return to the defensive status of a quasi-embryonic tactile consciousness. Reading is what Kierkegaard would have called an "absolute paradox," since its mode of existence is passive, hidden, enclosed, involuted, but its intent is active, oriented toward discovery, based upon the presumed capacity of the reader to "annihilate himself" and open himself to the creative power of the *other.*

Proust's response to this paradoxical situation is to simulate openness to exterior reality and receptiveness to that which menaces the integrity of his ego while he forges a logic of domination and control that allows for no real communication with the outside. Thus, in a digressive discussion of the decoration of rooms, Proust initiates his argument polemically, by taking exception to those people who surround themselves with familiar objects and works: "Je laisse les gens de goût faire de leur chambre l'image même de leur goût et la remplir seulement de choses qu'il puisse approuver. Pour moi, je ne me sens vivre et penser que dans une chambre où tout est la création et le langage de vies profondément différentes de la mienne, d'un goût opposé au mien, où je ne retrouve rien de ma pensée consciente, où mon imagination s'exalte en se sentant plongée au sein du non-moi" (167). But this plunge into the heart of the *other,* which carries with it the force of alienation and subjective dispossession, soon gives way to its opposite: the violent appropriation of the room's identity in an act of mastery or imprisonment whose closest psychological equivalent is a phantasmic rape. I now quote the conclusion of the paragraph on room decoration, in which the original rationale of the polemical discussion is overshadowed by a coherent sexual metaphorics. Here, Proust describes a hypothetical impersonal hotel somewhere in the provinces—its noises, smells, and cold atmosphere. We enter the room:

> Le soir, quand on ouvre la porte de sa chambre, on a le sentiment de *violer* toute la vie qui y est restée éparse, de la prendre hardiment par la main quand, la porte refermée, on entre plus avant, jusqu'à la table ou jusqu'à la fenêtre; de s'asseoir dans une sorte de *libre promiscuité* avec elle sur le canapé exécuté par le tapissier du chef-lieu dans ce qu'il croyait le goût de Paris; de *toucher partout la nudité* de cette vie dans le dessein de *se troubler soi-même* par sa propre familiarité, en posant ici et là ses affaires, *en jouant le maître* dans cette chambre pleine jusqu'aux bords de l'âme des autres et qui garde jusque dans la forme des chenêts et le dessin des rideaux l'empreinte de leur rêve, en marchant pieds nus sur son tapis inconnu; alors, *cette vie secrète, on a le sentiment de l'enfermer avec soi* quand on va, tout tremblant, tirer le verrou; de *la pousser devant soi dans le lit et de coucher enfin avec elle* dans les grands draps blancs qui vous montent par-dessus la figure, tandis que, tout près, l'église sonne pour toute la ville les heures d'insomnie des mourants et des amoureux. (167–68; my emphasis)

For the reader of the *Recherche* this passage has a prophetic ring: it foreshadows the nature of the relationship between Marcel and Albertine. In *La Prisonnière* and *La Fugitive* the efforts of the protagonist are directed toward the impossible possession of a creature who fictively incorporates the *non-moi* of the provincial hotel room: Albertine also contains a "soul" and "dreams" that are the target of jealous investigations. Just as the desired mastery of the room is accomplished by an act of violence, in the same way Albertine can be possessed only through force, only by the kind of domination that betrays a fundamental insecurity in the hero's psychological constitution. If we read the above paragraph allegorically, keeping in mind its prefigurative status for the novel, we find that the process of reading vacillates between the unhappy consciousness of a fall into alterity (in opening a book, we plunge into the enigmatic otherness of signs) and the rhetorically fallacious but inevitable gesture by which we deny the existence of the *other* as such. In the latter volumes of the *Recherche* this pattern emerges as the alternation between anxiety and repose within the protagonist's imagination. When Albertine is correctly deciphered as elusive figure of ambivalence, Marcel loses his sense of self and gives in to a profound depression; when he naïvely assumes that he can empty her of her meanings and render her semiologically inactive, he enjoys a short-lived, illusory triumph. Thus, that which reading seems to promise as the logical result of its unfolding—the unveiling of truth in the luminosity of a successful hermeneutics—is in fact the hopeful projection of a subjectivity that prefers not to abdicate its control over the complexity of the sign or become overwhelmed by the rhetoric of lying.

If we turn now to the second part of "Journées de lecture," in which Proust elaborates a theory of reading grounded in "ce miracle fécond d'une communication au sein de la solitude" (174), we bring to the text an ironic awareness of the considerable price one has to pay to remain happily ensconced in the fragility of a protective solitude. On the one hand, it is impossible not to agree with Proust that the silent atmosphere of meditation is inherently and objectively more conducive to the exercise of reading than is the superficial context of conversation. We can also agree, on a pragmatic level, that it is a mistake to expect too much of reading, a mistake to confuse the book learning of the dilettante with the more profound efforts of an artist to find his own language, to make the transition from what he has learned of another author to what he now must discover within himself.[20] On the other hand, however, we must not forget that the choice of solitude as opposed to conversation is in fact the expression of a deeper desire: that of a pure narcissism which would constitute itself in the transparency of self-contemplation. Psychologically, conversation represents a major threat to the author of "Journées de lecture," since it implies an actual encounter with opinions which the self might not master easily. Hence, the scientifically objective presentation of the final pages of the essay acts as a mask hiding the "chemins fleuris et détournés" of the self's (hidden) rhetoric. But the masking effect is only partially successful, and at every twist and turn of his discourse, Proust returns to his obsessive metaphorics of possession and penetration. Indeed, it seems impossible to describe the process of reading without resorting to the figuration of sexual desire. When we read an isolated phrase of a writer, we see a small corner of a domain whose entirety we wish to visit and appropriate: "Dans chaque tableau qu'ils [les poètes] nous montrent, ils ne semblent nous donner qu'un léger aperçu d'un site merveilleux, différent du reste du monde, *et au coeur duquel nous voudrions qu'ils nous fissent pénétrer*" (177). Later in the same passage, Proust characterizes artistic "vision" as an essentially erotic relationship linking the reader to the beckoning surface of esthetic objects: "Cette apparence avec laquelle *ils nous charment et nous déçoivent et au-delà de laquelle nous voudrions aller*, c'est l'essence même de cette chose en quelque sorte sans épaisseur—mirage arrêté sur une toile—qu'est une vision. Et cette brume que nos yeux avides *voudraient percer*, c'est le dernier mot de l'art du peintre" (177-78; my emphasis). The basis of rhetorical discourse is its charm, which is always a charm of deception. We are made to believe the unbelievable—for example, that reading can be accounted for in theoretically neutral terms—whereas we will always "go beyond" the sense of the poetic structure itself, constructing our own subjectively rooted meanings, in an effort to impregnate the already-filled text—with ourselves.

The subversion of theoretical clarity by rhetorical association through which "Journées de lecture" deconstructs itself demonstrates that literary language cannot originate in a "pure" inwardness. The ideal of solitary communication is a desire, and the ideal of a prose free from referential imprisonment is ironized by the erotic/culpable relationship of the self to the reality from which it seeks to hide. If, in studying Proust's intellectual debt to Ruskin, we adopt the historical-psychological scheme proposed by Bloom and Terdiman for the evolution of modern literature, according to which an increased inwardness and loss of reciprocity with the world separates the unhappy son from his happier father, we must add a restriction: it is only on the conscious and declarative theoretical level that the son seems to succeed in eliminating the father's influence—in Proust's case by an intelligent equation of idolatry with the superficial outwardness of conversation. But in the act of writing, in the very movement of turning inside, Proust becomes engaged in the rhetoric of idolatry and can only repeat Ruskin's pattern of possession-taking. From the standpoint of theory, Proust creates a metaphorics of depth as the logical expression of a clear conceptual scheme; in Ricardou's terminology, "depth" is used as a mere ornament. But in fact, as was evident in the paragraph on the provincial hotel room, underlying the rational argument of Proust's discourse is a deeper depth, *la profondeur en tant que schème ordinal*. There is, first of all, at the most fundamental generative level, a desire of depth from which the coherent eroticism of the passage derives. If Proust "goes beyond" Ruskin, it is not because he has a better theory, but because he sinks into the abyss of possession/dispossession and assumes the desperate task of imprisoning a forever escaping sign. "Journées de lecture" is an especially important early text because, in describing the central scene of reading, it also demonstrates the apparently effortless transition from an isolated, self-centered privileged moment to the narration of that moment as an "allegory of reading," wherein the alternative recognition of and fall into idolatrous rhetoric takes on the temporal progression of a fiction. Within the scene of reading are the seeds from which the *Recherche* as a novelistic structure takes form. It is the morphology of this birth that the following chapter will undertake to examine.

# 4
# The Birth
# of Narration

## FANCY AND IMAGINATION: ALLEGORY AND SYMBOL

In asking the question, What is the origin of Proustian narration? I do not presuppose the possibility of discovering a precise point of articulation at which the critic of Ruskin, and later, of Sainte-Beuve, suddenly transforms himself into a creative author. On the one hand, our present knowledge of the genesis of the *Recherche,* as derived from textual study of *cahiers* and *carnets,* tends to show that the isolation of one such central point as opposed to another would be no more than the indication of a given reader's subjective preference. Proust's method of composition is that of addition and superposition, not of division and discrimination, so that very often a *cahier*'s contents will include analytical commentary as well as novelistic developments. On the other hand, as I have demonstrated in the two preceding chapters, Proust's reading of Ruskin renders problematic the traditional theoretical distinction between creation and criticism. It is true that Proust "criticizes" his predecessor, and it is true that his conception of reading as elaborated in "Journées de lecture" grants a privileged status to the creative act. In this narrow sense, there is no need to separate Proust from Ruskin on a strictly discursive-theoretical level: Proust only repeats the Ruskinian paradigm of imaginative possession-taking and thus in no way challenges or overcomes the ruling dichotomies and hierarchy of esthetic values that characterize Romanticism. But the rhetorical/deconstructive level of Proust's writing tells a different story. This was especially evident in the ironical juxtaposition of the Balbec-en-terre episode to its counterpart in "Journées de pèlerinage," where the desire to take possession of the hidden significance of the sign was revealed as illusory. In the same vein, but on a deeper psychological plane, we saw that the ideal of communication in the womb of silence, which assumed the phantasmic structure of a penetration, in fact masked the aggressiveness of a frustrated dominance and foreshadowed the alternations of imprisonment and escape in the latter sections of the *Recherche*.

Our examination of reading in Proust leads to a hypothesis which has been hinted at in an earlier development but which needs to be dealt with explicitly now: namely, that the deconstruction of possession-taking is at the core of Proustian narration, or, to use the terms of Paul de Man, that the *Recherche as* narrative form is the "allegory" of this deconstruction.[1] In some sense, then, the impossibility of penetrating the sign to master its meanings leads to a narrative deployment of this impossibility. But what is the structure of this deployment, how does it function, how does our knowledge of its manifestation give us a better understanding of Proust's novel? Can we legitimately name such a narrative and define it with theoretical rigor? To answer these questions, it is necessary to shift terminology from the psychologically based duality of fancy versus imagination to a more formal language we recognize as immanent to the specific field of esthetics. What concerns us now is the *modality* of narration and no longer the state of mind or subjective attitude that "determines" the choice of a given artistic construct. But in moving from the psychology of the subject to the descriptive domain of literary theory, although we change registers and use different tools of investigation, we remain within the same circle of essential problems, within the same generative dichotomies. I propose now that we make a terminological substitution faithful to the logic of Romantic esthetics that will allow us to open up the question of narration. Let us replace the couple *fancy* and *imagination* by its analogue in the domain of representational theory, *allegory* and *symbol*. In so doing, we will eventually justify the use of the term *allegory* in association with narrative structure and will deepen and complete earlier remarks concerning the contradictions between the theory and practice of Proust's novel.

The explicit link of the imagination to symbolism and of the fancy to allegorization is to be found in the theoretical reflections of many Romantic writers, with an almost exclusively positive valuation placed on the first couple, and a negative connotation attached to the second. A discourse of symbols is recommended as the highest and worthiest to poets, whereas allegory is relegated to the secondary status of uninspired ornamental illustration. I shall begin with two statements by Coleridge, the first from *The Statesman's Manual,* the second from his *Miscellaneous Criticism:*

Now an allegory is but a translation of abstract notions in a picture-language, which is itself nothing but an abstraction from objects of the senses; the principal being more worthless even than its phantom proxy, both alike unsubstantial, and the former shapeless to boot. On the other hand a symbol . . . is characterized by a translucence of the special in the individual, or of the general in the special, or of the universal in the general; above all by the translucence of the eternal through and in the temporal. It always partakes of the reality which it renders intelligible, and while it enunciates the whole, abides itself as a living part in that unity of which it is the representative. The other are but empty echoes which the fancy arbitrarily associates with apparitions of matter, less beautiful but not less shadowy than the sloping orchard or hillside pasture seen in the transparent lake below.

The Symbolical cannot perhaps be better defined in distinction from the Allegorical, than that it is always itself a part of that, of the whole of which it is representative. —"Here comes a sail"— (that is a ship) is a symbolical expression. "Behold our lion" when we speak of some gallant soldier, is allegorical. Of most importance to our present subject is this point, that the latter (allegory) cannot be other than spoken consciously, —whereas in the former (the symbol) it is very possible that the general truth may be unconsciously in the writer's mind during the construction of the symbol; and it proves itself by being produced out of his own mind, —as the Don Quixote out of the perfectly sane mind of Cervantes, and not by outward observation or historically. The advantage of symbolic writing over allegory is, that it presumes no disjunction of faculties, but simple dominance. [2]

The theoretical discourse of Coleridge is organized in a series of neatly defined polarities that function on the philosophical, rhetorical, semiological, and psychological levels. Philosophically, the symbol is characterized by its "essential" quality, whereas allegory is "arbitrary." Rhetorically, this means that the symbol translates into synecdoche—the figure of part-whole relationships in which there is a shared essence (in Coleridge's example, the sail "symbolizes" the ship by being itself a portion of the ship's materiality)—whereas in allegory the link between tenor and vehicle must be inferred by the reader (when we say "Behold our lion" we must supply the common element "courage" that relates a gallant soldier to a beast of prey). Semiologically, the fact that allegory functions according to arbitrary or "abstract" association implies a separation between *signifiant* and *signifié* that can lead to erroneous interpretation. The symbol, on the other hand, would seem to escape misreading in that sign and meaning

are bathed in a superior "translucence." Perhaps it would be more precise
to say that the structure of allegorical representation presupposes on the
part of the reader a certain "foreknowledge" of cultural contexts that
would allow him to bridge the gap between the phenomenality of a given
picture language and its authorially intended significance, while Coleridge
wishes us to believe that the meanings of the symbol unfold in an organic
manner from the core of its manifestation in substance. Although in some
cases poets do not consciously realize the implications of their symbolism,
it is assumed that readers can get at these implications without recourse to
"outward observation" or historical fact, through an act of magical intuition. Finally, in terms of psychology, the semiological constitution of
allegory as a split sign causes, within the writer and the reader, an unpleasant "disjunction of faculties," while symbolical discourse, with its presumed fusion of *signifiant* and *signifié,* can be mastered by the author and
controlled by the reader in an act of "simple dominance."

As is well known, Coleridge's reflections on the nature of poetic language derive from German early Romantic theories.[3] The play of dichotomies that appears in the above quotations can be traced back to
various literary sources, and the juxtaposition and analysis of these sources
can lead to a coherent set of programmatic values whose totality defines
the deepest currents of Romantic thought.[4] Such a study is beyond the
scope of the present limited inquiry. I will merely emphasize here the
fundamental system of polarities generated by the couple symbol-allegory
during this period and will underline certain complexities inherent in the
system that add a note of ambivalence to the clear-cut appearance of
critical distinctions.

The consensus among German Romantic writers concerning the merits
of the symbol and the disadvantages of allegory is most obvious if one
renders it visible in a schematic tableau. Following is a nonexhaustive but
representative sample of opinions:[5]

| AUTHOR | SYMBOL<br>(positive value) | ALLEGORY<br>(negative value) |
| --- | --- | --- |
| A. W. Schlegel | "Organic" | "Mechanical" |
| H. Meyer | Fusion of *signifiant* and *signifié* | Separation of *signifiant* and *signifié* |
| Humboldt | "Penetration": profound joy of reaching the inner signifi-cance of things | "Cold admiration": superficial pleasure in the deciphering of an enigma |
| Hegel | "Warm, Full, Serious, Sub-stantial" | "Cold, Empty, Non-substantial" |
| Goethe | "Laconic density of signifi-cance" | "Discursive expansive-ness" |

| AUTHOR | SYMBOL *(positive value)* | ALLEGORY *(negative value)* |
|---|---|---|
| Goethe *(cont.)* | "Unconscious mode of production" | "Conscious mode of production" |
| | "Productive of potentially infinite interpretation" | "Understandable and finite significance" |
| Creuzer | "Unmediated vision" | Mediated representation |
| | "Instantaneous totality of a light-ray falling from heaven" | "Progression in a series of moments" |

The central point at which all these valuations converge is the semiological structure of the two opposed modes of discourse. It is agreed generally, in accordance with the later definition of Coleridge, that the symbol "abides itself as a living part in that unity of which it is a representative," while the meaning of an allegorical representation is only imperfectly and conventionally incorporated in a "picture language" with which it relates abstractly, artificially. To express this difference of formal properties the Romantics used a metaphorics of sexuality. Since the nature of allegory is that of separateness and semantic *difference,* it is termed "mechanical," "cold," "empty," whereas the fused essence of the symbol evokes "organicity," "warmth," "depth," "penetration." The ultimate dream of Romantic thought is thus to lift the barrier between sign and meaning, to attain a level of transparent communication where there is a *melted* totality of significance expressed by Creuzer as an "unmediated vision." The temptation is to equate the language of symbolism with the instantaneousness of a metaphysical revelation, and call this moment of illumination the "nature of poetry." I now quote from one of Goethe's reflections:

> Es ist ein grosser Unterschied, ob der Dichter zum Allgemeinen das Besondere sucht oder im Besondern das Allgemeine schaut. Aus jener Art entsteht Allegorie, wo das Besondere nur als Beispiel, als Exempel des Allgemeinen gilt; *die letztere aber ist eigentlich die Natur der Poesie: sie spricht ein Besonderes aus, ohne ans Allgemeine zu denken oder darauf hinzuweisen.* Wer nun dieses Besondere lebendig fasst, erhält zugleich das Allgemeine mit, ohne es gewahr zu werden, oder erst spät. (my emphasis)[6]

Not only is the mode of production of the symbol unconscious (the poet expresses, within the particular, a general truth of which he is unaware), but its mode of reception as well: we are told that if the reader "grasps the particular," he "immediately" obtains the general. His consciousness either remains forever ignorant of the deeper message of the symbol or else learns it at some later point. But it is important to probe the consequences of Goethe's categorical statement. On the one hand, since the "nature of poetry" is that of an unmediated unconscious communication, Time as difference or separation is abolished. The lifting of the barrier between *signifiant* and *signifié,* image and meaning, the particular and the general, allows the two poles to merge and lose their identity *as* poles. On the other hand, however, Goethe is unable to abandon completely the problem of conscious or rational understanding. The differential between the immediate effect of the symbol's power and the perception of the significance of this power can only be described in terms of a temporal jump ("oder erst spät"). That is: the inner structure of the symbol can be accounted for in atemporal terms, but the reading of the symbol—the manner in which we approach its meaning from the "outside" of our rationality—reintroduces a temporal horizon.

## THE "MADELEINE" AND TEXTUAL TEMPORALITY

The relevance of the symbol-allegory controversy to Proust's work becomes evident if we reread the famous "madeleine" episode in the light of the organizing polarities pictured on the preceding pages. It will be remembered that the ecstatic discovery of past time in its lived totality allows the narrator-protagonist of the *Recherche* to begin the unravelling of his remembrances, to set in motion the narrative of his childhood: before he tasted the cake dipped in tea and understood its significance as unifying link between his present and past selves, he was only able to visualize, in schematic abstraction, the isolated screen-memory of the "drame du coucher." The narrator explains that the revelation of the madeleine episode takes place through the power of involuntary memory, which, unlike purely conscious memory, conserves the essence of past events. Proust's *mémoire involontaire* is structured according to the symbolical mode: it is based upon a "translucence" of the general in the particular and the fusion of *signifiant* and *signifié.* The "édifice immense du souvenir" is potentially present in the "goutelette presque impalpable" of the tea (I, 47); the taste of the cake allows a smooth transition from the merely sensual to the transcendentally meaningful. Further, the entire episode takes place under the aegis of possession-taking. Recent psychocritical readings have revealed the subterranean roots of the passage—the congruence of the "petite madeleine"'s shape with the vulva, the "cannibalistic" undertones of the communion of the self with maternal substance, the narcissistic aggression of the protagonist toward an exterior body he must assimilate while attempting to conserve his own integrity and desired inviolability.[7]

Rhetorically, the text is constructed according to manipulations of *contenant* and *contenu,* beginning with the introductory paragraph, in which the narrator asserts his belief in the possibility of releasing the souls of one's dead ancestors held captive in the "inferior" forms of plants and animals: when passing near such enclosures, we manage to "entrer en possession de l'objet qui est leur prison." The souls escape from their confinement, having conquered death, "et reviennent vivre avec nous" (I, 44). In a similar way, the truth of past experience contained within the materiality of the madeleine is released when the protagonist unlocks its significant potential in the combined actions of tasting and remembering. But in a second movement, that which has been freed from the bonds of oblivion becomes re-imprisoned within the subject. The liberated souls come to "live with" the self, while it is equally clear that the truths inhabiting the madeleine are in fact the hidden proof of Marcel's inner continuity and abiding personal identity. The episode as a whole produces an apotheosis of self-satisfaction and self-sufficiency by grounding the meaning of reality itself in a moment of subjective appropriation. As was the case for the symbol according to Goethe, the functioning of involuntary memory implies the suspension of time: the revelation-illumination happens instantaneously, so that the protagonist loses his conception of self-limitation:

> Et bientôt, machinalement, accablé par la morne journée et la perspective d'un triste lendemain, je portai à mes lèvres une cuillerée du thé où j'avais laissé s'amollir un morceau de madeleine. Mais à l'instant même où la gorgée mêlée des miettes du gâteau toucha mon palais, je tressaillis, attentif à ce qui se passait d'extraordinaire en moi. Un plaisir délicieux m'avait envahi, isolé, sans la notion de sa cause. Il m'avait aussitôt rendu les vicissitudes de la vie indifférente, ses désastres inoffensifs, sa brièveté illusoire, de la même façon qu'opère l'amour, en me remplissant d'une essence précieuse: ou plutôt cette essence n'était pas en moi, elle était moi. J'avais cessé de me sentir médiocre, contingent, mortel. (I, 45)

A detailed analysis of the passage would show that the entirety of the madeleine experience is related in the terms of Romantic symbolism. Proust is speaking the same language as Goethe and Coleridge, and he is pushing to its logical limits the discourse of translucence and unmediated vision. The esthetic theory of the *Recherche* is quite simply a Romantic theory. But it is far less simple to justify the use of this theory in relation to the novel it attempts to found. Because the symbol has the power of instantaneous enlightenment, the Romantics most often associated it with the short, semantically dense form of lyric poetry, whereas, in the words of Creuzer, the "progression in a series of moments" that one finds in epic poetry or the novel seems more aptly attributable to the rationally controlled, "extended" mode of allegory. This raises a series of interrelated questions. Did Proust create a *roman poétique,* in which the conscious allegorical explanatory function of the novel was subsumed within an all-encompassing symbolism? Does the narrative line "unroll" itself from inside the symbol without causing the trauma of a disjunction or a fall into differential time? Does the madeleine episode truly *contain,* wrapped within itself, the future events of the novel, such that these events can be said to partake of the essence of the originative "goutelette presque impalpable"? And finally, in a general sense, can it be shown that the narrative reality of the *Recherche* corresponds with the premises of Proust's esthetics, or is there a conflict between theory and practice that cannot be reduced to the status of a subsidiary, inessential contradiction, but requires its own interpretation?

In the final paragraph of the madeleine passage (I, 47–48) the narrator tells us that as soon as he has recognized the taste of the cake and located its origin in the past, the entire "world" of Combray suddenly emerges in its essential truth. This emergence occurs according to the logic of association. From the initial discovery—that the core experience causing his present felicity took place at the home of Tante Léonie—the narrator's unconscious memories then allow him to visualize first the concrete reality of "la vieille maison grise sur la rue, où était sa [de Tante Léonie] chambre" (I, 47), then the town of Combray in its lived daily appearance ("la ville, depuis le matin jusqu'au soir et par tous les temps, la Place où on m'envoyait avant déjeuner, les rues où j'allais faire des courses, les chemins qu'on prenait si le temps était beau"). Rhetorically, as Gérard Genette has observed with analytical depth,[8] the metaphorical process of analogy that grounds the madeleine experience gives way, at this precise point, to a metonymical movement: in Proust's words, the room of Tante Léonie "vint comme un décor de théâtre *s'appliquer au* petit pavillon donnant sur le jardin" (my emphasis). In a strict sense, we are indeed within the modality of juxtaposition, or metonymy, but the elements being juxtaposed all derive from the same source. The narrator seems to be saying that the transition from the atemporal ecstasy of metaphorical *correspondances* to the deployment of the world in which involuntary remembrance functions does not involve any insuperable difficulties or fundamental contradictions. Indeed, in the concluding sentence of the description, when the miraculous expansion of the original taste sensation into the "differentiated" universe of Combray is evoked for the last time, the narrator makes use of a significant simile:

> Et comme dans ce jeu où les Japonais s'amusent à tremper dans
> un bol de porcelaine rempli d'eau, de petits morceaux de pa-
> pier jusque-là indistincts qui, à peine y sont-ils plongés, s'étirent,
> se contournent, se colorent, se différencient, deviennent des

fleurs, des maisons, des personnages consistants et reconnaissables, de même maintenant toutes les fleurs de notre jardin et celles du parc de M. Swann, et les nymphéas de la Vivonne, et les bonnes gens du village et leurs petits logis et l'église, et tout Combray, ses environs, tout cela qui prend forme et solidité, est sorti, ville et jardins, de ma tasse de thé. (I, 47-48)

The small bits of paper that the Japanese place in a bowl of water produce beautiful forms and cause us to react in astonishment: we are amazed that so little can contain so much. In the same way, the narrator is not unwilling to push the *contenant-contenu* structure to its limit, in saying that the town and gardens of Combray "come out of" his teacup. The comparison is convincing enough in the context of the passage as a whole, but it is necessary to keep in mind that the Japanese papers are the tricks of a *jeu de société*. They are "preprogrammed" (in a highly rational way) to unfold in a given manner, and the fascination they cause is akin to that generated by fireworks: we admire a certain technical mastery but are simultaneously aware that the game has been fixed. In further developments of this chapter I shall be concerned with the thorny problem of the reliability of the narrator's voice. We know Proust's esthetic theory, its subordination of narrative difference to symbolical-analogical instantaneousness, but we need to determine whether Marcel's declarations are trustworthy statements or whether their highly tuned rhetoric of persuasion hides a desire to eliminate textual complexity and ambivalence, to preestablish our reaction patterns as we read the novel.

## THEORIES OF PROUSTIAN NARRATION

### Genette

Although Proustian narration has been described, on occasion, in systematic fashion,[9] the best recent codification of the diverse techniques to be found in the *Recherche* is certainly that of Gérard Genette, in *Figures III* ("Discours du récit"). More than other modern critics, Genette is conscious of Proust's narrative idiosyncrasies, of the way in which the author of the *Recherche*, despite an apparent adherence to the Realist model of fiction-telling, in fact stretched and disfigured the conventions that formed his readers' comfortable frame of reference. Proust's major contribution to the transformation of the nineteenth-century novel is in his manipulation of temporal structures, which Genette describes with analytical rigor.

First, Genette deals with the order of Proustian narration—with the relationship between what Christian Metz has called "le temps de la chose-racontée" and "le temps du récit."[10] In the *Recherche*, we must make a

distinction between the chronology of events that take place in the protagonist's life and the sequence in which these events are told by the
narrator. We find, in Proust's novel, that the narrator very often antici-
pates in his telling of events, that he "jumps ahead" of the protagonist's
present experience. Genette calls this technique *prolepse* ("toute man-
oeuvre narrative consistant à raconter ou évoquer d'avance un événement
ultérieur" [82]), and goes so far as to affirm: "Reste que la *Recherche du
temps perdu* fait de la prolepse un usage probablement sans équivalent
dans toute l'histoire du récit, même de forme autobiographique" (106).
The two major implications of this peculiarity are (1) that there is a not-
able lack of "suspense" in the novel, since the narrator is constantly foreshadowing future experiences, and (2) that the novel thereby looks like a
demonstration or logical proof of certain ideas important to the narrator.
When, in the madeleine episode, the link is made between the taste sensation of the cake and the subsequent rediscovery of the "essential" Combray and its inhabitants' lives, there is also a characteristically Proustian
parenthetical remark: "(quoique je ne susse pas encore et dusse remettre
à bien plus tard de découvrir pourquoi ce souvenir me rendait si heureux)"
(I, 47). What is being anticipated here is nothing less than the Matinée
Guermantes at the end of the novel, when the eruptions of involuntary
memory lead to the decision to write. Such proleptic remarks give us the
impression of great authorial control. Although the protagonist does not
know what awaits him in the future of his fictional existence, the narrator
does, and seems to manipulate all events according to a retrospective
understanding. It would appear, on the whole, that Proust is less interested in creating a "believable" hero with whom we could suffer and
empathize than in using this hero to illustrate certain "laws" of human
conduct that can be commented upon from "above," in dispassionate disinterest. This would imply that Proust makes strategic use of novelistic
patterns, sometimes with a great degree of *désinvolture,* but that he does
not necessarily "believe in" the novel, at least in its traditional form. In
an uncanny, ironical way, the *Recherche* questions and undermines the
very techniques Genette analyzes with such painstaking lucidity.

Proust's disdain for narrative conventions is not limited to the strict
chronology of the *récit*'s "order." It extends to other levels of fictional
temporality defined by Genette as "durée" and "fréquence." If we examine first the duration or speed of narration in the *Recherche*—that is,
"le rapport entre une durée, celle de l'histoire, mesurée en secondes, mi-
nutes, heures, jours, mois et années, et une longueur: celle du texte,
mesurée en lignes et en pages" (*Figures III*, 123)—we discover an interesting evolution. As the novel progresses from the early stages of childhood and adolescence toward the later scenes of adult life, there is a
remarkable deceleration (*ralentissement*) in the rhythm of the *récit,*

accompanied by the increasingly isolated or insular appearance of long textual blocks that are merely juxtaposed to each other, without being linked in a temporal flow. In speaking of the *discontinuité croissante* of Proustian narration, Genette observes:

> Le récit proustien tend à devenir de plus en plus discontinu, syncopé, fait de scènes énormes séparées par d'immenses lacunes. . . . Il semble bien que Proust ait voulu, et dès le début, ce rythme de plus en plus heurté, d'une massivité et d'une brutalité beethoveniennes, qui contraste si vivement avec la fluidité presque insaisissable des premières parties, comme pour opposer la texture temporelle des événements les plus anciens et celles des plus récents: comme si la mémoire du narrateur, à mesure que les faits se rapprochent, devenait à la fois plus sélective et plus monstrueusement grossissante. (128)

In his chapter entitled "Fréquence" Genette explains the technical reasons for the brutal and brusque construction of the novel's fragmentary episodes. By "frequency" Genette means the "système de relations . . . entre [les] capacités de 'répétition' des événements narrés (de l'histoire) et des énoncés narratifs (du récit)" (146). There are four possibilities of interaction, at least in theory: I can tell one time what happened once, tell $n$ times what happened $n$ times, tell $n$ times what happened once, or tell once what happened $n$ times. Genette demonstrates that the Proustian récit is characterized by a highly original, unorthodox concatenation of the first and the fourth possibilities, which he terms, respectively, the *singulatif* and the *itératif*. Whereas in the Balzacian novel the temporal rhythm of narration is that of alternation between well-defined dramatic scenes and the accelerated movement of the "récit sommaire" (170), in Proust the balancing effect is between the *singulatif* and the *itératif*, where most often the former is integrated into the latter, "réduit à le [l'itératif] servir et à l'illustrer, positivement ou négativement, soit en respectant le code, soit en le transgressant, ce qui est une autre façon de le manifester" (167).

In studying the various narrative sequences of the *Recherche,* Genette uncovers a general characteristic pattern. On the one hand, single events rarely exhibit the power of dramatic action and reversal, since they are most often subsumed within the synthetic, assimilative envelopment of the iterative; and on the other hand, each individually definable iterative passage is a unit unto itself that does not melt into the higher harmony of an overall narrative continuity. Thus, in the case of the love of Swann for Odette or Marcel for Gilberte, Genette speaks of an evolution by "paliers itératifs, marqués par un emploi très caractéristique de ces *dès lors, depuis, maintenant,* qui traitent toute histoire non comme un enchaînement d'événements liés par une causalité, mais comme une *succession d'états* sans cesse substitués les uns aux autres, sans communication possible. L'itératif est ici, plus que de l'habitude, le mode (l'aspect) temporel de cette sorte d'oubli perpétuel, d'incapacité foncière du héros proustien (Swann toujours, Marcel avant la révélation) à percevoir la continuité de sa vie, et donc la relation d'un 'temps' à l'autre" (169). It is apparent from this observation that the technical possibilities and limits of the iterative mode play out the personal psychological drama of the novel's narrator-hero, which can be described, succinctly, as a dilemma of domination or control. The iterative, as Genette suggests, is a method of abstraction: by relating a series of repeated actions in one *énoncé narratif,* the writer presumes to master the variety of phenomena and neutralize the differences among common elements.

Genette's narratological study of the *Recherche* has two contradictory effects: it answers questions and solves problems on the purely descriptive level of scientific observation by codifying Proust's novelistic techniques, and it raises other questions, points to other problems that lie outside the purview of literary theory, in the realm of interpretation. In the specific case of the narrative techniques just discussed, Genette is principally concerned with defining *prolepse, singulatif, itératif, ordre, durée, fréquence,* and with illustrating their functional logic in the fabric of the *récit.* When matters of interpretation arise, as in the discussion of the narration's *discontinuité croissante,* the theorist does indeed disappear for a moment so that the critic can speak, but the critic's role is limited and his conclusions circumspect. In contrasting "la fluidité [temporelle] presque insaisissable des premières parties [du roman]" to "le rythme heurté, d'une massivité et d'une brutalité beethoveniennes" of the latter sections, Genette couches his analysis in the form of a hypothesis: *"comme si* la mémoire du narrateur, à mesure que les faits se rapprochent, devenait à la fois plus sélective et plus monstrueusement grossissante" (my emphasis). According to this modestly phrased remark, the "fluidity" of the beginnings and the later violent narrative discontinuities both belong to the realm of memory. Discontinuity as such would not represent the ironization or deconstruction of Proust's *mémoire involontaire* so much as a distortion of its laws. In other words, without stating his opinion explicitly, Genette implies that the shift in narrative register is not tantamount to a fundamental reversal of modality. This would mean, from the perspective of the terminology we are developing, that the symbolic mode of unmediated vision and possession-taking is capable of subsuming within itself the fragmentary episodic forms of the novel's final volumes. There would be no need to introduce a second theoretical term—"allegory"—in binary opposition to the symbol, since the latter provides the central explanatory core from which all narrative effects are derivable.

But if Genette's implicit argument is true, and if the structure of involuntary memory indeed accounts for the novel in its totality, the passage from fluidity to discontinuity must itself be fluid, not discontinuous. Genette has not proven this point, but merely raised it in the formulation of a "conditional" afterthought. We must turn elsewhere for a deepening of perspective on the relationship of the poetry of memory to narration: it is not in Genette's detached analytical narratology that the significance of *discontinuité croissante* can be discovered.

### Feuillerat and Spitzer

In the early years of Proust criticism, the problem of narrative discontinuity was discussed with less scientific rigor and more subjective involvement than is the case currently. One could be tempted today to dismiss much of what was written on the narrative form of the *Recherche* before 1960 as too general, too imprecise, and too full of questionable value judgments for serious consideration. Yet it would be a mistake not to recognize in some of these studies a powerful intuitive prefiguration of the deepest theoretical questions now at the forefront of critical attention. A case in point is Albert Feuillerat's *Comment Marcel Proust a composé son roman* (New Haven: Yale University Press, 1934), a sometimes brilliant, sometimes exasperatingly simplistic account of the Proustian novel's constitutive contradictions. Unlike many modern critics, for whom Marcel Proust has become an untouchable talisman, Feuillerat has no exaggerated respect for the author of the *Recherche*. He is unhappy with Proust for succumbing to certain stylistic and compositional idiosyncrasies and is not unwilling to voice his disappointment in categorical terms. Like Genette, Feuillerat devotes considerable intellectual energy to an examination of "le discontinu du développement proustien" (109), but unlike his narratologist successor, he immediately condemns this method for its destructive consequences within the esthetic whole of the novel.

Feuillerat is the first important critic of Proust to have made use of early drafts of the *Recherche* in his interpretation of the definitive version. In his perusal of the *placards*, he noticed what has now become common knowledge among *proustiens*—namely, that Proust's method of composition was generally that of addition, only rarely that of suppression or condensation, and that the originally planned three-volume novel as advertised in the 1913 Grasset edition of *Du côté de chez Swann* grew beyond its set bounds during and after the First World War to such an extent that it seemed a completely "new" book had been conceived by 1918. According to Feuillerat, these far-reaching revisions destroyed the structural balance of the *Recherche*'s narrative form, added muddy complexities to its thematic network, and substituted a tone of hyper-rational disenchantment to the "atmosphère de rêve éveillé" (262) characteristic of its earlier volumes, especially *Swann*.

Feuillerat's thesis is quite clear: Proust's novel consists of two mutually exclusive styles or "manières." The first, chronologically (and in the order of the critic's personal preference), can be described by the words "demi-éveil," "impressionnisme," "inconscient," "mémoire"; the second, that of the subsequent *enrichissements*, by the terms "rationnel," "intelligence," "conscience critique," etc. (120-30). Feuillerat suggests that the excesses of the narrator's psychological probing are already to be found in the "Gilberte" episode of *A l'Ombre des jeunes filles en fleurs*: "Cette clairvoyance et cette attitude calculatrice, cette façon qu'a le narrateur de tenir constamment la main sur les leviers de la machine psychologique sont quelque chose de très nouveau" (121). In a further development, when discussing the narrator's microscopic analysis of Charlus and Albertine, Feuillerat uses the terms "monstrueux" and "excroissances" (256) to describe the disproportionate fictional space occupied by these two characters in the final volumes of the *Recherche*. In effect, Feuillerat and Genette are in agreement about the *fact* of "monstrous" expansion in the later sections, but Genette ascribes this tendency to a quasi-"optical" effect of memory ("la mémoire du narrateur, à mesure que les faits se rapprochent, devenait à la fois plus sélective et plus monstrueusement grossissante"), whereas Feuillerat refuses to subordinate the phenomena of narrative discontinuity to the act of remembrance as such. On the contrary, the earlier critic contends that the extreme concentration on psychological motivation characteristic of *Sodome et Gomorrhe, La Prisonnière*, and *La Fugitive* undermines and dismantles the esthetic theory based upon *mémoire involontaire*. This would imply that what we have called the symbolic mode is operative only in those parts of the novel that are untainted by the "excroissances" of the later volumes, and that we may need to reintroduce its rationally controlled binary opposite—allegory—to account for those "monstrueux gonflages" produced by the narrator's increasingly sceptical and defensive relationship to the paralyzing reality he attempts to comprehend/imprison. Feuillerat leaves us with the impression that the *Recherche* is a "double" work that cannot be reduced to any form of transcendental esthetic unity.

In presupposing the superiority of the symbolical mode over the allegorical, Feuillerat implies that the "excessive" generalization of the latter (its disregard for the particular truths of fictional characterization) is in some way inimical to the integrity of the *Recherche* as novelistic *récit*. In a strict sense, what we are calling "allegory"—the rational typology of human motivations—corresponds more closely to what Leo Spitzer, in a brilliant stylistic study composed in 1928, called the *traité* or *moralité* than to the *récit*.[11] Indeed, when Spitzer writes: "Proust passe constamment du récit au traité: le récit ne fournit plus alors qu'un exemple pour des expériences générales. Innombrables sont les phrases qui oscillent entre la moralité et le récit" (460-61), he means that the telling of a story according to the logic of an imaginary chronology and the construction of a more or less "believable" plot is subordinated to a series of "laws" that govern and encompass the totality of human conduct. Like Feuillerat, Spitzer recognizes within Proustian fiction a fundamental irreducible duality, but he realizes that this duality is expressed most dramatically in a properly narrative form, and that the moralizing tendency in Proust produces an ordering of fictional events radically opposed to that which we find in the nineteenth-century novel.

### Rogers

Spitzer's early study indicates in passing what B. G. Rogers develops in great detail in his cogent analysis of Proust's narrative techniques. Although Rogers' conception of the novel is somewhat narrowly Aristotelian —based upon the notions of plausibility and "probability" in plot and character depiction—his analysis of narrative forms is an original and solidly documented interpretation of the depths of Proustian ambivalence. In his statement of purpose, Rogers writes:

> The object of this study is to examine Proust's whole ouput in the light of two opposing tendencies which characterize it, dictating choice both of 'genre' and technique; the one consisting of reflections, aphorisms and general conclusions in the manner of La Bruyère and classical moralists, —a strain which dispenses altogether with fictionalisation, or subordinates it to the secondary role of illustration and example; the other comprising all the traditional preoccupations of the novelist, with conventional attitudes and techniques which place the ordering of a fictional story above comment and observation. (*Proust's Narrative Techniques*, 10-11)

Rogers explains the paradox of Proustian narrative in terms of a disparity between esthetic theory and the actual practice of writing, and locates the origin of this paradox in the preface of *Contre Sainte-Beuve,* where the future author of the *Recherche* makes "an intellectual argument—against intelligence."[12] That is: Proust argues for the superiority of sensation over rational intelligence, of what we have called the "symbol" over "allegory," but he does so rationally and consciously, so that he is in fact enveloping the symbolic object in an allegorical discourse. In the later narrative system of the *Recherche*, this means that the "probable" organic unfolding of imaginary events is imprisoned within what Rogers calls explicitly an "allegorical demonstration": "By means of convincing *characters*, like the Combray figures or the Duchesse de Guermantes, of carefully planned *situations*, like Marcel's successive contacts with different aspects of life which nearly all prove disappointing, and by means of *plot*, the unexpected revelation of art as the key to Marcel's vocation, *A la Recherche* is an allegorical demonstration of an argument, carried out in fictional terms" (98).

In using "fictional terms" to convey an allegorical message, Proust subjects these terms to various degrees of distortion. The specificity of Proustian narration is best described as a *modal incompatibility* [13] in which the apparent form of the *Recherche* as "symbolic-poetic" novel is constantly deformed by the special exigences of the allegorical. Because allegory abstracts from the particular and generalizes from individual occurrences, it requires a broad field of vision that can only be provided by a narrator possessing absolute or near-absolute understanding. Yet the fictional terms in which the novel is developed do not lend themselves to such all-embracing knowledge, since the narrator-hero, who tells his story in the first person, is presumably not omniscient. The consequences of this primordial contradiction, according to Rogers, are several. (1) Proust, in introducing what amounts to an omniscient narrative voice, undermines his theory of "the subjectivity of all experience and judgment . . . [and] the individual's imperfect perception of knowledge" (*Proust's Narrative Techniques*, 128). (2) In those scenes in which the narrator-hero finds himself, purely by chance, a witness to extraordinary and fundamentally important theatrical displays of hidden character, "there is little attempt to do more than arrange a situation capable of revealing certain information that Marcel would not normally possess, involving almost always a concordance of circumstances often lacking in plausibility" (133). [14] (3) Marcel is an unsubstantial, shadowy "hero" because the narrator most often relates his story from the retrospective point of view of acquired understanding, and not from the standpoint of the young man *as* he experiences reality: the narrator is, in a sense, the "truth" of the protagonist's "errors" and most often lets the reader know immediately how his former self has strayed from the narrow path of understanding (139–43). (4) Because the "moralizer" dominates the hero and examines his actions from afar, the "progressive" or "imperfect" flow of novelistic time (that of Marcel engaged in events whose significance is as yet obscure) is drained of its dramatic potential: "The author uses his undramatic methods of telling often dramatic parts of his story to underline the ideas behind the 'demonstration' the whole work constitutes" (148). (5) There is a visible movement within the *Recherche* toward ever-greater allegorical control, which causes the *récit* to lose whatever organic continuity it exhibited in the earlier volumes and to become increasingly fragmentary and episodic (152).

Viewed in themselves as general conclusions, the five remarks I have isolated from Rogers' analysis concur with the terminologically more precise work of Genette: we recognize in numbers 4 and 5, for instance, what Genette calls respectively *prolepse* and the *discontinuité croissante* of Proustian narration. Yet, as I have suggested, the major achievement of Rogers consists of his discovery that these five narrative effects derive from a central cause: the modal incompatibility of the symbolical *récit* and the allegorical *traité* or *moralité*.

My use of Rogers' work here is strategic. I am unconcerned with how "believable" or "convincing" characters, situation, and plot may be in the *Recherche,* but I do find it important that the superimposition of an allegorical demonstration on a symbolic-organic novelistic form causes the very notion of "believability" to vacillate and even lose its relevance. Similarly, I do not find it bothersome in the least that Marcel is an "unconvincing" hero, an unsubstantial shadow-figure; but I do think that the reasons for his strange passivity (grounded by Rogers in Proust's authorial preference for retrospective omniscient narration) deserve serious attention. Ultimately, Genette is more prudent than Rogers despite the veneer of a certain "modernism," in that he notes, but does not truly analyze, the split between narrator and protagonist, which is the narrational objective correlative of the modal dichotomy separating allegory from symbol. Rogers takes the risk of making the link between these two levels and of affirming that the *Recherche*'s use of a hero in a symbolic *récit* is ironized by the narrative mastery of an allegorical-rational discourse. But some further questions need to be answered: Can we verify by detailed textual analysis the hypothesis of the symbol-allegory duality as formulated by Rogers? Is there a definable episode in Proust that plays out and illustrates the antinomies between hero and narrator? Is it possible to find a specific textual origin of the *discontinuité croissante* in Proustian narration? I propose to search for answers to these questions in the reading of two passages that reflect and complete each other, the one from *Jean Santeuil* and the other from the *Recherche.*

## "DE L'AMITIÉ AU DÉSIR" AND "LE BAISER REFUSÉ": THE PROBLEMATICS OF ALLEGORICAL NARRATION

I have chosen to compare a short fragment of *Jean Santeuil* entitled "De l'Amitié au désir" by the Pléiade editors[15] to the episode of *A l'Ombre des jeunes filles en fleurs* known as "Le Baiser refusé" (I, 929–34). The two texts tell the same story and relate to each other as preliminary sketch to final draft. In studying them simultaneously, we can observe the evolution of Proust as a novelist; in particular, we can verify the coexistence of the *récit* and the *traité* in the organization of the first passage and the emergence of a mimetic and "probable" *récit* in the second. "Le Baiser refusé" is a rewriting of "De l'Amitié au désir" in which the moralizing point of view of the omniscient retrospective narrator is abandoned in favor of the limited perspective of the protagonist Marcel: the scene is constructed dramatically, according to the logic of suspense. We as readers experience the fictional events from within the mind of Marcel and are subjected to the same shock of painful recognition as he when, at the end of the passage, Albertine refuses to grant him the kiss he expected, seemingly with justification, to receive. On the surface, the comparison of the early fragment to its later form demonstrates clearly and unequivocally Rogers' contention that Proust gradually assimilated the stock-in-trade of the nineteenth-century novelist; and if we care to agree with the critic's Aristotelian-prescriptive judgment, we can go a step further and declare the second episode "superior" to its imperfectly (i.e., non-novelistically) conceived model. But these conclusions need to be questioned more closely. This is why I shall now examine the structure and meaning of both texts, without assuming from the outset that "De l'Amitié au désir" is intrinsically inferior or nugatory. The matter of central importance is not the presumed "progress" of Proust as novelist, but the significance of the *traité*'s disappearance, coupled with the *récit*'s corresponding expansion.

"De l'Amitié au désir" and "Le Baiser refusé" both have a tripartite textual organization that can be described as the following sequence: (1) presentation of an initial, potentially dramatic situation, and description of a physical and emotional context in which the protagonist discovers the accessibility of a desired woman (called Valentine in *Jean Santeuil* and Albertine in the *Recherche*); (2) the protagonist's dreams of domination and possession of the woman, which assume the form of an apotheosis of self-sufficiency and narcissism; (3) the explicit deconstruction of these dreams, by which the narrator indicates his ironical relationship to the protagonist. I will respect this ordering of events in my own analysis, and will read both passages in simultaneous juxtaposition, so as to render their formal and semantic propeties clear by the evidence of contrast.

### Context

"De l'Amitié au désir" (Page 837) The first paragraph of the passage describing the evolution of Jean Santeuil's sentiments for Valentine is a classical exemplification of the generalizing potential that characterizes the *traité*. In the opening sentence the narrator tells us: "Les circonstances et les lieux se prêtent souvent à la réalisation parfaite de nos désirs, mais elle ne s'y produit pas." The following six-page development will be an illustration of this formula, a proof of its veracity. Like the seventeenth-century *moralistes,* Proust begins with an abstract declaration that contains implicitly the particular arguments later to be deployed in its behalf. Thus, we can expect that there will be a minimum of suspense, since we know in advance the inevitable outcome of the text. In this case, we are told, far before the "circonstances" and the "lieux" are presented in fictional detail, that the realization of Jean's desires for Valentine will not be possible. The purpose of the text as a whole will be to reveal the psychological laws, the emotional-sentimental mechanisms that cause the protagonist to fail in his quest for the physical possession of his beloved. Valentine is not important in herself—she is not "particularized" or even given a name until very late in the passage (841)—but she is, rather, the individual woman chosen by the writer to represent or incorporate a general truth. In the sentences immediately following the introductory statement, we read: "Un jour vient où la femme que nous aimons vient passer deux jours sous notre toit, dans une solitude complète. Elle dîne seule avec nous. Puis nous allons nous promener, nous rentrons, nous la conduisons seuls à sa chambre. Nul témoin, nulle gêne." Not only is Valentine reduced to the status of an example (she is one of a potentially infinite series of women who can replace each other as the temporary incarnations of "la femme que nous aimons"), but the events leading up to the protagonist's subsequent efforts at seduction—the arrival of the woman at Jean's home, the dinner, the nocturnal walk, the episode in the bedroom—these circumstances which would be exploited and manipulated for dramatic effect by the traditional novelist, are presented here in skeletal form, enveloped in the controlled abstraction of the Moralist's "eternal present." Finally, since the narrator is unconcerned with the painstaking creation of a fictional *cadre,* he wastes no time in justifying the undisturbed solitude of the two young people. Jean and Valentine are together and alone, in a quasi-magical isolation, according to the logic of the daydream: "nul témoin, nulle gêne" is the unexplained precondition of their intimacy.

"De l'Amitié au désir" can be described, in Rogers' language, as the "allegorical demonstration of an argument, carried out in fictional terms," if we understand the argument to be the impossibility of possession-taking and the fictional terms to be the love of Jean for Valentine. The characters Jean and Valentine are subordinated to the demonstration, which unfolds with clarity and rigor. The narrator dominates his fictional universe and manipulates it according to a preconceived plan, so that the conclusion of the text is an echo and a confirmation of the introductory statement.

Yet within the first paragraph the reader can sense a certain tension between the omniscience of the narrator and the more limited perspective of the protagonist: this tension will be responsible for the complex interference of *traité* and *récit* later on in the development of the passage. At the precise moment in which narrative mastery is most apparent (while the negative result of Jean's amatory efforts is being signalled proleptically) there is a subtle shift in point of view that causes the reader to identify with the inner thoughts and desires of the protagonist. Whereas in the earlier sentences of the paragraph, the "on" or "nous" was unambiguously that of the moralizing voice speaking from a guarded esthetic distance, this tends to change when the narrator passes from a general discussion to the specifics of the fictional situation: "Ainsi d'elle, cette maison où il n'y a que *nous deux,* cette chambre éclairée par la lune où personne ne peut *nous* voir, ne recouvrant qu'une chaste causerie" (my emphasis). Here, the solitude of the young man and woman, the moonlit room, the security of the unobserved alcove, prompt Jean to imagine the possibility of a smooth transition from a "chaste causerie" to what he calls, in the following sentence, "l'initiative de quelque caresse": that is, the *nous,* although still principally and intentionally that of the Moralist, is now contextually ambivalent. The narrator utters the phrase itself, but it is as if he had penetrated the mind of Jean to do so, as if his generalized "nous" were borrowed from the personal "nous" of the two lovers. This melting together of the abstract and the concrete, of allegorical demonstration and novelistic illustration, is not just a matter of grammatical-semantic coincidence (here, the single form and double meaning of the pronoun "nous"), but more importantly, the rhetorical form of Jean's desire to possess Valentine: a metaphorical fusion of irreconcilable forces.

Although the text as allegorical narration sets out to prove that the controlled distance of a "chaste causerie" is unrelated to "l'initiative de quelque caresse," Jean is convinced, through the illusory evidence of circumstance, that the latter can be born from the former, that the former is merely the removable mask of the latter. Thus, our reading of "De l'Amitié au désir" oscillates between the foreknowledge we have of Jean's sentimental failure and the delusion we share with the protagonist (as we follow his reasoning in its progressive textual presentation) that this failure is avoidable and even improbable. In order that the passage function as an esthetically coherent unit, it is necessary for us to *forget* the last sentence of the first paragraph (the Moralist's conclusion)—"nous refermons la porte sur cette chambre qui se prêtait et dont nous n'avons pas profité"— and assume, with Jean, that the specific instance described in the following paragraphs will contradict this law, that the door will remain open, that Valentine will open herself to his insistent desires.

**"Le Baiser refusé"** (I, 929–31) Unlike "De l'Amitié au désir," which is the isolated fragment of a highly episodic, discontinuous whole, "Le Baiser refusé" is a well-defined scenic totality with an obvious contextual significance: within the flow of narrated events that constitute *A l'Ombre des* *jeunes filles en fleurs,* it is the moment of "crystallization" of Marcel's love for Albertine and thus is the dramatic culmination of the volume. Until this scene, the narrator tells us, the days Marcel spent waiting for Albertine "passaient sans rien m'apporter de décisif, sans avoir été ce jour capital dont je confiais immédiatement le rôle au jour suivant, qui ne le tiendrait pas davantage; ainsi s'écroulaient l'un après l'autre, comme des vagues, ces sommets aussitôt remplacés par d'autres" (929). "Le Baiser refusé" is the unexpected eruption of the *singulatif* into this iterative monotony, the momentary cessation of time's *éc(r)roulement* and the suspension of Habit's work. But the narrator is careful to insert the scene's radical disjunction into the precise frame of verisimilitude: he explains with an almost excessive carefulness how it is that the "circonstances" and the "lieux" of Marcel's encounter with Albertine lend themselves to amorous activity. The first sentence of the passage is so full of descriptive detail as to seem a parody of novelistic plausibility: "Environ un mois après le jour où nous avions joué au furet, on me dit qu'Albertine devait partir le lendemain matin pour aller passer quarante-huit heures chez Mme Bontemps et, obligée de prendre le train de bonne heure, viendrait coucher la veille au Grand-Hôtel, d'où avec l'omnibus elle pourrait, sans déranger les amies chez qui elle habitait, prendre le premier train" (929). This explanation is much more than a concession to the Realistic canon, however, and the mere fact that Proust should be so overtly conscious of the question of *vraisemblance* needs to be examined in itself. Two pages later, when Marcel is alone with Albertine, he asks her if this projected stay in the Grand-Hôtel is more than a rumor:

> Oui, me dit-elle, je passe cette nuit-là à votre hôtel, et même, comme je suis un peu enrhumée, je me coucherai avant le dîner. Vous pourrez venir assister à mon dîner à côté de mon lit et après nous jouerons à ce que vous voudrez. J'aurais été contente que vous veniez à la gare demain matin, mais j'ai peur que cela ne paraisse drôle, je ne dis pas à Andrée qui est intelligente, mais aux autres qui y seront; ça ferait des histoires, si on le répétait à ma tante; mais nous pourrions passer cette soirée ensemble. Cela, ma tante n'en saura rien. . . . Venez tôt, pour que nous ayons de bonnes heures à nous. (931)

Verisimilitude in this context is not principally a novelistic effect destined to make the reader believe in the probability of related events: instead, it stands as an enigma that the protagonist must interpret. The combination of circumstances elaborated by the narrator seems too good to be true. It is indeed very fortunate for Marcel that the Grand-Hôtel is more convenient as a point of departure for the train than the home of

Albertine's friends, and it is even more fortunate, if not suspicious, that Albertine should have a slight cold, so that she will not dine in public but in the privacy of her room. Inevitably, Marcel begins to believe that the young woman's visit has an ulterior motive and that the excessively well-concatenated signs of "plausibility" derive, in fact, from Albertine's awkward attempts to avoid social criticism. The contrast here is between *paraître* ("j'ai peur que cela ne paraisse drôle") and *être:* the protagonist will be tempted, progressively, to assume that he can pierce the veil of Mlle Simonet's adherence to etiquette and discover the erotic core of her secretive, as yet unknown being. What counts in "Le Baiser refusé" is not *vraisemblance* as novelistic technique but Marcel's deciphering of its meaning and testing of its limits: ultimately, he wishes to know if all this *vraisemblance* is *vraisemblable*—or if it is an artificially constructed barrier whose purpose is to protect the two lovers from the curious eyes of the outside world.

In the early sections of *A l'Ombre des jeunes filles en fleurs,* Albertine appeared alternately as a well-behaved middle-class girl devoted to her aunt and as a mysterious figure whose facial expressions, gestures, and language implied her initiation in the hidden domain of sexuality. It never occurs to Marcel that the object of his affection might be both of these seemingly incompatible persons: instead, he assumes that she is either one or the other. The words "nous jouerons à ce que vous voudrez" have the ring of an unmistakably erotic intention, so he begins to assume that the "true" Albertine lives in a realm of sexual pleasure now open to him. This assumption causes him to forget the negative lessons of his previous experiences with Gilberte and to think, as he once did in childhood dreams, that love is "une entité non pas seulement extérieure, mais réalisable" (931). As was the case at the end of the introductory paragraph to "De l'Amitié au désir," where the protagonist had begun to believe that a "chaste causerie" was perhaps the transparent guise of a future "initiative de quelque caresse," here Marcel sees *within* the Albertine of bourgeois social convention the Albertine of his own thoughts, who can grant him unimaginable favors. According to a structural manipulation with which we are now familiar, we see that the *contenant* (the well-behaved everyday girl) hides a more profoundly meaningful *contenu*, which, when possessed by the protagonist, will allow for a perfect merging of the real and the imaginary. This is precisely the opposite movement of the Balbec-en-terre episode, in which *contenant* and *contenu* were split apart into irreconcilable, mutually antagonistic units. The promise of possession-taking, ironized in that earlier section of *A l'Ombre des jeunes filles en fleurs,* reemerges here in the euphoric form of a desire whose accomplishment seems logical and inevitable:

Tandis que la Gilberte que je voyais aux Champs-Elysées était une autre que celle que je retrouvais en moi dès que j'étais seul, tout d'un coup dans l'Albertine réelle, celle que je voyais tous les jours, que je croyais pleine de préjugés bourgeois et si franche avec sa tante, venait de s'incarner l'Albertine imaginaire, celle par qui, quand je ne la connaissais pas encore, je m'étais cru furtivement regardé sur la digue, celle qui avait eu l'air de rentrer à contre-coeur pendant qu'elle me voyait m'éloigner. (931)

## The Dream of Possession

"De l'Amitié au désir" (Pages 837-40) With the first sentence of the second paragraph—"Cette troisième fois Jean était assis devant son lit"—the narrator passes from the *traité* to the *récit*, from the iterative to the singulative. The following pages tell how Jean's feelings change from an unfocused tenderness to a powerful, almost violent desire: the atmosphere is that of a highly charged eroticism. As is often the case in Proust's writing, the sensually appealing female figure is associated with the colors red and pink, and her presence in bed with undone hair is an obvious enticement: "Les draps montaient jusqu'à sa figure d'un rose écarlate qui faisait mieux ressortir les cheveux défaits" (837); "il regardait cette figure fine et rose dans la vie, si pleine, si charnelle, si écarlate" (838). When Jean pretends to have sprained his wrist, Valentine responds by massaging his hand: "Elle passait doucement sa main grasse, brillante et chaude sur son poignet, et tout d'un coup dans ses yeux il eut l'idée qu'elle sentait qu'elle lui faisait plaisir et le faisait pour cela, dévoilant sous son aspect indifférent et aimé le consentement à lui faire plaisir d'une autre manière" (838). Predictably, Jean takes the massage to be a sign of Valentine's previously repressed wish to be loved and possessed: he sees it as part of a continuous, coherent set of sexual signals whose significance is unambiguous. At this point, Jean believes in the tranquil and "translucent" coexistence of *signifiant* and *signifié* in the organization of love's symbols. He thinks he can infer from his own pleasure that of the young woman, and that the present divergence between the modest insignificance of light physical touch and what he imagines to be the natural culmination of the scene is a matter of *appearance* only: "Elle sentait *visiblement* ce qu'il éprouvait et continuait sans laisser voir qu'elle le faisait pour cela, avec une *apparente hypocrisie* qui le rendait fou" (838; my emphasis). By concluding (prematurely) that the semiological constitution of "love" is that of a melted significant unity, Jean achieves a sense of absolute certainty that allows him to turn away from Valentine and concentrate on his own feelings. Perhaps the most striking single aspect of the long development on pages 838 and 839 is that the blatantly sexual ambiance of seduction gives way, gradually, to a very different mood. It is now assumed that Valentine can be possessed, and that "fact" renders her further presence inessential. From now on, the narrator will begin to describe the "rebirth" of Jean, which is in fact a triumph of absolute subjectivity and narcissistic self-admiration.

At first, the text seems to be constructed according to a perfect correspondence between the emergence of a "new" Albertine from the old and the progression, within Jean, from former indifference to current dèsire. In this sense, it is not surprising or exceptional to find the sentence: "Et alors le désir que généralement il ressentait tout simplement comme un besoin, sans rien d'autre, *naissait* au fond de tout ce qui était pour lui justement cette femme jusqu'ici, quelque chose au sein de quoi il n'y avait aucun désir, aucune complicité ou consentement possible, aucun rêve de ce genre, de l'amour platonique fini, et du charme gardé" (838; my emphasis). The narrator is saying that Jean's feelings are the result of a change in conception: since Valentine has changed and revealed her inner self, thereby causing her lover to modify his interpretation of her actions, it is natural that Jean's desire should be born from nondesire, or what is called here "de l'amour platonique fini." The metaphor of birth is no more than an adequate illustration of the idea of "newness" in general, and does not yet attract attention to itself. But later on, as Valentine vanishes by stages from the narrator's field of vision, the reader begins to realize that what is at sake is nothing less than the protagonist's "self-birth." The text slips, by degrees, from the original notion of possession of *other* (Valentine) to possession and origination of self. Jean is no longer a masculine figure attempting to penetrate the openness of the female vessel, but by the twist of a remarkable inversion, is himself the openness his desire wishes to penetrate.[16] This narcissistic self-sufficiency is psychologically regressive, but masks itself as the newness of discovery. The narrator tells us that Jean's recently acquired "understanding" of love is tantamount to a Ruskinian *Open Sesame* whereby one enters into a form of life beyond life, where one finds the hidden object of one's quest—oneself:

> C'était comme si la vie eût tout d'un coup changé et si le monde était plus riche qu'il ne croyait. . . . tout d'un coup elle [la vie] s'entr'ouvrait et lui montrait en son fond quelque chose qu'il ne connaissait pas et qui le remettait à une de ces heures où dans l'enfance nous croyons que la vie comporte de l'inconnu et du nouveau, du délicieux et de l'enivrant, ou dans nos rêves où nous pensons que ce que nous avons senti jusqu'ici n'était pas la vie, que

c'était comme une mesure pour rien et qu'il y a quelque chose
hors de la vie que nous avons vécue et qu'au lieu de continuer elle
va commencer, comme si c'était un lieu où nous n'étions pas encore et où nous allons entrer. Ainsi il sentait que par la porte poussée par un hasard il répudiait ce qui n'était pas encore la vie, ses
sentiments sentimentaux pour elle qui s'attardaient en lettres, re-
proches, adoration, services rendus, froideur affectée et pénétraient
tout d'un coup dans la chambre magnifique de la vie qui aurait
peut-être pu toute sa vie lui rester fermée et auprès de laquelle il
aurait passé sans jamais la connaître. Mais maintenant il se sentait
entrer en lui-même, entrer dans des palais qu'il ne connaissait
pas, foulant en tremblant toute sa manière d'être jusqu'ici avec elle,
de la juger, de l'aimer, sentant que c'était un décor qui tombait.
(839)

This triumphant passage, like the madeleine episode of the *Recherche*
that it foreshadows, affirms the superiority of the symbolic mode over the
allegorical. The text is constructed on a series of clearly defined dichotomies that echo those of Romantic esthetic theory. The point of departure
is the narrator's assumption that Valentine is a symbol, not an allegorical
sign: that is, her appearance and her meaning converge; she is "readable."
Hence, the protagonist no longer need employ indirect and convoluted
means of manipulation and seduction to dominate her. The "lettres, re-
proches, adoration, services rendus, froideur affectée" that characterize
Marcel's relationship to Gilberte and Albertine seem unnecessary here,
since we are certain that Valentine has nothing to hide. Coldness of affected artifice gives way to the warmth of "la chambre magnifique de la
vie"; theatricality yields to an authentic intercommunication ("Et l'apparence charmante et froide d'elle tombait"). To borrow from Hum-
boldt's terms, the superficial pleasure in the deciphering of an enigma is
replaced by the penetrative joy of reaching the heart and inner significance of things.[17]

As is the case for the madeleine, the revelation of a metaphysical truth
depends upon the unpredictable mechanism of the unconscious: the
"porte poussée par un hasard" thrusts the protagonist, unawares, into an
unknown world whose higher reality he experiences in the ecstasy of
atemporality. The difference between "De l'Amitié au désir" and its complex metamorphosis in the *Recherche* is that the earlier text does not hide
its roots in regressive, nostalgic wishes as well as its later version. Indeed,
the rediscovery of past time, which is the consciously developed subject
of the madeleine episode, seems, on the surface, to be a matter worthy of
independent attention and examination. It is only recently, as we have
seen, that Serge Doubrovsky and Philippe Lejeune have demonstrated

that the psychological origins of the madeleine in maternal substance are at least as important as the ostensible thematic material of the passage. On the other hand, it is much easier to see in "De l'Amitié au désir" that "la chambre magnifique de la vie" and the powerfully expressed phrase "il se sentait entrer en lui-même, entrer dans des palais qu'il ne connaissait pas" indicate unequivocally the desire both to return to the womb and to create a personal mythology of self-generation. In the *Recherche,* the narrator succeeds rather better in masking the monstrous dimensions of his narcissism when he says, "Il est clair que la vérité que je cherche n'est pas en lui [le breuvage], mais en moi" (I, 45). We are only too willing to believe that the search for truth must arise from a profound analysis of self rather than from the reptitious tasting of an insignificant little cake. But if we superimpose "De l'Amitié au désir" on the later text, and if we equate Jean to Marcel, and Valentine to the madeleine (both being symbols in the Romantic sense), we must conclude that the turn inward is not the disinterested quest for some exterior, metaphysically superior force called "time," but that this quest is itself the esthetically sublimated form of a radical subjectivism that never progresses beyond the frustrated stasis of narcissistically organized mirror images.[18] Implicitly, "De l'Amitié au désir" takes the argument for truth one step farther than Proust can admit, and says, under the cover of a discussion of "love": "Il est clair que la vérité que je cherche en elle [Valentine], *c'est moi.* "

The world of symbolic *correspondances* created by the narrator of *Jean Santeuil* is that of an absolute transparency of significance. Valentine, having presumably revealed her feelings for Jean, joins the protagonist in a sphere of reciprocity that transcends language—"[dans] une vie où on va si bien vers l'inconnu qu'on y dit des choses qu'on est étonné d'entendre, que l'intelligence ne prépare pas . . . où les mots eux-mêmes s'offrent comme ailleurs la bouche ou les mains, pour se contenter seulement parce qu'ils résolvent de minute en minute l'état où on est" (840). Words, gestures, actions merge with each other in undisturbed harmony, as in the resolution of a musical chord. The differential structure of language is abolished, its temporal component negated. Proust has taken the symbolic mode to the extreme limit of its semiological potential, and has shown that the achievement of unmediated vision and penetrative imagination implies the pleasurable but indistinct and undefined *openness* of meaning: all signs within this scheme reflect each other and complete each other in an analogical parallelism. Before Jean proceeds to kiss Valentine, his confident mind has conjured up a paradise of intra-uterine plenitude, a "forêt de symboles" that he can enter and possess as he regains the integrity of his former being.

**"Le Baiser refusé" (I, 931–34)** The continuation of the episode is an obvious reworking of "De l'Amitié au désir": it contains the same elements as the earlier text, but combines them in a more dramatic way and emphasizes the importance of the physical surroundings in the Grand-Hôtel as Marcel prepares his evening with Albertine. Unlike Jean Santeuil, who never doubts for a moment that Valentine will succumb to him, the protagonist of the *Recherche* is not certain of his conquest at first ("Qu'allait-il se passer tout à l'heure, je ne le savais pas trop" [I, 932]). The passage as a whole is an account of the progressive optimism of his sentiments. No doubt the major reason for this difference is that "De l'Amitié au désir" describes the lovers in improbable dreamlike isolation, whereas Marcel, in "Le Baiser refusé," needs to confront the difficulties of his situation and overcome certain obstacles in order to attain the goal of intimacy. Significantly, what stands between Marcel and the realization of his desires is an intimidating foursome of female figures: his grandmother, the constellation of "jeunes filles en fleurs" friendly to Albertine, Mme Bontemps (Albertine's aunt), and Françoise. If the protagonist is to succeed in his sexual quest, he must manage to "conquer" or "eliminate" these women. In the first sentence of the long paragraph that stretches until the end of the scene, the narrator writes: "J'allais dîner avec ma grand'mère, je sentais en moi un secret qu'elle ne connaissait pas. De même, pour Albertine, demain ses amies seraient avec elle sans savoir ce qu'il y avait de nouveau *entre nous,* et quand elle embrasserait sa nièce sur le front, Mme Bontemps ignorerait que j'étais *entre eux deux,* dans cet arrangement de cheveux qui avait pour but, caché à tous, de me plaire, à moi" (931–32; my emphasis). The logic here is that of a calculated reversal. Whereas a group of women is in his way, Marcel acts as if he has introduced himself *between* Albertine and them, thus neutralizing whatever power they might otherwise exercise over him.

Proustian love is secretive and surreptitious because it must avoid the censorship of the mother-figure, who is present in all these women, not just in the grandmother. When Marcel finally concludes that Albertine's invitation necessarily signifies the offer of her person, we read: "Puis, tout à coup, je pensai que j'avais tort d'avoir des doutes, elle m'avait dit de venir quand elle serait couchée. C'était clair, je trépignai de joie, je *renversai* à demi Françoise qui était sur mon chemin, je courais, les yeux étincelants, vers la chambre de mon amie" (932; my emphasis). The comic tone of the description is deceptive, in that it causes the reader to concentrate on the visual externals of the scene, while the less visible significant core remains hidden. The *reversal* of Françoise is the consciously allowable and socially acceptable translation of an inexpressible, violent wish: the imaginary rape of the mother—which stands as the precondition for the possession of Albertine. The calm self-admiration of "De l'Amitié au désir" metamorphoses into a subject's will to power in "Le Baiser refusé" as soon as the mother-figure appears not just as the womb toward which one aspires, but also as the Fury whose demonic, omnipresent interdicts render impossible all independent joy.

Marcel's struggle to break links with the women who hover around him, enveloping him in a stifling protectiveness, takes on the form of a swelling of masculine potency and an increasing subjective control over the temporal and physical constraints of reality. His progress toward Albertine's room is related in sexually emblematic terms: he ascends by "lift" to the proper floor of the hotel, and when he arrives near the door, we hear "ces quelques pas que personne ne pouvait plus arrêter, je les fis avec délices, avec prudence, comme plongé dans un élément nouveau, comme si en avançant j'avais lentement déplacé du bonheur, et en même temps avec un sentiment inconnu de toute-puissance, et d'entrer dans un héritage qui m'eût de tout temps appartenu" (932). The reader recognizes a variation on the theme of *le nouveau* ("comme plongé dans un élément nouveau") which was more balatant and repetitious in "De l'Amitié au désir." We find that Marcel, like Jean, implicitly equates the penetration of the sexual act with the entrance into a world presumed new, but which is in fact the matrix. The equivalence of the forever existing primordial origin and its illusory appearance as "newness" is conveyed by the allusion to inheritance—where one obtains on a particular day, by rights, what one has always potentially owned.

Throughout the passage barriers are struck down so that Marcel can lift the taboo placed on possession-taking. Not only are new and old, present and past, devoid of true significance in this world of congruence between wish and accomplishment, but the categories of self and other, imaginary and real, melt into the fluid totality of the symbol. On the one hand, as we noted previously, Marcel presumes, even before he enters the room and sees Albertine, that the real woman "contains" his dream. In a similar fashion, he now pretends to master a reality which is tailor-made for the fulfillment of his desires. Thus, toward the beginning of the scene, Marcel thinks: "En tous cas, le Grand-Hôtel, la soirée, ne me semblaient plus vides; ils *contenaient* mon bonheur. . . . Les moindres mouvements, comme m'asseoir sur la banquette de l'ascenseur, m'étaient doux, parce qu'ils étaient *en relation immédiate avec mon coeur*" (932; my emphasis). Henceforward there is no point in speaking of a discrepancy between the inside domain of the subject and the "outside" world, since the two exchange properties freely, without conflict. But it is clear that if the Grand-Hôtel seems to "contain" the happiness of the protagonist, it is only because the latter has projected his feelings upon the hotel in the first place. To paraphrase Baudelaire, we might write that Marcel has "peopled his solitude"—which in this case translates as the humanization of his physical surroundings. As the episode develops, as the erotic tonality becomes more pervasive, there is a corresponding heightening of the subject's feelings of power which is, in fact, the monstrously extended deployment of the pathetic fallacy. "Le Baiser refusé" gradually turns into a critique of the egocentrical excesses that subtend and vitiate Romantic symbolism.

In the scene of seduction that concludes the passage, the narrator elaborates a logic of association whereby Albertine relates analogically to certain significant elements of nature. Albertine is not just "la substance précieuse de ce corps rose" (932), not just the schematically defined sign of feminine charm as was Valentine; rather, she fuses with her environment and becomes part of a vast system of symbols whose totality Marcel wishes to grasp and enclose within the expanding limits of his body. Rhetorically, the text is constructed on a series of metonymical juxtapositions that are felt by the reader to be the result of a higher poetic necessity. Although on a literal level it is true that Albertine is merely *next to* ("à côté de") a window that opens onto a valley illuminated by the moon's rays, that the ocean lies *next to* the valley, the patent effect of these chance spatial proximities is to convince us, emotionally, that Albertine shares the female "essence" of her surroundings. In the end, nature is Albertine and Albertine is nature. The protagonist, concerned with possessing an individual woman, rethinks his ties to the totality of natural phenomena. I quote from the early portion of the culminating dramatic scene:

> Elle [Albertine] me regardait en souriant. *A côté d'elle,* dans la fenêtre, la vallée était éclairée par le clair de lune. La vue du cou nu d'Albertine, de ces joues trop roses, m'avait jeté dans une telle ivresse (c'est-à-dire avait tellement mis pour moi la réalité du monde mon plus dans la nature, mais dans le torrent des sensations que j'avais peine à contenir) que cette vue avait rompu l'équilibre entre la vie immense, indestructible qui roulait dans mon être, et la vie de l'univers, si chétive en comparaison. La mer, que j'apercevais *à côté de la vallée* dans la fenêtre, les seins bombés des premières falaises de Maineville, le ciel où la lune n'était pas encore montée au zénith, tout cela semblait plus léger à porter que des plumes pour les globes de mes prunelles qu'entre mes paupières je sentais dilatés, résistants, prêts à soulever bien d'autres fardeaux, toutes les montagnes du monde, sur leur surface délicate. (933; my emphasis)

Feminine properties and attributes are *extensive:* they fill textual space from the inside to the outside, from the "joues trop roses" of Albertine to the "vallée" (dream-symbol of womanhood), to the "seins bombés des . . . falaises." Masculine force is *inclusive:* Marcel borrows (or more precisely, steals) from nature and attempts to *contain* its torrential flow within himself. The key word of the passage is "ivresse." The "drunkenness" that takes hold of the protagonist is a form of solipsistic madness that allows for the unjustifiable but poetically seductive inversion of human and natural qualities. We know, of course, that the "reality of the world" does not reside in the irrepressible sensations of Marcel, and that the sea, the window, the cliffs, and the moon are not as easy to carry as feathers for his eyes. But we "know" this through the laws of intelligence, which are not the laws of sensation or memory according to Proust the esthetic theorist. Yet it is difficult to accept this all-too-considerable poetic license, and it is especially difficult to assume that Marcel is to be taken seriously as his "mad" use of the pathetic fallacy grows out of all proportion.

In a later reflection, just as the protagonist is leaning over to kiss Albertine, we hear: "La mort eût dû me frapper en ce moment que cela m'eût paru indifférent ou plutôt impossible, car la vie n'était pas hors de moi, elle était en moi" (933). It is easy enough to see the outlandish character of this final manipulation of the *contenant-contenu* structure, and we can conclude, before the surprise ending of the episode, that the relationship between narrator and protagonist is decidedly ironical in this context. But the irony stretches much farther, in that the passage as a whole, like its early form in "De l'Amitié au désir," mimics and demystifies certain aspects of the madeleine episode, notably the capacity of the cake dipped in tea to "hold up" the "immense edifice of memory" (like the eyelid of Marcel that carries the entire natural world) and the ecstatic feeling of the narrator that his fundamental discovery (of lost time in the madeleine sequence, of the "truth of love" in "Le Baiser refusé") has lifted him above the constraints of mortality:

> Mais, quand d'un passé ancien rien ne subsiste, après la mort des êtres, après la destruction des choses, seules, plus frêles mais plus vivaces, plus immatérielles, plus persistantes, plus fidèles, l'odeur et la saveur restent encore longtemps, comme des âmes, à se rappeler, à attendre, à espérer, sur la ruine de tout le reste, *à porter sans fléchir, sur leur goutelette presque impalpable, l'édifice immense du souvenir.* (I, 47; my emphasis)

> Mais à l'instant même où la gorgée mêlée des miettes du gâteau toucha mon palais, je tressaillis, attentif à ce qui se passait d'extraordinaire en moi. Un plaisir délicieux m'avait envahi, isolé, sans la notion de sa cause. Il m'avait aussitôt rendu les vicissitudes de la vie indifférentes, ses désastres inoffensifs, sa brièveté illusoire, *de la même façon qu'opère l'amour, en me remplissant d'une essence précieuse: ou plutôt cette essence n'était pas en moi, elle était*

*moi. J'avais cessé de me sentir médiocre, contingent, mortel.*
(I, 45; my emphasis)

### The Refused Kiss and the Birth of Narration

"Le Baiser refusé" (I, 934) The conclusion of the text is abrupt and devastatingly clear. If it can be said, as I have indicated throughout, that the rhetorical fabric of the passage is woven in reversals and inversions (with an especially insistent, obvious use of the *contenant-contenu* manipulation), then the culmination of the scene can be called a reversal of the reversals, an inversion of the inversions. In refusing the protagonist the kiss he assumes is his by the natural right of "inheritance," Albertine demonstrates an inviolability far more profound than the virginal purity that would result from a slavish respect for social convention. She has flaunted convention merely by her presence in the Grand-Hôtel and by her invitation to Marcel: the reason for her denial must lie elsewhere. The mistake made by the protagonist is to believe in the elaborate traces of *vraisemblance* that inhabit the text—all pointing to the apparent availability of Albertine as possessable creature: "Mais je me disais que ce n'était pas pour ne rien faire qu'une jeune fille fait venir un jeune homme en cachette, en s'arrangeant pour que sa tante ne le sache pas, que d'ailleurs l'audace réussit à ceux qui savent profiter des occasions" (934). Ironically, it would seem that Albertine invited her young friend precisely in order to "do nothing." Marcel cannot understand the significance of this strange idea because he has been convinced, by the logic of verisimilitude, to think of Albertine as a product of nature, as a "fruit rose inconnu" (ibid.) that he can taste and whose essence he can assimilate and control.

The ending of the passage deconstructs the conception of Albertine as Romantic symbol associated with the processes of natural growth and replaces it with that of the allegorical sign based upon the noncoincidence of *signifiant* (Albertine's deceiving appearance as possessable entity) and *signifié* (her secret, incomprehensible desires and actions). Albertine is inviolable because her semiological structure is that of an unbridgeable disjunction: by definition, she cannot be reduced to the stability of a melted significant totality. Yet Marcel attempts just such a reduction when he "reads into" her artifice and finds the underlying permanence of a light source: "Dans l'état d'excitation où j'étais, le visage rond d'Albertine, éclairé d'un feu intérieur comme par une veilleuse, prenait pour moi un tel relief qu'imitant la rotation d'une sphère ardente, il me semblait tourner, telles ces figures de Michel-Ange, qu'emporte un immobile et vertigineux tourbillon." There are two possible, mutually exclusive interpretations of this beautiful description. The first (that of the protagonist) originates in an "état d'excitation" that builds analogical links between the inside and the outside—the "feu intérieur" within Albertine's face and the "sphère ardente" of the sun that it reflects microcosmically. The face "turns," but this movement is the euphoric combination of immobility and "vertige." For Marcel, to penetrate Albertine would be equivalent to possessing the sun's rays and suspending the temporal flux of its revolution while simultaneously enjoying the impression of its whirlwind speed: such is the dream he has constructed. The second interpretation—an ironization of the first—would show that the "état d'excitation" is the cause of the naturally balanced unity of opposites that falls apart when submitted to the rigors of analysis. In fact, the roundness of Albertine's face contains a *night-light* ("veilleuse") that has its source, not its nature, but in man's inversion of natural laws. The "feu intérieur" is a pure innerness which we misread as the *analogon* of the sun. If Albertine relates to "la rotation d'une sphère ardente," it is only insofar as we detach that sphere from its place in the order of things and allow it to be the pureness of a tropological turning, independent of all heliocentrical hierarchy. Thus the episode contains the mechanism of its own deconstruction, but this mechanism becomes apparent only when the extreme delusion of the protagonist forces us to examine the rhetorical complexity of the narrative argument.

"Le Baiser refusé" is more than an isolated scene in the series that constitutes Marcel's developing liaison with Albertine: it is the prefigurative pattern of Proustian "love" as such, the fixed mold according to which all individual successive loves of the protagonist can be described and understood. The passage begins with the false supposition that Albertine is somehow intrinsically different from the other female figures of Marcel's entourage, that the possession of her pink sensuality can guarantee the protagonist's entrance into a "new" and authentic world of symbolic *correspondances*. It turns out that she is instead the perfect incarnation of the avenging mother. The ringing of the bell at the conclusion of the scene is the poetic equivalent of castration: "J'allais savoir l'odeur, le goût, qu'avait ce fruit rose inconnu. J'entendis un son précipité, prolongé et criard. Albertine avait sonné de toutes ses forces." Albertine joins the grandmother and Françoise as upholders of the taboo on possession-taking; she is merely one of the many forms of the mother in the *Recherche*. The remainder of the novel will prove the radical impossibility of merging with maternal substance despite the indefatigable efforts and blind determination of Marcel to manage this forbidden feat.

But it would be a simplification to say that masculine energy is defeated by a feminine defensive barrier. This is the overt meaning and blatant irony of the episode, but underneath is a more convoluted configuration. The unconscious level of the text has already transformed Marcel into a woman before the "castration" takes place. The final metamorphosis of the *contenant-contenu* manipulation—the interiorization of "life" and the "world" by the expanded subjectivity of the protagonist ("comment le monde eût-il pu durer plus que moi, puisque je n'étais pas perdu en lui, puisque c'était lui qui était enclos en moi")—assumes the form of a phantasmic pregnancy. If Marcel is forever blocked from opening and penetrating the womb in masculine fashion, he will disguise himself as a woman and give birth to the fictive entity of his forthcoming book. It is at this deep psychological level that "Le Baiser refusé" rewrites the madeleine episode—which is also based on the apotheosis of the narcissistic self and on the interiorization of substance in an imaginary pregnancy: "Un plaisir délicieux m'avait envahi . . . *de la même façon qu'opère l'amour, en me remplissant d'une essence précieuse* (I, 45; my emphasis). The surface difference in subject matter that seems to separate the scenes into the thematically diverse domains of "art" and "love" becomes irrelevant when we realize that the "delicious pleasure" of the madeleine experience operates according to the structure of love, and that "love" itself is the rhetorical strategy whereby the self, constantly frustrated in its extension toward the other, gives birth to itself and justifies its art.

"Le Baiser refusé," when superimposed on the madeleine episode, shows unequivocally the regressive character of the self's quest for auto-determination and thus tends to put into question the widely held assumption that Proustian narration is the fluid and unproblematic "natural" unfolding of the act of remembrance. Indeed, if on the one hand the *récit* is said to originate in the retrospection of an organizing consciousness, but if this consciousness is deluded in its affirmation that the essence of truth can be assimilated like the maternal body into the inclusiveness of a superior masculinity, then it follows that the "organic" structure of the symbol is inadequate as a representation of Proustian narration and that one must search elsewhere for a suitable explanatory model. The conclusion of "Le Baiser refusé" leaves us with the following hypothesis, which we shall need to verify progressively: that the "birth" of narration is (1) the non-natural, nonorganic, disjunctive, and discontinuous movement whereby the illusory promises of the symbolic mode are revealed in the artifice of their poetic beauty; (2) the passage of the protagonist into a world where the atemporal merging of subject and object is repeatedly undermined; (3) the paradoxical "opening" into a textual space that is beyond the logic of mimesis or verisimilitude. It is into this strange space, only hinted at in "Le Baiser refusé," that Jean enters in the final pages of "De l'Amitié au désir."

"De l'Amitié au désir" (Pages 840–42) The last two paragraphs of the passage constitute a brusque conclusion of the *récit* and a return to the *traité*. Like Marcel in his relations with Albertine, Jean has misread Valentine, has misinterpreted the signs of sensual openness she has offered in such profusion: she does not allow him to kiss her and threatens to ring (presumably for help, but the scene being completely *invraisemblable,* the two lovers being alone, one wonders what purpose this ringing could serve). But the episode does not stop here. Unlike "Le Baiser refusé," which suddenly terminates on a note of irony, "De l'Amitié au désir" continues, as Jean attempts to understand Valentine's reasons for rejecting him. The narrator shifts from the presentation of Jean's dramatically heightened emotions to the rational analysis of Valentine's contradictory nature: mimesis gives way to the mode of hypothesis.

The narrator does not propose one universal law that would explain Valentine's surprising refusal, but a series of psychologically complex suppositions in the form of interlaced clauses all originating in the words *peut-être* and *soit que.* Readers of the *Recherche* are familiar with this technique; it consists of giving multiple motivations for a particular act or event, and is a favorite method of the classical *moralistes* in their dissection of human passions. In this context, the hypothetical form of the narrator's logic is an admission of Valentine's enigmatic status and a demonstration that she cannot be represented in terms of the organicity and significant unity of the Romantic symbol. Valentine is, rather, the incarnation/personification of the arbitrariness of the sign. The "reasoning" of her refusal as reconstructed by the narrator is based upon the insuperable separation of appearance from reality, *signifiant* from *signifié.* The assumption underlying the entirety of the narrator's argument is that Valentine is unable to make the concept of "possession" merge with the act itself, unable to think of the relationship between word and meaning as being structured by the essential sharing of properties of a synecdochic union. I quote now a portion of Proust's intricate and undisciplined early prose:

> Peut-être dans l'enchevêtrement de ses mauvais instincts et de ses bonnes moeurs, de sa courtisanerie et de sa vertu, croyait-elle que "la possession" n'était pas un mal . . . comme si la notion [de] possession n'était pas pour elle la même chose que la possession même, approuvant la totalité de l'une, repoussant de la seconde jusqu'à ce qui de si loin et en si innocent pouvait en rapprocher, pouvant commencer par une telle caresse du moment qu'elle pouvait consister en quelque chose qui n'est pas forcément une caresse (le massage), à faire du plaisir, mais se refusant aussitôt à ce qui constituait pour elle les actes même les plus simples et les plus innocents du plaisir même, soit qu'elle [fût] familiarisée avec l'idée sans que cela eût diminué sa crainte de la chose, soit qu'elle eût un goût spécial pour la chose qui lui en permettait tout ce qui d'elle était pour elle autre chose et portait un autre nom, mais reculait dès que la notion de la chose apparaissait. (840–41)

In this awkwardly worded but deeply reflective text, the narrator explains what Jean cannot understand: the structure of Valentine's thoughts and the ground for her nonpossessable being. The protagonist of *Jean Santeuil,* like Marcel in the *Recherche,* experiences alternately the effects of his beloved's "mauvais instincts" and "bonnes moeurs," of her "courtisanerie" and "vertu," but is unable to conclude that this *enchevêtrement* of opposing qualities has a definable semiological basis in the form of allegorical discontinuity. In the *traité* the protagonist merely illustrates the systematic ideas of the narrator and is most often blocked from access to the latter's insights. Hence it is not surprising that when, in the last paragraph of the passage, the point of view shifts to the limited perspective of Jean, there should be a return to the illusory promises of symbolic rhetoric. Psychologically, Jean's reasoning is based upon sublimation. Although he recognizes his defeat at possession-taking in reality, he wishes to continue conceiving of Valentine in terms of organic continuity, and manages to do so by replacing her concrete sensuality with a purely imaginary substitute:

> La Valentine qu'il avait depuis deux ans devant ses yeux, était effacée. Maintenant elle était pour lui, dans une chambre close, sur des draps blancs, ressortant mieux sous ses cheveux défaits, une tête cramoisie, *symbole magnifique et luxuriant* de plaisirs qu'à vrai dire il n'avait pu goûter matériellement, mais de la révélation de l'existence desquels la vie désormais se trouvait pour lui enrichie. (841; my emphasis)

The remainder of the passage develops according to the logic of recuperation whereby the negativity of existential actions is transformed into the positive enrichment of a fictional projection. In becoming a symbol or idol, Valentine loses her threatening power of "castration" and the text resolves itself into a dreamworld to the second degree: now Jean can *adore* his phantom creature—which is safer and more comfortable than any attempt to penetrate her essence.

"De l'Amitié au désir" plays out the contradictions that will be operative and textually productive in the *Recherche.* The episode relates the impossibility of possession-taking but refuses to respect the semiological consequences of its own clear revelations. The narrator knows that Valentine is not just a creature exhibiting traits of ambivalence, but the allegorical figure of ambivalence itself—a pure enigmatic significance surface hiding an unknowable inner core. But the protagonist is unable to accept the corollary to this fact: that Valentine exists, not in the mode of reality or even dreamed reality, but in the form of a potentially infinite hypothesis that cannot be reduced to the "natural" components of the symbol. The discrepancy between the narrator's knowledge of the un-knowability of the allegorical sign and the protagonist's blindness to this irrecuperable negative understanding causes the text to vacillate between two irreconcilable modes of discourse that do not merge into some higher narrative unity but nevertheless presuppose each other's functioning and thrive on mutual antagonism.

*A la recherche du temps perdu* is the point of intersection of the *traité,* which is allegorical-hypothetical, and the *récit,* which is symbolical-probable. The simultaneous reading of "De l'Amitié au désir" and "Le Baiser refusé" has allowed us to verify Rogers' contention that the novel contains what amounts to a modal incompatibility. But it is not true that the more profoundly authentic moments of the *Recherche* correspond with the dominance of the symbolic *récit* and the disappearance of the *traité,* which Rogers relegates to the secondary status of the "non-novel-istic." On the contrary, as we have just observed in the ending of "De l'Amitié au désir," adherence to the symbolic mode is the result of the protagonist's misreading of the allegorical sign, of his refusal to dwell within the non-natural domain of the hypothetical. And in "Le Baiser refusé" the ironization of possession-taking is also a deconstruction of the verisimilitude that characterizes the traditional *récit:* if Marcel understood what was happening to him, he would recognize that the logic of the *récit* is not that of Albertine as allegorical figure, that she *as* sign is impenetrable and therefore incompatible with the very structure of the symbol. If the form of the Proustian text were the direct, transparent expression of the allegorical semiology incorporated by Albertine, it would be pure *traité;* and if the narrator were able to dominate or espouse the structure of alle-gory, one could imagine his discourse as that of a moralizer's proleptic control. But narrative control is achieved at the expense of the essence of the allegorical sign—which is unknowable. Once the narrator moves from the stage of hypothetical reasoning to the formulation of laws, he has falsified the very basis of his argument and gained an illusory mastery. Proleptic technique in the *Recherche* derives from the transformation of the hypothetical into the factual. In expressing general atemporal truths, the narrator denies the temporal differential structure of allegory.

Ironically, it is the protagonist who, precisely through his repeated errors of interpretation, abides closer to the negative semiological truth of allegory than does the so-called "omniscient" narrator. Since the alle-gorical sign is composed of a disjunction between *signifiant* and *signifié,* since we cannot infer the latter from the former or "see" the meaning of the sign through the transcendental magic of symbolic "translucence," the act of reading emerges as the only method of communication between the two poles of significance. And because the core of the allegorical sign is strictly impenetrable, while reading is necessarily structured as the deciphering of an enigma, as the illumination of the hidden, reading becomes an interminable misreading, the forever frustrated attempt of the protagonist to possess an elusive object. The origin of the *discontinuité croissante* in the Proustian text and of the succession of isolated "paliers itératifs" is in the reading of the allegorical sign, which can only produce infinite repetition, infinite variations on the same theme. What we call the *récit* is the mechanism of repeated failures to stop the process of reading. The erroneous interpretations inscribed within the structure of allegory extend outward to generate, nonorganically, a "progression in a series of moments": narration.

# 5
# The Self
# in/as Writing

It is impossible to study Proust's narrative technique as a closed system of purely formal relationships. The *discontinuité croissante* of the *Recherche* is not fundamentally a phenomenon of abstract design (even if it is shown to foreshadow the experimental, fragmentary organizational patterns used by the *nouveaux romanciers*) but derives its deeper meaningfulness from the modal incompatibility at the core of the novel. The conflict between the desire of a subject to penetrate and possess the essence of the symbol and the allegorical-hypothetical narration of the failure of this desire produces the appearance of discontinuity which it is the duty of the theoretician to describe as an objective aspect of the *Recherche*'s structural identity. But one must not forget, in arriving at the clarity of terminological distinctions, that what we call technically "narrative form" is based upon the concretely elaborated drama of the self. When I juxtaposed "De l'Amitié au désir" to "Le Baiser refusé" in order to analyze and locate within the novel the generation of narration *as* discontinuity, I expressed the dichotomy between symbol and allegory in sexual terms, according to the love context of the passages. "Penetration," "possession," "narcissism," "imaginary rape," "birth," "intra-uterine plenitude"—the repetition of these words and others of the same semantic constellation suggests that an interpretation of Proustian narration is inseparable from the problematic constitution of the self *in* fiction. And if it can be said rightfully that there is an evolution within the *Recherche* toward an ever-greater fragmentation of episodic material, this manifestation of a formal difference must correspond in some way with the development of the *je* who lives the imaginary events and tells the story of the novel. With the "discovery" of Albertine—or more precisely, of Albertine as allegorical figure who demonstrates the split between *signifiant* and *signifié* and the impossibility of Ruskinian/Romantic possession-taking—there is a movement toward a generalized increased innerness, whereby the self retreats progressively from the outward "conversational" concerns of social intercourse to a more private, enigmatic existence as jealous decipherer of his beloved's secret, unimaginable activities.

Since the publication of *A la recherche du temps perdu* readers have had difficulty understanding the significance of the latter sections of *Sodome et Gomorrhe, La Prisonnière,* and *La Fugitive,* for two fundamentally related reasons: (1) the sudden shift from a Balzacian or, some would prefer to say, Saint-Simonian kaleidoscopic description of Parisian aristocratic mores to a claustrophobic concentration on the relationship of two people is in itself puzzling and disconcerting; (2) the extreme minuteness with which the narrator examines the involuted psychological "laws" acted out in this relationship seems to indicate, on the part of the author, a painful personal obsession. It is as if Proust, reacting to the pressure of some existential conflict of his own, had decided to abandon the elaborately conceived imaginary universe with its individualized characters and places of the earlier volumes and reduce his fictional space to the anaerobic void of the prison room that alternately contains and lets escape its unhappy inmate. One reason readers have felt an uncomfortable estrangement from the *Recherche* at this point of its turning inward is that they are suddenly confronted with a world no longer characterized by multiplicity, but by an infinitely variable and repeatable pattern of duplicity. Human behavior does not offer a spectacle of chaotic and exalting productive energies, but shrinks to a cycle of either/or propositions that succeed each other without transition or intercommunication. Near the midpoint of *Sodome et Gomorrhe* Proust writes: "Si multiple que soit l'être que nous aimons, il peut en tous cas nous présenter deux personnalités essentielles, selon qu'il nous apparaît comme nôtre ou comme tournant ses désirs ailleurs que vers nous. La première de ces personnalités possède la puissance particulière qui nous empêche de croire à la réalité de la seconde, le secret spécifique pour apaiser les souffrances que cette dernière a causée. L'être aimé est successivement le mal et le remède qui suspend et aggrave le mal" (II, 833). These sentences foretell concisely the subject matter of *La Prisonnière* and *La Fugitive,* which constitute a monstrous expansion of the oscillation between calm (Marcel confident of his domination over Albertine) and anguish (Marcel aware that he cannot comprehend the *otherness* of Albertine's lesbian links to unknown women).

In the penultimate volumes of the novel, the tendency toward omniscient narration disappears, and the *je* who relates fictional events no longer pretends to extend his sensory and intellectual apprehension of reality beyond very precisely established limits. Just as the thematic material of the *récit* loses diversity and becomes the simplified structure of a polar opposition, in a similar way the property of narrative to subsume the outside world in the grammatical form of *il* and *elle, ils* and *elles,* recedes in favor of a dialogic system, in which only *je* and *tu* prevail. On all levels of form and meaning, *La Prisonnière* and *La Fugitive* develop fugal variations on the related motifs of duality, dichotomy, duplicity, and ambivalence: the universe of these volumes is that of emotional conflict and impossible choices. By passing abruptly from the macrocosm of society to the microcosm of Marcel's mind in its attachment to the elusive Albertine, by insisting so heavily on the metaphor of "sickness" to describe the process of love, by placing the reader squarely within the obsessional repetitions of the self's doomed quest for stability, Proust opens up the question of the relationship between fiction (esthetic distance) and autobiography (adherence to self, closeness to personal desire). Like Marcel, we as readers are placed in an either/or situation: is the *Recherche* a fiction, is it an autobiography? Does it evolve from fiction to autobiography? Is it legitimate to extend the idea of modal incompatibility to the ambiguous copresence of these two narrative forms? In the following pages, I will study the "inner development" of the *Recherche:* its progressive change of thematic emphasis and tone that results from the ever-expanded significance of the Marcel-Albertine dialogue; the contagious "spreading" of homosexuality that begins with Albertine but soon includes many of the novel's principal characters; and, perhaps most striking of all, the gradual domination of reality by the "mad" imagination of the protagonist. At stake throughout is the precise nature of the relationship between Proustian selfhood and the act of writing, between psychological vulnerability and the impulse to create.

In recent years, a group of Proust scholars has devoted itself to the minute examination of the *carnets* and *cahiers* from which the *Recherche* grew to attain its novelistic unity. Since Madame Mante-Proust gave her permission for Proust's manuscripts and typescripts to be placed at the Bibliothèque Nationale and made available for textual study, much progress has been made in determining the chronological sequence of the notebooks, and therefore, in establishing the patterns of internal *genesis* through which sketches of episodes and fragmentary notes gradually become scenes of the novel.[1] The more one delves into the details of this literary-genetic problematics, the clearer it becomes that whatever "fluid" appearance of transitional and contextual *armature* the *Recherche* possesses in the definitive Pléiade edition was achieved at the expense of great authorial effort. Anyone who spends time in the Salle des Manuscrits of the Bibliothèque Nationale unfolding Proustian *paperoles* knows that the novel is like a surrealistic marriage between an accordion and a patchwork quilt: one has to admire Proust and his editors for their success in imposing a linear sequence on the ramifications and bifurcations of the original drafts.

Although much painstaking work remains to be done before we can trace in detail the origin and development of the final version of the *Recherche* from its embryonic beginnings, we now know, in a general, schematic way, the basic stages of this evolution. Proust first wrote a series of disorganized notes in 1909—half-theory, half-novel—which we call *Contre Sainte-Beuve* for the sake of convenience but which is much more than a polemic with the noted nineteenth-century critic. Then, from 1910 to 1912 he composed a first version of the *Recherche* divided into three parts: *Du côté de chez Swann, Le Côté de Guermantes,* and *Le Temps retrouvé.* In 1913 *Du côté de chez Swann* was published by Grasset, but in 1914 came two events which completely upset the tripartite format of the book: the First World War, whose obvious effect for writers was to curtail drastically the printing of literary works; and Proust's homosexual liaison with his chauffeur, Alfred Agostinelli. Critics of Proust are unanimous in concluding that the combination of these two crises—the one public, the other private—led to a profound *remaniement* of the *Recherche* and produced, in fact, what amounts to a "new" novel.

During the war years, Proust incorporated into his fictional creation what seems to be a rather transparently transposed autobiographical account of his relationship with Agostinelli, in the guise of the Marcel-Albertine drama of *La Prisonnière* and *La Fugitive.* Alfred Agostinelli becomes Albertine, and the insertion of Albertine into an already voluminous text caused certain organizational problems. Maurice Bardèche has shown that the tome *A l'Ombre des jeunes filles en fleurs* is a "composite" made up in part of what was to be the second volume of *Du côté de chez Swann* in the Grasset edition and in part of a new section composed after 1914 in which Albertine plays a major role. The practical difficulty faced by Proust as organizer of an esthetic totality was that of integrating into what already existed of his novel not only the principal episode concerning Albertine but also preparatory scenes that would render this episode inevitable and necessary within the overall framework of the fiction. Bardèche has hypothesized (though, as he freely admits, without the solid evidence of textual proof) that "Proust, après une période d'abattement et d'inactivité, a repris ses cahiers à la fin de 1914 et qu'il a écrit d'abord le cahier qui contient le premier jet d'*Albertine disparue* [*La Fugitive*], puis qu'il a écrit ensuite, probablement en 1915, les 'préparations' dont il avait besoin, à savoir le chapitre des 'jeunes filles' dans le premier séjour à Balbec, la

visite d'Albertine à Paris, enfin le second séjour à Balbec avec Albertine"
(*Marcel Proust romancier,* II, 75). The notebook (numbered 54 in the catalogue of the Bibliothèque Nationale) which contains the initial transcription of *Albertine disparue* is described by Bardèche as "un cri, le cri du
désespoir, l'improvisation de la fureur et de la folie, sur le moment, dans
les semaines ou les mois qui suivent [la mort d'Agostinelli dans un accident d'avion], et . . . se termine par le calme après les soubresauts, puis la
stupeur de l'oubli" (73). If the earlier scenes were indeed added *after* the
writing of the Agostinelli/Albertine tragedy as such, they were conceived,
in all probability, to attenuate what could be judged an excessively autobiographical tone and to immerse Albertine into the already consistent
fictional context of the previous volumes. If Albertine were to be one
character among others at first, one among several girl-flowers, her subsequent emergence as unique object of the narrator's attention might appear
less brusque than if she were given no "introduction."

Despite these efforts at fictional framing and integration, when the
reader reaches the penultimate volumes of the *Recherche* he is thrust into
a radically different, essentially unsuspected atmosphere of claustration
that has nothing in common with the euphorically constituted universe of
Balbec with which Albertine is poetically associated. It is as if, in changing
from landscape artist to portrait painter, Proust had discovered that the
young flower-girl of the beach and fresh air, originally appreciated as the
esthetically pleasing unit of a larger composition, when isolated and imprisoned, could only serve to magnify the anxieties of the protagonist and
render him incapable of the wider perspective within which he had depicted the metamorphoses of natural processes. In *La Prisonnière* the narrator tells us that Albertine, like an exotic animal in a cage unhappy with
its domesticated state, has "lost her colors" and become "gray."[2] But this
grayness is the projection of Marcel's feelings, which have withdrawn into
the protectiveness of a self-inflicted, self-woven cocoon: Albertine *is* precisely what Marcel thinks she is; her existence has passed from the natural
to the artificial/hypothetical. Hence the impression one receives when
reading that there has been a shift in modality in the novel, that the
symbolic/probable logic of the fictional *récit* has given way to the absolute implausibility of a psychologically complex relationship centered in
the compulsions of a self who resembles very closely the person Marcel
Proust. Yet the question of whether the *Recherche* is autobiographical or
not cannot be a mere matter of impressions: we need to determine with
some theoretical precision to what degree Proust's novel fits the requisite
conditions of autobiography, to what degree it stretches and distorts the
classical mold in which it is cast.

The distinction between autobiography and fiction is itself problematical, as will be apparent from later developments in this study, but

generally we call a work autobiographical if it adheres closely to the actual events of an author's life and limits itself to a reorganization of these same events, while a fiction transmutes the real material into imaginary constructs that lose partially or completely their air of recognizable correspondence to the lived experience from which they are drawn. The fundamental criterion for discrimination is resemblance or lack of resemblance to existential reality. Now this criterion obviously lacks any objective or scientific rigor, since one reader's perception of the analogical "closeness" of copy to model can differ from another's. Let us suppose, however, that the merely relative value of the criterion of resemblance is sufficient for descriptive purposes and that we can use it to study the evolution of Proust's creative writing. We note inevitably a paradoxical fact: namely, that the use of third-person narrative in *Jean Santeuil* accompanied a highly personal subject matter (the hero of the abortive novel being quite clearly the young Marcel Proust, and his activities and adventures basically those of the author), whereas the later choice of the first person for the *Recherche* came when Proust had become capable of delineating an independently coherent fictional world, and therefore, on the surface at least, had gained an ironical distance from self. The passage from *il* to *je,* which would seem to be that of objective detachment to subjective involvement, is exactly the opposite for Proust, and there is a remarkable *loss* of resemblance between life and imaginary events as the author assumes the autobiographical voice. Gérard Genette has explained this contradiction in psychological terms, as the result of Proust's inner personal development. He writes of

> l'assomption tardive, et délibérée, de la *forme* de l'autobiographie directe, qu'il faut immédiatement rapprocher du fait, apparemment contradictoire, que le contenu narratif de la *Recherche* est moins directement autobiographique que celui de *Santeuil:* comme si Proust avait dû vaincre d'abord une certaine adhérence à soi, se détacher de lui-même pour conquérir le droit de dire "je" à ce héros qui n'est ni tout à fait lui-même, ni tout à fait un autre.
> La conquête du *je* n'est donc pas ici retour et présence à soi, installation dans le confort de la "subjectivité", mais peut-être exactement le contraire: l'expérience difficile d'un rapport à soi vécu comme (légère) distance et décentrement, rapport que symbolise à merveille cette semi-homonymie plus que discrète, et comme accidentelle, du héros-narrateur et du signataire. (*Figures III,* 256–57)

The logic of Genette's argumentation is based upon an irrefutable fact: the *Recherche* is less self-indulgent and less self-glorying than *Jean Santeuil.* For this reason, it is tempting to conclude that the transition from the early work to the novel involves the achievement of a higher degree of fictionality, which is tantamount to a greater esthetic distance. The use of *je* should not be interpreted reductively, as mere confession, but is a formal strategy whereby the author makes the reader aware of a discrepancy between the empirical and the fictional self. Indirectly, Genette is warning us against committing the error of naïve readers, which consists in confusing the *signifié* of a literary text with its referent. Since this confusion has been made all too often in the case of Proust,[3] one can only agree with the critic's appeal to our vigilance. Yet one cannot avoid questioning the somewhat hidden reductiveness of Genette's own reasoning: is it legitimate to suppose that a text must be *either* autobiographical/confessional *or* fictional/removed from reality? Could it not happen that an imaginative work is simultaneously the one *and* the other, an oscillating movement between these two poles? And might it not be just as naïve to bracket the referentiality of a text in the name of disinterested formal analysis as it is to participate uncritically in the referential illusion as such?

I do not believe much is gained or solved if we affirm, with Genette and Germaine Brée, that first-person narration in the *Recherche* is the result of a conscious esthetic choice rather than the sign of confession or "confidence directe."[4] This hypothesis amounts to isolating the text in the realm of an abstract, self-sufficient fictional space where existential force is simply replaced by the free play of forms. What Genette, Brée, and many other readers of Proust note in passing rather than examine deeply is the *perversity* of saying *je* when one may or may not, may and may not "mean what one says." There is much discretion but no accident involved in the "semi-homonymie . . . du héros-narrateur et du signataire": the name of the protagonist and narrator is Marcel, like that of the author, or at least it seems to be if the short passage in *La Prisonnière* (III, 75) staging the act of nomination is itself readable. I will interpret the implications of this passage later in the present chapter, but for the time being it is sufficient to say that the semi-identity of "Marcel" and Marcel Proust poses considerable problems and in no way presupposes the victory of fiction over autobiography. On the contrary, the use of one name to designate two disparate literary functions implies that the *Recherche* thrives on ambivalence and on the transgression of distinct boundaries.

To understand the significance of Proustian modal transgression, it is necessary to define in mutual opposition autobiography and fictional/novelistic prose and to determine exactly the structure and limits of each. There can be no subversion without the fixed existence of a law, no crossing of boundaries unless frontiers have been traced with clarity. The best recent, theoretically consequent attempt to describe autobiography that provides us with just such clarity is that of Philippe Lejeune in *Le*

*Pacte autobiographique* (Paris: Seuil, 1975). The originality of Lejeune's methodological approach resides in its displacement of the criterion that distinguishes autobiography from fiction: instead of resemblance/lack of resemblance of the written account to the real model, Lejeune prefers to use the concept of *identity*. What matters is not the degree of "similarity" (in itself impossible to ascertain) of a text to its referent, but, quite simply, whether or not the author, narrator, and protagonist are "identical." After all, it is possible to conceive of a novel that is closer to life than a poorly researched or badly organized autobiography, but it is impossible to confuse the presence of the author's signed name on the cover page with its absence, just as it would seem, a priori, impossible not to determine unequivocally whether there is sameness or difference of names in the triad "author-narrator-protagonist." The criterial shift from resemblance to identity brings with it an elimination of vagueness and relativity and an appreciable gain in concreteness. As Lejeune explains at the very beginning of his essay, his point of departure is the *experience* of reading through which a literary text is made to function. To read an imaginative work is to actualize its significant potential. The author and the reader contact each other through the medium of the printed word, which has not just intellectual, but social and "legal" consequences. In Lejeune's terms, "l'auteur se définit comme étant simultanément une personne réelle socialement responsable, et le producteur d'un discours" (23). This means that the author's signature and the designation "autobiography" have the force of a pact or contract whereby the reader is assured of the identity of that which he is about to peruse. Referentiality and responsibility are two facets of the same question for Lejeune, and it is the absolute verifiability of the *nom propre* that guarantees the stability of the critic's theoretical distinctions.[5]

Within Lejeune's system of classification, *A la recherche du temps perdu* appears to be a hybrid form. Marcel Proust's name is on the cover page of his book, but there is no explicit indication as to whether he, as author, viewed his work as a novel or as an autobiography. Lejeune tentatively places the *Recherche* in the category of the *pacte romanesque*, but, like Genette, he is confronted with the bothersome passage of *La Prisonnière* in which Albertine "names" the protagonist-narrator: "Elle retrouvait la parole, elle disait: 'Mon' ou 'Mon chéri', suivis l'un ou l'autre de mon nom de baptême, ce qui, en donnant au narrateur le même prénom qu'à l'auteur de ce livre, eût fait: 'Mon Marcel', 'Mon chéri Marcel' (III, 75; quoted in *Le Pacte autobiographique*, 29). The apparent identity Marcel—Marcel Proust tends toward the autobiographical, but this supposed identity is expressed hypothetically, through an authorial intervention that only reinforces the essential functional separation between author and narrator characteristic of fiction, not autobiography. Hence

Lejeune's conclusion: "Cette bizarre intrusion d'auteur fonctionne à la fois comme pacte romanesque et comme indice autobiographique, et installe le texte dans un espace ambigu" (ibid.). The *Recherche* is a text which defies theoretical classification and puts into question the clarity of consciously elaborated distinctions. It adopts the form of classical autobiography without assuming full referential responsibility for its writing, but it nevertheless contains an autobiographical clue or hint ("indice autobiographique") that makes it impossible for the reader-detective to abandon following the traces of a disguised but insistent empirical/confessional discourse. Marcel Proust is *and* is not to be heard in the voice of his narrator: *je* is both self and other, in the simultaneity of textual undecidability.

If we conclude, with Lejeune, that the *Recherche* occupies an "espace ambigu" between fiction and autobiography, the next logical step of our own interpretive process would appear to be a determination of the structure and meaning of this ambiguity. We would need to find what literary-textual effects arise as a result of deviance from the norm of autobiographical *identity*. But to pursue such an investigation immediately would imply that Lejeune's theoretical system is itself not open to question and not subject to the disruptions of formal or semantic multiplicity. Before reading the *Recherche* as subversion of an established theoretical rule, we need to see how the rule came to be established. Specifically, we must examine the origin of the *nom propre* that grounds the classificatory scheme of the critic.

At the center of Lejeune's argument is a disagreement with certain fundamental ideas of the linguist Emile Benveniste. In reading the essay "Le Pacte autobiographique," it is not difficult to pass over the disagreement because Lejeune's personal and analytical style are not those of a strident polemicist: indeed, his suggestion is merely to "nuancer" (21) Benveniste's observations with a few of his own reservations. But the nuances are, in fact, changes of extraordinary importance that are relevant to the problematic position of Proust as (pseudo-) autobiographer.

In the fifth section of *Problèmes de linguistique générale* (Paris: Gallimard, 1966), entitled "L'homme dans la langue," Benveniste discusses the nature of pronouns and the question of "subjectivity" in language, both of which have an obvious direct bearing on the expression of selfhood in writing. He distinguishes initially between nouns in general and the pronouns *je* and *tu* by saying that the former "refer to a constant and objective notion" whereas the latter have no "definable object" of reference (252). Unlike the *il,* which shares the objective status of nouns, *je* and *tu* are "des signes 'vides' non référentiels par rapport à la réalité', toujours disponibles, et qui deviennent 'pleins' dès qu'un lecteur les assume dans chaque instance de son discours" (254).[6] This means that when I pronounce the word *je,* I am referring not to the outside reality of some conceptual totality but to "l'acte de discours individuel" *in* which I have identified myself: "La réalité à laquelle . . . [je] renvoie est la réalité du discours. C'est dans l'instance de discours où *je* désigne le locuteur que celui-ci s'énonce comme 'sujet'" (260). And finally, the problem of self-consciousness is seen by Benveniste as possessing a *dialogic* structure—that of the mutual reflexiveness of *je* and *tu:* "La conscience de soi n'est possible que si elle s'éprouve par contraste. Je n'emploie *je* qu'en m'adressant à quelqu'un, qui sera dans mon allocution un *tu.* C'est cette condition de dialogue qui est constitutive de la *personne,* car elle implique en réciprocité que je devient *tu* dans l'allocution de celui qui à son tour se désigne par *je*" (260).

The notions of self-consciousness, subjectivity, and personality are not conceptually rigorous postulates allowing us to analyze and classify the variations and vicissitudes of the self's development; rather, these very notions are derivative. It is because there exists an original dialogic situation, it is because language continually actualizes itself in repeated *instances de discours,* that we have personality, subjectivity, and self-consciousness. Benveniste's theory of language is situational and dynamic. I speak in context and determine myself as "subject" in the very process of addressing my interlocutor. Each time I utter a word I fill the void of the empty sign *je,* and in the linguist's terms, I "appropriate" the entirety of language in my discourse (*Problèmes,* 262). Proust's passage on naming in *La Prisonnière* is strangely suitable to this scheme, in that the identity of the narrator-protagonist emerges in a dialogue as a quasi-literal "appropriation." Albertine, in waking, says *"Mon"* or *"Mon* chéri," followed by the *prénom* hypothetically associated with that of the book's author. But Proust goes one step beyond Benveniste, because he not only affirms that personality and subjective identity are the effects/results of dialogue, but also that the self owes its identity to the *other; je* becomes *je* only when it has been possessed by *tu.* Marcel is Marcel only *in* the mouth of Albertine, so that it might be more truthful to say that *je* is appropriated *by* language, when language is understood as the totality of the dialogic situation.

Lejeune's theory of autobiography bypasses the complexities of dialogic exchange and anchors the *je* in the unambiguous referential verifiability of the *nom propre.* In effect, Lejeune refuses to consider *je* and *tu* as empty signs that become filled in the repeatable act of linguistic utterance. Instead, he declares that they are "already" attached to a proper noun, and that this noun can always be identified:

> C'est dans le *nom propre,* que personne et discours s'articulent avant même de s'articuler dans la première personne, comme le montre l'ordre d'acquisition du langage par les enfants. L'enfant parle de lui-même à la troisième personne en se nommant par

son prénom, bien avant de comprendre qu'il peut lui aussi utiliser la première personne. Ensuite chacun se nomme "je" en parlant; mais pour chacun, ce "je" renverra à un nom unique, et que l'on pourra toujours énoncer. (*Le Pacte autobiographique*, 22)

It is thus by an appeal to empirical reality—the order of language acquisition in children, which is observable and scientifically describable—that Lejeune justifies the referential identity and stability of *je*. We will always know who *je* "is" because *je* has a name. This may seem comforting at first, until we inquire as to the origin of the name. What Lejeune is really describing is a double alienation: the first, occurring when the child speaks of itself in the third person as an object, using its "given" name; the second, when it must make use of the generalized term *je,* by which it passes into the trans-subjective realm of language. The primary difficulty in Lejeune's system is that it is too secure in its attachment to the commonsense boundaries of everyday reality. We are told that the proper name guarantees autobiographical identity. But in what sense can we associate the vacillations of the appropriating/dispossessing process of naming with the unproblematical notion of *le propre,* understood as that which one owns and does not need to question? The answer is far from evident, and cannot be studied in theoretical isolation, but needs elaboration in concrete textual analysis. Finally, it is necessary to conclude that Lejeune achieves theoretical-formal clarity at the expense of psychological insight. The postulation of the *nom propre* as foundation of his system obscures the more basic and complex issue of the modality of the *je*'s textual presence or absence. How the self is appropriated by the act of writing, how its obsessional patterns of existence leave traces in the text—these matters exceed the problematics of *identity* and *property,* but need to be investigated if the relationship of the *Recherche* to autobiography is to be understood.

## AUTOBIOGRAPHY AND ALLEGORY

When we say, with excessive simplicity, that autobiography is "the expression of the self in writing," we assume that the self is a totality which can be analyzed into constituent elements and represented by an explanatory narration. In most classical autobiographies the question to which the literary text is an answer can be paraphrased, How did I become who I am now? The writer selects certain events from his past that assume, retrospectively, a paradigmatic importance, because they seem to have foreshadowed or determined his present character. The mere fact that the autobiographer chooses to relate a given action or anecdote and to suppress others that occurred during the same period implies that he has, at least in general terms, an idea of who he "is." Rousseau's account of the sexually pleasurable spanking at the hands of Mlle Lambercier (*Confessions,* I) and Proust's description of the "scène du baiser" at Combary both establish, *in nuce,* a psychological pattern that remains visible throughout the authors' lives and which, in its varied realizations, constitutes the stable entity we call "personality" or "selfhood." But this attempt to anchor the diversity of an existence in a concept—which involves, in literary creation, the retrospective imposition of thematic continuity on the potentially infinite multiplicity of episodic material—is not necessarily the only method available to the writer of confessional discourse, although it is the most familiar to the reading public of the nineteenth and twentieth centuries.

Because so much of Romantic and modern literature concerns itself with crises of identity, it has become natural to speak of the self as an hypostatized unit of meaning which encounters obstacles along its path to fulfillment, which can be "unhappy" with respect to the harmony it seeks, but which never loses its appearance of a closed structural unit. In the *Recherche,* it seems on the surface that Proust has inherited this notion of the self and that the problems of the *moi* that inhabits the pages of his book need to be examined in the light of Romantic and post-Romantic literary tradition. Until now, I have interpreted Proust as if this were indeed possible, especially in my comparison of Ruskin's (Romantic) esthetic theory to the strategies of writing transposed from the English critic and incorporated in the *Recherche.* Even when Proust deconstructs Ruskin, as in his ironical manipulations of possession-taking, we could say that the novelist *se pose en s'opposant,* and thus does not disengage himself entirely from the cultural context of his age, even if he undermines some of its most tenacious philosophical and rhetorical foundations. But if we declare, for example, that Proust chooses the allegorical mode rather than the symbolic, it is not sufficient to contrast the two and conclude that allegory is simply that which the symbol is not: we need to examine, positively, what allegory is, and to do so, we are compelled to take into account its origin. I propose now to evoke the question of the relationship of the self to allegorical discourse, with reference to the cultural framework of the Middle Ages. When Proust studied Ruskin, he was able to discover the extent to which Romanticism borrowed its theoretical terminology and esthetic justification from the Middle Ages. There are unmistakable traces of medieval thought and form in Proust's novel, even in certain areas that have struck many critics as being the most "original." What we now seek to examine is the point at which the modernism of a twentieth-century *roman psychologique* intersects with the special psychological style of medieval allegorical representation.

Allegory first flourished during the transition period between late classical antiquity and the early Middle Ages, when, as C. S. Lewis notes, the Greco-Roman gods had begun to "sink into personifications," men had started to conceive of their inner lives as a moral struggle between opposing vices and virtues, and the spoken word, the conversational norms of *lógos* (speech) and *dialégesthai* (talking) had given way to the world of silent reading.[7] Allegorical representation in general attempts to render visible the inner dramas of consciousness: it is, to use the felicitous phrasing of Lewis, "the subjectivism of an objective age" (*Allegory of Love,* 30). But what happens, precisely, when the allegorist concentrates his attention on the hesitations and contradictions of the mind? What does he discover?

> The gaze turned inward with a moral purpose does not discover *character.* No man is a "character" to himself, and least of all while he thinks of good and evil. Character is what he has to produce; within he finds only the raw material, the passions and emotions which contend for mastery. That unitary "soul" or "personality" which interests the novelist is for him merely the arena in which the combatants meet: it is to the combatants . . . that he must attend. . . . For such a man allegory will be no frigid form. It is idle to tell him that something with which he has been at death-grips for the last twenty-four hours is an "abstraction"; and if we could be free, for a little, of our own *Zeitgeist,* we might confess that it is not very much more abstract than that "self" or "personality" on whose rock-bottom unity we rest so secure and of which we would so much rather hear him talk. (61)

This analysis of things medieval awakens an uncanny resonance in the reader of the *Recherche.* There is a striking similarity between Proust's theory of multiple personality (the characters of the novel exhibit contradictory facets when they appear in different contexts: Albertine is not a "unitary soul" but a succession of women disseminated in time and space[8]) and the conception of the mind as "arena" where combatants meet. Indeed, if the individual human being whom I am observing contains forces contending for mastery, then I will see, alternately, one force then the other emerging victorious, but never a totalized "self" that would incorporate or definitively eliminate the elements engaged in battle. What is called *psychomachia* in the Middle Ages is the very form of Proustian psychology.[9] Furthermore, it is now apparent that the reduction of the *Recherche*'s scope from that of macrocosmic outward description to microcosmic dialogic structure, in which the *il* disappears and the *je-tu* of

Marcel-Albertine dominates, corresponds to the abandonment of traditional novelistic properties (i.e., among other things, of the "rock-bottom"
self) and the assumption of an *allegorical* narration.

Proust's spiritual closeness to his predecessors in the domain of literary
allegory emerges most clearly when one compares the *Recherche* to certain masterpieces of the Middle Ages that exhibit a quasi-encyclopedic
scope in their depiction of the intricacies of human passion. Perhaps the
most obvious choice is the *Roman de la Rose*, since the thematic material,
like that of *La Prisonnière* and *La Fugitive*, is derived uniquely from the
central problem of love. As in the *Recherche*, Guillaume de Lorris's allegory involves, on the one hand, the limitation of the hero's role to that of
neutrality and "passive" observation, and on the other hand, a splitting of
the heroine into various personified forces. As Lewis explains in his elegant interpretation of the *Roman*, "The lover of the *Romance* is concerned not with a single 'lady,' but with a number of 'minds' or 'aspects'
of that lady who alternately help and hinder his attempts to win her love,
symbolized by the Rose" (118). I believe it is not a matter of coincidence
that Albertine is first presented as a "jeune fille en *fleurs*"—that is, as a
woman who has been transformed into a flower within the mind of the
narrator-protagonist. She is the Rose whom Marcel wishes to possess and
keep within his grasp.[10] In the *Roman*, there is a concentric scenic organization that places the heart of the woman at the farthest remove from the
hero's initial point of departure: the progression of the allegory is from
outside to inside, from superficial exteriority to deep interiority. Lewis
writes: "*Litteraliter*, the scene is at first a river bank outside a walled
garden; later the interior of the garden; and later still, a rose-plot surrounded by a hedge inside the larger garden. . . . *Allegorice*, therefore, the
scene is at first, the river of life in general, in early youth; later, the world
of courtly society; later still, the mind of a young girl living in the world
of courtly society" (119). This tripartite structure corresponds somewhat to
Proust's original conception of his novel, which divided the imaginary landscape of his fictional world into L'Age des Noms (the period of childhood
dreams and fantasies), L'Age des Mots (the experience of disenchantment in society), and L'Age des Choses (the recuperation of existential
loss in the transcendance of recovered time). As the *Recherche* evolved
away from this scheme, because of the introduction of Albertine, the
third stage of the series came even closer to its unconscious model in the
*Roman*, since the metaphysics of *Le Temps retrouvé* was now deferred
considerably: taking its place as the logical step inward after the encounter
with society is the confrontation with the "heart" and "mind" of Albertine. *La Prisonnière* and *La Fugitive*, the most "modern" volumes of
Proust, the pages that seem to demand the existence of Samuel Beckett

to carry out their implications and mine their considerable resources, are also the "oldest" from the standpoint of literary history. The one critic of Proust who establishes the link between the *Roman de la Rose* and the *Recherche* is Hans-Robert Jauss, in his impressively researched and articulate *Zeit und Erinnerung in Marcel Prousts 'A la recherche du temps perdu': Ein Beitrag zur Theorie des Romans* (Heidelberg, 1955). Jauss is now best known for his solid contributions to *Rezeptionsästhetik,* which he has made in a series of articles dealing with classical and modern periods of French and German literature.[11] But he is by training a *Romanist* in the broadest humanistic sense of the term, and a distinguished medievalist. Jauss's analysis of Proust, as the title of his book indicates, concentrates on time and memory in the *Recherche:* the major thrust of his argument is a demonstration of the perfect correspondence between thematic content and novelistic form in the "fictionalization" of time and memory. I will discuss this in more detail toward the end of the present chapter. In general, Jauss is sensitive to the convergence of philosophical-esthetic problems and matters of technique. In the early part of his interpretation, he establishes the fact that Marcel is not a unitary personality, but divided into "successive selves." Therefore, it would seem that the protagonist's perception of reality and of the temporal process must be fragmentary, sporadic. The question then arises, How is it that a broken or diversified "subject" can live Time as *Durée?* Jauss's answer entails an important reference to medieval allegory:

> Die Zeit, die "Marcel" in ihrer Dauer nicht wahrnehmen kann, kleidet sich für ihn in verschiedene "Formen" und nimmt in all dem, was in der reinen Phänomenologie der Veränderung konstant bleibt oder kontinuierlich wiederkehrt, allegorisch-mytische Gestalt an. . . . Hier weist Prousts "Psychologie in der Zeit" auf eine ältere, mittelalterliche Tradition zurück. Isofern bewusstseinsimmanente Vorgänge wie "Vergessen", "Gewohnheit", "Betrübnis" im Laufe der Erzählung sichtlich über den innerseelischen Bereich hinauswachsen und sich, wenn nicht geradezu als Figurationen der Zeit, so doch als überpersönliche Mächte enthüllen können, fühlt sich der Betrachter plötzlich an die allegorischen Figuren im *Roman de la Rose* erinnert, wo ähnliche Wesenheiten wie *Oubli, Habitude, Chagrin* erscheinen und zugleich als "Potenz" wirksam sind. (155)

> (Time, which "Marcel" cannot perceive in its duration, clothes itself for him in various "forms" and takes on, in all that which, in the pure phenomenology of change, remains constant or

continually recurs, an allegorical-mythical shape. . . . Here, Proust's "psychology in time" points back to an older, medieval tradition. Insofar as events immanent to consciousness such as "Forgetfulness," "Habit," "Sorrow" visibly grow, in the course of the narration, beyond the inner domain of the mind, and, if not exactly as figures of Time, nevertheless as transpersonal Powers manage to reveal themselves, the observer suddenly is reminded of the allegorical figures in the *Roman de la Rose*, where similar entities such as *Oubli, Habitude, Chagrin* appear and at once function as "powers.")

In a precise and detailed tableau, Jauss gives an overview of the "Figurationen der Zeit" that lift themselves above the "mere phenomenology of temporal change" and that serve as abstract chapter headings for the episodic textual blocks of the novel. He shows, convincingly, that many scenes of the *Recherche*, which are, on the literal-representational level, descriptions of social events or of artistic revelation, in fact illustrate the general laws of allegorical forces such as *Chagrin, Jalousie, Beauté, Mort, Vice, Oubli,* and *Vieillesse* (157–58). Yet when Jauss writes that time "clothes itself" for Marcel in various forms, we must be careful to add that it is the narrator, not the protagonist, who is capable of making the conceptual jump from the immanence of temporal flux to the transcendence of allegorical abstraction. The narrator, not Marcel, organizes retrospectively his lived experiences in a coherent pattern. If we limit ourselves to the perspective of Marcel, we see that the relationship of allegorical sign to meaning involves disjunction and noncommunication, so that, as we have seen before, the process of deciphering allegorical representations never achieves the final stasis of a generalized understanding.

Jauss is conscious of Proust's interest in the semiological status of allegory and cites the passage in *Du côté de chez Swann* that describes the noncharitable appearance of Giotto's Charity as an example of a constant Proustian "truth": "Der Knabe [Marcel] kann die eigentümliche Schönheit dieser Fresken noch nicht begreifen und wird erst später verstehen lernen, dass gerade in der Nicht-Teilhabe der Person an der Tugend, die durch sie hindurchwirkt, nicht nur der ästhetische Wert, sondern darüberhinaus auch die 'psychologische' oder zumindest 'psysiognomische' Wahrheit dieser Darstellungen beruht" ("The young boy [Marcel] cannot yet comprehend the peculiar beauty of these frescoes and will only later learn to understand that it is precisely in the nonparticipation of the person in the virtue that works through him that not only the esthetic value, but beyond that, even the 'psychological' or at least 'physiognomical' truth of these representations lies" [157]).[12] The all-important factor in the *Recherche* is that the protagonist, by gradually realizing that the "person" he loves (whether Gilberte, the Duchesse de Guermantes, or Albertine) does not participate in the virtue (or vice) that works through her, is therefore unable to reach what Jauss calls "das personale Du" ("the personal you"), but finds himself trapped in the magic circle of inconceivable and invisible *forces occultes*.[13] Marcel intuits obscure energies beyond Albertine that she only temporarily personifies, and it is to these energies that he bows down, as in the worship of primitive gods. Jauss's analysis touches on, but does not develop, the possible link between allegorical personification and archaic forms of magical religion, according to which the phenomenal world is traversed by invisible divine forces that act upon us and affect our individual destinies ("... als *Potenz wirksam* sind").

## ALLEGORY AND THE MAGIC OF OCCULT FORCES

The basis for the analogy between allegory, a highly self-conscious and structured literary mode of expression, and primitive worship of occult forces may seem at first flimsy and far-fetched, especially if we conceive of literary stylization and transposition as an intellectual "victory" over our animal nature and the brute material conditions of existence. But modern psychology—specifically, the branch of psychoanalytic research— has taught us that the work of art is in fact a complex sublimation of instinctual drives, and that the imaginary transmutation of psychic forces into esthetic forms disguises but does not abolish the elementary patterns of aggression and eroticism that dominate the functioning of the unconscious. For our purposes, this means that the turn inward toward microcosmic dialogue and allegorical representation is not uniquely a matter of consciously chosen technique, but also the esthetic manifestation of an unconscious psychological structure. Our task of interpretation needs to proceed further, in order to uncover the coherent design of which the *forces occultes* are but a significant fragment. We can gain assistance in this inquiry from Angus Fletcher, who in the sixth chapter of his *Allegory: The Theory of a Symbolic Mode,* discusses the "psychoanalytic analogues" of allegorical writing—obsession and compulsion. Fletcher draws heavily on Freud's *Totem and Taboo* and Otto Fenichel's *The Psychoanalytic Theory of the Neuroses* in his effort to paint the psychological portrait of the allegorist.[14] Having elaborated, in the earlier chapters of his treatise, the structural peculiarities of literary allegory, especially the discontinuity of its episodic form, Fletcher then attempts to show that the mental constitution of the obsessional/compulsive neurotic corresponds to these peculiarities. The validity of such a methodology based strictly upon analogy can be disputed a priori, but its compelling results are worth examining. This is certainly true for readers of the *Recherche,* who recognize in Fletcher's portrait the distinctive traits of Marcel Proust:

it is as if Proust had "posed" for the critic and served as model for his theory. In the analysis that follows, I will be referring not only to Fletcher, but also to the crux of *Totem and Taboo* for a detailed examination of some major points. The establishing of analogical links between obsessional actions, the archaic mental lives of primitive men, and allegorical discourse will provide a theoretical framework for our reading of the psychologically dense conclusion of *Sodome et Gomorrhe.*

The sixth chapter of *Allegory* is a broad development of the thesis that Fletcher had introduced in the opening pages of his study: namely, that "anxiety . . . is the most fertile ground from which allegorical abstractions grow" (37). He notes, for example, that the formal "rigidity" of allegory is often expressed by the compulsiveness of the hero: Aeneas in Virgil's epic is an obvious example. And compulsiveness, in turn, is linked quite closely to rituals of purification and atonement, which generally assume an ethical or social content in the work of art but which derive from the conflicts of the author's empirical self. In discussing the notions of compulsion, obsession, ritual, and magic, Fletcher refers, logically enough, to Freud's *Totem and Taboo,* which relates explicitly, as its subtitle indicates, "some points of agreement between the mental lives of savages and neurotics." Notably, the psychological concept of *ambivalence,* to which Freud devotes a long and analytically precise development, is shown to resemble the constitutive dichotomy of the *tabooed* object, which is both sacred, consecrated, and uncanny, dangerous, forbidden, unclean. The neurotic who feels ambivalence toward his parents or lover or siblings treats them as if they were "taboo," as if they possessed "peculiar magic powers" that could be conveyed by them through the medium of inanimate objects (*Totem and Taboo,* 20). What Jean-Pierre Richard calls "l'objet herméneutique" (in *Proust et le monde sensible*) of Proustian fiction—whether literally a physical object, such as the madeleine, or an immaterial essence, like Vinteuil's musical phrase—always contains a magical energy source which, when the protagonist perceives, touches, or consumes it, enters into the latter's body and transforms him. This is because the *objet herméneutique* is in fact the esthetic fictionalization of the fearsome energies emanating from the maternal and paternal sides of the Oedipal triangle. To eat the madeleine, for example, is to consume and interiorize maternal substance—to be possessed by the "wirksame Potenz" (Jauss) of the Mother.

Throughout *Totem and Taboo,* Freud describes the taboo situation in dynamic terms, as a *transferral* or *displacement* of a quasi-electric charge. The person who has transgressed the taboo prohibition "himself acquires the characteristic of being prohibited—the dangerous charge is transferred to him" (22). Hence neurotics' irrational fear of touching objects which, they believe, contain "magic power": "Obsessional prohibitions are extremely liable to displacement. They extend from one object to another along whatever path the context may provide, and this new object then becomes, to use the apt expression of one of my women patients, 'impossible'—till at last the whole world lies under an embargo of 'impossibility.' Obsessional patients behave as though the 'impossible' persons and things were carriers of a dangerous infection liable to be spread by contact on to everything in their neighborhood" (27).

One of the most interesting similarities between the mental lives of savages and the aberrations of neurotic sickness is the confusion between the imaginary and the real that is common to both. The neurotic, like the savage, believes that a real object contains a supernatural force that he has, in fact, projected onto it. Perhaps even stranger, he assumes that the mere utterance of a word that has been "prohibited" is as potentially dangerous as the touching of a tabooed object. This is because for him words and things do not belong to different spheres of existence, but both participate in the *mana* (occult power) communicated by the *extensiveness* of contagious magic. When Fletcher writes: "The *magic of names*, which more than any other linguistic phenomenon, dominates the allegorical work, is likewise an essential ingredient in the neurosis. Names are felt to be adequate substitutes for things, even better than adequate since it is easier to manipulate names than things" (293–94), we think immediately of the role of naming in the *Recherche*, of the fact that for the young protagonist the words *Balbec, Florence, Venise, Quimperlé,* and so forth were felt to be just as real as, perhaps more real than, the everyday environment of Combray.

When taken to an extreme, the tendency to overvalue the imaginary at the expense of present reality leads to what Freud calls the "omnipotence of thoughts," which Frazer described thus in *The Golden Bough:* "Men mistook the order of their ideas for the order of nature, and hence imagined that the control which they have, or seem to have, over their thoughts, permitted them to exercise a corresponding control over things."[15] Here we recognize the error of Marcel, who, in "Le Baiser refusé," superimposed the possessive logic of his desire on the contextual reality of the scene, and thereby performed a monstrous inversion of the order of his thoughts and the order of nature. As in the case of savages and neurotics, Marcel accomplished this inversion through an *association of ideas*—the merging of Albertine with the eroticized feminine natural elements with which she "communicated" metonymically/contagiously: the valley, the sea, the "seins bombés" of the surrounding cliffs. "Le Baiser refusé" can be read as the fictional staging of an obsessional neurosis, in which the "mad" confusions and reversals of the protagonist's mental projections have exemplary significance. But the narrative control of ironical esthetic distance is equally evident in the dramatization of events. The narrator and the reader understand, and do not share, Marcel's delusion: the excessive rhetoric of the text leads them to anticipate the deconstruction of possession-taking and the clear demonstration of the ego's false assumption of his thoughts' omnipotence. We sense, in the split of ironical narrator from "mad" protagonist, that Proust was able, on important occasions, to recognize his own, esthetically transposed neuroses and analyze them clinically. The point of fundamental disagreement between the obsessional/ compulsive psyche of Proust and the mental lives of savages lies in the former's high degree of self-consciousness. Frazer and Freud do not speak of primitive people who simultaneously worshipped occult forces in fear and trembling and yet uncovered, "agnostically," the baseless superstitions on which their credence was founded.

According to Freud, the fixed traits in the "psychological constellation" (29) that defines obsessional neurosis all center in emotional ambivalence. Like the primitive man who both reveres and fears a tabooed object, the obsessional neurotic both wishes to touch, and fears to touch, the object of his desires:[16] "The conflict between these two currents cannot be promptly settled because—there is no other way of putting it—they are localized in the subject's mind in such a manner that they cannot come up against each other. The prohibition is noisily conscious, while the persistent desire to touch is unconscious and the subject knows nothing of it" (29–30). Because the unconscious desire is very strong, the neurotic must develop his conscious defenses to a great extent in order to remain in control of his mental life. The consequence of this is an often admirable development of the intellect accompanied by ineradicable traces of archaic magic and superstition. Fenichel describes such a pattern cogently, as the "cleavage of the ego":

> Compulsive thinking is not only abstract, it is also *general,* directed toward systematization and categorization; it is theoretical instead of real. The patients are interested in maps and illustration rather than in countries and things. . . . The overvaluation of intellect often makes compulsion neurotics develop their intellect very highly. However, the high intelligence shows archaic features and is full of magic and superstition. Their ego shows a cleavage, one part being logical, another magical. The defensive mechanism of isolation makes the maintenance of such a cleavage possible. (*The Psychoanalytic Theory of the Neuroses,* chap. 14, quoted in Fletcher, *Allegory,* 296)

Each element of Fenichel's analytic description corresponds to aspects of Proust's personality as we know it from biographical evidence and to essential qualities of the *Recherche*. The tendency toward systematization and categorization takes on the form of "laws" and allegorical abstraction in the novel; the interest in maps and illustration was constant in Proust's life (as, for example, his well-known fascination with the *Indicateur des chemins de fer*[17]). The "archaic features" of his intellect come to the surface in his work at crucial moments, as in the introductory sentence to the madeleine episode already cited in this study: "Je trouve très raisonnable la croyance celtique que les âmes de ceux que nous avons perdus sont captives dans quelque être inférieur, dans une bête, un végétal, une chose inanimée, perdues en effet pour nous jusqu'au jour, qui pour beaucoup ne vient jamais, où nous nous trouvons passer près de l'arbre, entrer en possession de l'objet qui est leur prison" (I, 44). The defensive mechanism of isolation is found not only in the author's progressive retreat from the constraints of everyday existence, in his decision to live an "inverted" life, sleeping during the day and working at night in a cork-lined room, but also in the often-criticized "passivity" of Marcel, who does not live energetically, but manages, often with complete implausibility, to be present, as observer, when the exemplary events of the fiction are staged. The cleavage of the ego into two isolated, noncommunicating spheres is the psychological *analogon* of the splits and disjunctions, formal and semantic, which I have discussed in earlier sections of this study. The separations of the *Recherche* into *roman poétique* and *roman analytique* (Feuillerat), into *récit* and *traité/moralité* (Spitzer, Rogers); the paradoxical coexistence of narrative "omniscience" and the dispossessive force of sequential iteratives (Genette); the breaking of the dreamed unitary sign "Balbec" into the irreconcilable, mutually distant Balbec-en-terre and Balbec-plage (deconstructions of Ruskinian possession-taking)—these and other fictional transpositions reflect and confirm the obsessional/compulsive neurosis whose "wirksame Potenz" informs the *Recherche*.

At present, we can better comprehend what Genette correctly called "l'expérience difficile d'un rapport à soi vécu comme (légère) distance et décentrement." The pronoun *je* is the locus of a primary ambivalence. It designates both protagonist and narrator, but splits them into opposing, noncommunicating functions. The erroneous dreams of the protagonist—his belief in semiological transparence and in the omnipotence of thoughts—contrast with the conscious control and logical mastery of the narrator, and the two, in Freud's words, "cannot come up against each other." Most importantly, it is clear that the double function of the *je*, in which the narrative voice pretends to account for, analyze, and morally judge the protagonist, allows Proust to open the floodgates of his unconscious while simultaneously exercising rational restraints. The "reprehensible" qualities of Marcel—his laziness, indecisiveness, weakness, openness to erotic and alcoholic seductions—can be depicted more easily because the narrator is always in the position to condemn them. The cleavage of the ego, in becoming the splitting of the fictional self, both confirms the imprisonment of Marcel Proust in the moral dualism of psychological ambivalence and provides the author with the necessary technical means to experience the alternating frustrations (personality-loss) and imaginary exaltations (narcissistic triumphs) of this dualism in the very process of writing.

Proustian solipsism has a distinctive textual structure that is produced by the force of desire. In the beginning, the ego, lacking stability and definition, searches beyond itself for fulfillment, which it obtains, fleetingly and precariously, by an act of coercion (Marcel resorts to emotional blackmail in receiving the balm of the maternal kiss in Combray). But whatever happiness results from the kiss and the presence of the mother cannot be complete or real because it does not involve reciprocity of sentiments: it takes place, as the narrator says, through an "abdication" (I, 38) of parental authority, through the weakness of acquiescence that the young protagonist knows he has caused and about which he will feel perpetually guilty. The original "scène du baiser" establishes the pattern for Marcel's later loves, which are never exercises in reciprocity, but always exasperated efforts at domination and seduction that are doomed to ultimate failure. The impossibility of possession-taking demonstrated in "Le Baiser refusé" can be explained by the fact that Albertine's body is haunted or *possessed* by the phantom of the mother, who is a tabooed object. The mother is both sacred and forbidden, loved and hated, because she gave herself to the protagonist, but only incompletely and in the mode of a frustrating contiguity: she slept in the same room with him, but not in the same bed; he conquered her presence, but not her person. By withdrawing into the background and by not asserting the power of his authority, the father allowed his son to come within touching distance of the barrier against incest, within an excessively close distance of that which is prohibited by Law. If the narrative of the *Recherche* repeatedly relates the same allegorical message, which I have called the *impossibility* of possession-taking, it is because Marcel's loves are all disguised repetitions of the initial encounter with the taboo against incest, which becomes, in Freud's terms, an obsessional prohibition "liable to displacement." Since the mother cannot be possessed, all women lie "under an embargo of 'impossibility'."

One reason for the encyclopedic scope of Proust's novel is that subjective desire never ceases to function and to seek objects onto which it projects itself. Another way of stating this is that Marcel never really learns from his experiences. "Le Baiser refusé" is an unheeded lesson that does not impede the protagonist from further entanglements with the enigmatic Mlle Simonet. In a general sense, the *Recherche* is a novel of dis-illusionments, a fictional machine that unravels the illusory beauty of dreams. *Le Côté de Guermantes* tells the story of a noble name's loss of prestige.[18] *Sodome et Gomorrhe* relates the process whereby the individualized towns of Normandy become subsumed under the levelling generality of Habit.[19] But each destruction is followed by a rebuilding that forgets the very causes of destruction. Hence Marcel's attachment to Albertine despite all that has preceded, despite the sobering "laws" of love illustrated by the liaisons with Gilberte and the Duchesse de Guermantes, and by Swann's unhappy affair with Odette. What the protagonist cannot learn, because it would be too painful, is that the forever reborn quest for new objects to desire is an egocentric strategy of protection that hides the fact that there is nothing worth desiring but the self.

Most often, the narrator remains blind to the absoluteness of his narcissism and orients his discourse toward a description of the disconcerting qualities of Albertine. He wishes to depict himself as a lover whose principal anguish results from the nearly indecipherable "multiplicité entremê-lée des détails réels et des faits mensongers" (II, 734) that characterizes his beloved's speech. In fact, however, Albertine's evasiveness corresponds to the protagonist's violent will to dominate at all costs; her lies are no more perverse or complex than those used by Marcel to neutralize her power and contain her energy. One senses that Marcel's "love" for Albertine would be accomplished only if she ceased to exist, only if she became the purely fictional/hypothetical material of a dream that exteriorized the self's desire to merge with itself in perfect closure. In one short but unconsciously revealing sentence, the narrator comes close to admitting this: "Une partie de moi à laquelle l'autre voulait se rejoindre était en Albertine" (II, 731). Albertine is the object of Marcel's affections, but only insofar as she "contains" or incorporates his subjectivity, only to the extent that she vanishes as independently constituted entity.

I have suggested earlier that the "turn inward" toward dialogic confrontation between Marcel and Albertine, which is also a turn away from the realm of *mondanité,* involves a shift from the esthetic distance of classically conceived fiction to the more intimate form of a personal/confessional discourse that one might be tempted to call "autobiographical." But two questions need to be answered before we can determine the nature of this shift: First, does the change from fiction to autobiography, from mimesis of the exterior world to self-adherence, actually occur at a given, definable point of the text? And, second, how does the self become inscribed in the text? What are the levels of readability that emerge from its inscription? I shall discuss these matters in an analysis of the fourth and final "chapter" of *Sodome et Gomorrhe* (II, 1112-31). The interpretation of this rich and powerful text will lead to a concluding section on the role of

Albertine in *La Prisonnière* and on her relationship to the problematics of autobiographical and allegorical modes of writing.

## "BRUSQUE REVIREMENT VERS ALBERTINE" (II, 1112-26)

In the pages preceding the concluding chapter of *Sodome et Gomorrhe,* the narrator-hero evokes memories that come to him as he rides on the little train toward La Raspelière (II, 1075-1112). The passage as a whole is transitional, in that it recapitulates, in the generality of an iterative presentation, Marcel's comfortable feeling of sociability during his outings at the country home of the Verdurin. But at the same time, the superficial pleasure of these conversational encounters cannot hide their essential emptiness. In the end, Marcel is compelled to recognize that habit has destroyed the spontaneity with which he formerly perceived the beauties of Normandy's natural environment. Now, the names of the small towns along the line of the "Transatlantique" are no longer poetically suggestive, but the flat, uninteresting signs of an unchanging conventional significance. Thus, the name "St.-Pierre-des-Ifs," which the protagonist had associated with the pictorial experimentation and technical innovations of Elstir, ultimately announces only "qu'allait apparaître un quinquagénaire étrange [Charlus], spirituel et fardé, avec qui je pourrais parler de Chateaubriand et de Balzac" (1108). This process of disenchantment, by which the magic of names yields to a sober and somber literalism (and which Brichot's etymologies only serve to reinforce by the authority of "scientific" accuracy), is a variation on the degradation of metaphoric inauguration into the "death" of cliché. And the fourth chapter of *Sodome et Gomorrhe,* like the "Soirée chez la marquise de Saint-Euverte," is structured according to a dramatic opposition between the erosion of habit ("l'usure métaphorique") and the possibility of a rebirth of significance ("la métaphore vive"). Marcel's apparently complete detachment from Albertine at the beginning of the passage corresponds precisely to Swann's "mélancolique indifférence" (I, 322) in the introductory paragraph to the "Soirée," and the "brusque revirement vers Albertine" announced by the chapter subheading is just as surprising, just as involuntarily motivated, as the sudden "reappearance" of Odette in the guise of Vinteuil's *petite phrase.* In both cases, Proust allows the text to come to a dead end before giving it a new life. But the structural congruence of the two episodes only serves to emphasize their diametrical difference in tone. Whereas in the "Soirée" the irruption of metaphorical transfer creates the euphoric pattern of light imagery and the emotional pathos of rediscovered love, in *Sodome et Gomorrhe* Marcel's brusque return to Albertine occurs in a moment of anguish, as the result of a haunting revelation.

As the fourth chapter opens, Marcel is pondering the strategy he will use to rid himself definitively of Albertine. He has told his mother that he has decided not to marry Albertine, and now he imagines that the time is ripe for the unveiling of his decision to the object of his passion—or rather, to the woman whom he used to love, before he achieved his present state of detachment (1112-13). Marcel believes that his break with Albertine will be made easier by his present interest in Andrée, whom he does not wish to marry, but who will presumably acquiesce to all his desires and provide him with the protective tranquillity of affection he needs. Marcel imagines a conversation in which he tells Andrée that he loves another woman, but requests nevertheless that she "console" him from the "sadness" of this imaginary relationship. The logic of the protagonist is based upon artifice and the sentimental advantages of mendacity: "Je souriais intérieurement en pensant à cette conversation, car de cette façon je donnerais à Andrée l'illusion que je ne l'aimais pas vraiment; ainsi, elle ne serait pas fatiguée de moi et je profiterais joyeusement et doucement de sa tendresse" (1113). The first section of the chapter is written with the assumption that exterior reality—here, the thoughts and emotions of desired or indifferent women—can be controlled by an act of subjective will which, in fact, remains hypothetical. Here, the self conceives of the outside world as a mere extension of his own consciousness. Marcel's concern that Andrée not become bored with him is the transparently disguised mirror-image of an egocentrism that he himself creates.

It is against the backdrop of the extreme conscious control exercised by Marcel over his present and imagined future life that the discovery of Albertine's lesbianism occurs, precipitating the text into an inversion of all the preconceived ideas on which the stability of the self had been based. When Albertine, ready to leave the train, wishes to finalize plans for the next day's social calendar, Marcel objects that to return once more to La Raspelière will only be a waste of time ("du temps absolument perdu" [1113-14] unless it were possible to have Mme Verdurin arrange for the playing of some of Vinteuil's works. Ironically, at precisely the moment of the conversation in which Marcel assumes Albertine will be least interested and have little to say, she responds that she knows the best friend of Mlle Vinteuil, whom the reader recognizes as the high priestess of Sapphism at Montjouvain (I, 159). Thus, all the protagonist's hypothetical projects regarding the discarding and elimination of Albertine from his mind prove illusory, since the woman he had thought to master now appears, *stricto sensu,* unknowable. Albertine's revelation triggers the mechanism of involuntary remembrance, so that the "image tenue en réserve pendant tant d'années" (1114) of Montjouvain now emerges from the depths of the unconscious to occupy center stage. Proustian *mémoire involontaire,* which is glorified in *Le Temps retrouvé* as the key to artistic salvation and held to be intrinsically superior as a method of knowledge to

the conscious memory of fact, assumes the function of a much darker
"truth" here—the truth of anguish and suffering: "Nous pouvons avoir
roulé toutes les idées possibles, la vérité n'y est jamais entrée, et c'est
du dehors, quand on s'y attend le moins, qu'elle nous fait son affreuse
piqûre, et nous blesse pour toujours" (1114). The awakening of the
Montjouvain image has a paradoxical double effect: it causes the protagonist to sink into profound guilt (he associates the remembrance of
the scene of cruelty and desecration with his own "cruel" abandonment
of his grandmother during her illness and death), and it opens to him a
completely new world of unexpected relationships between women whom
he had kept categorically separate in his mind. He experiences "la joie
d'une belle découverte" (1116) as he begins to understand retrospectively
the constellation of hints and clues pointing to Albertine's sexual identity,
hints which he had passed over as insignificant when they first appeared,
but which now illuminate each other in a coherent design called "homosexuality." But this purely intellectual joy is superficial when compared
to the depression and pessimism that now seem to be his lot:

> C'était une *terra incognita* terrible où je venais d'atterrir, une
> phase nouvelle de souffrances insoupçonnées qui s'ouvrait. (1115)

> Mais nulle journée maintenant ne serait plus pour moi nouvelle,
> n'éveillerait plus en moi le désir d'un bonheur inconnu, et pro-
> longerait seulement mes souffrances, jusqu'à ce que je n'eusse plus
> la force de les supporter. (1117)

> Moi qui ne m'étais jusqu'ici jamais éveillé sans sourire aux choses
> les plus humbles, au bol de café au lait, au bruit de la pluie, au
> tonnerre du vent, je sentis que le jour qui allait se lever dans un in-
> stant, et tous les jours qui viendraient ensuite ne m'apporteraient
> plus jamais l'espérance d'un bonheur inconnu, mais le prolonge-
> ment de mon martyre. (1117)

The entire scene is constructed on a series of reversals and substitutions.
There is no middle ground for compromise, only the stark opposition of
mutually antagonistic perceptions and imaginings. Vice has superseded
virtue; ugliness has blotted out all remnants of beauty: "Derrière Albertine, je ne voyais plus les montagnes bleues de la mer, mais la chambre de
Montjouvain où elle tombait dans les bras de Mlle Vinteuil avec ce rire où
elle faisait entendre comme le son inconnu de sa jouissance" (1117). And
later in the episode: "La passion mystérieuse avec laquelle j'avais pensé
autrefois à l'Autriche parce que c'était le pays d'où venait Albertine . . .
je l'éprouvais encore mais, par une interversion de signes, dans le domaine

de l'horreur" (1119). More than any other contextually defined scene of the *Recherche*, the fourth chapter of *Sodome et Gomorrhe* is the transcription of what Freud calls emotional *ambivalence*. The inversion of signs into horror takes place because hate of Albertine has temporarily dislodged love for Albertine. Albertine is herself the magic vessel of powerful energies, the mana both coveted and feared by the protagonist.

In *Totem and Taboo*, Freud explains the psychological reasons for the elaborate precautions taken by primitive peoples against coming into contact with their rulers. The king cannot be touched because the populace has attributed to him "dangerous magical power which is transmitted by contact like an electric charge and which brings death and ruin to anyone who is not protected by a similar charge" (41). But paradoxically, some tribes believe that the sin of entering the king's house and thus coming within range of his power can be atoned for by the touch of the king. In Freud's words: "Here we are met by the remarkable fact that contact with the king is a remedy and protection against the dangers provoked by contact with the king" (42). The paradox becomes explainable when we realize that the powers possessed by the ruler of a community are accompanied by taboo restrictions that make his life uncomfortable and artificially closed to fundamental pleasures. The community has projected onto him both love and hate, which he simply *returns* to the community in actions which appear contradictory, but which derive from a common origin. In the same way, Albertine, who is described in the conclusion of *Sodome et Gomorrhe* as a malevolent or diabolic agent, is simultaneously the calming curative force that can grant Marcel a peaceful "convalescence" from pain: "Elle m'offrait justement—et elle seule pouvait me l'offrir—l'unique remède contre le poison qui me brûlait, homogène à lui d'ailleurs, l'un doux, l'autre cruel, tous deux également dérivés d'Albertine. En ce moment Albertine—mon mal—se relâchant de me causer des souffrances, me laissait—elle, Albertine remède—attendri comme un convalescent" (1118).

Throughout the episode, the protagonist's anxieties crystallize around the now mysterious Albertine: his conscious powers of reasoning are directed at surmising her lesbian relationships, past and present, and at reassuming control over her errant desires. Since she is the center of his preoccupations, she seems also to be the origin of his pain and the source of wished-for recuperation from suffering. But when the narrator writes, "Elle *seule* pouvait [m']offrir . . . *l'unique* remède contre le poison qui me brûlait" (my emphasis), he is blind to the true origin of his troubles, which the recent revelations of Albertine merely obscure. In fact, Albertine is not alone or unique. She is the ghost of Marcel's mother. The narrator wishes us to believe that Albertine has become the "object-choice" for his love. He wishes to be taken seriously in his concentrated attention on one person: he needs to convince himself that he can love one woman for herself, that he can shed the suffocating influence of maternal protectiveness that has shielded him from any true encounter with reality. If Marcel is to "marry" Albertine, he must emancipate himself from the mana of the mother. This does not (cannot) occur because the overpowering magic force of the mother is contagious (extensive). Albertine is, from the very beginning, a surrogate mother.

The staging of the scene is significant. After learning of Albertine's acquaintance with Mlle Vinteuil's friend, Marcel convinces Albertine to spend the night in the Grand-Hôtel. When she descends from her room to be with the protagonist, she must speak softly "pour ne pas éveiller ma mère, de qui nous n'étions séparés que par cette cloison dont la minceur, aujourd'hui importune et qui forçait à chuchoter, ressemblait jadis, quand s'y peignaient si bien les intentions de ma grand'mère, à une sorte de diaphanéité musicale" (1118). The inversion of signs, the descent into anguish, take place because there has been a change in the structure and significance of the narrow partition separating Marcel's room from that of the maternal figure. In happier days (the first visit to Balbec in *A l'Ombre des jeunes filles en fleurs*), Marcel could knock on the wall and be heard easily by his grandmother. The immediacy of communication, which Proust expresses beautifully in the phrase "diaphanéité musicale," is a transparent reference to the peacefulness of the womb and to the closeness of the unborn child and his mother. The womb is a "cloison" that protects without separating, a barrier only against the threats of the outside, not against inner tranquillity. The grandmother in the *Recherche* is the mother before the separation of birth. In the episode we are analyzing, the partition has taken on a radically different meaning: it has become the barrier against incest, which, in the protagonist's mind, merges with the interdict against all possession-taking. Even asleep, the mother renders communication difficult for the lovers: she will always haunt them, her image will always come between the desires of the protagonist and their realization. Albertine cannot compete successfully with Marcel's mother because the two women are associated, in the mind of the protagonist, with the outside world of hostility, the asphyxiating atmosphere of the world beyond the womb. Indeed, when Marcel thinks of the mysterious life of Albertine in Trieste, where she plans to spend the Christmas holidays with Mlle Vinteuil's friend, he also remembers his original frustration of non-inclusion at Combray: "C'était de Trieste, de ce monde inconnu où je sentais que se plaisait Albertine, où étaient ses souvenirs, ses amitiés, ses amours d'enfance, que s'exhalait *cette atmosphère hostile, inexplicable,* comme celle qui montait jadis jusqu'à ma chambre de Combray, de la salle à manger où j'entendais causer et rire les étrangers,

dans le bruit des fourchettes, maman qui ne viendrait pas me dire bonsoir"
(1121; my emphasis).

The neurotic's defensive mechanism of withdrawl or isolation described
by Fenichel originates in a feeling that reality is equivalent to the unknown or "inexplicable." The loss of the womb's security is not be to
overcome by direct confrontation with the hostile forces of life, but remains an ineradicable memory of absolute negativity. But since this memory is too painful to be accepted in its irrevocability, the self devises
strategies of *indirection* whereby it attempts to re-create, fictively, within
the very domain of real hostility, the benevolent conditions of the matrix.
This can be accomplished only if the violence of coercive persuasion takes
place, only if the self makes of its weakness (sickness) a method of domination. In the conclusion of *Sodome et Gomorrhe* Marcel is only initially
the victim of Albertine's revelation: he converts his anguish into strength
by assuming the pose of the unjustly afflicted invalid, by weaving a lie in
which he traps his beloved. Just as in "la scène du baiser" Marcel persuaded his mother to grant him the nocturnal kiss by writing her a note
and expressing his suffering, in the present episode he manages to gain the
sympathy of Albertine and keep her with him by inventing a story that
has no basis in reality, by creating a literary dimension that is added on,
as hypothetical supplement, to his existential predicament. He justifies
asking Albertine to sleep at the Grand-Hôtel in these terms:

> Pour que vous compreniez, il faut que je vous dise une chose que
> vous ne savez pas. Quand je suis venu ici, j'ai quitté une femme
> que j'ai dû épouser, qui était prête à tout abandonner pour moi.
> Elle devait partir en voyage ce matin, et depuis une semaine, tous
> les jours je me demandais si j'aurais le courage de ne pas lui télé-
> graphier que je revenais. J'ai eu ce courage, mais j'étais si malheur-
> eux que j'ai cru que je me tuerais. C'est pour cela que je vous ai
> demandé hier soir si vous ne pourriez pas venir coucher à Balbec. Si
> j'avais dû mourir, j'aurais aimé vous dire adieu. (1118)[20]

Like Scheherezade, whose execution is deferred as long as she produces
imaginary tales and entertains the king, Marcel can hope to avoid suffering
at the hands of his ruler, Albertine, as long as he transforms her from the
possessor of magical, unknown energies into the passive reader of his in-
vented experiences. On the deepest psychological level, the Proustian impulse to create fiction is based on a desire to deny the death sentence
imposed on our dreams by birth into the world and to reestablish, in the
privacy of a room, the central position of unmediated communicability
that had been lost in reality. Like Scheherezade, Proust understands that

the most efficacious and devious method of avoiding imprisonment is not to attempt escape into the unknowable outside, but to build his own labyrinthine prison of lies and deceit, an inner and inverted kingdom in which he can catch the consciousness of his prisoner-readers.

## THE OMNIPOTENCE OF THOUGHTS (II, 1126–31)

The last three paragraphs of *Sodome et Gomorrhe* read like the transcription of a neurosis: they are an undisguised cry of pain in which all pretense of guarding esthetic distance yields to pitiless self-examination and open confession. The masks of fictional transposition fall. We hear, behind the narrator's commentary, the voice of Marcel Proust, who analyzes his own psychological makeup with a quasi-clinical rigor. Proust recognizes and explains unequivocally that he is unable to love a woman *as* a woman—that is, as a physical presence to be desired for itself and possessed. Rather, he intuits through and beyond the real object of his desire an imaginary constellation of forces which he worships and whose elusive essence he attempts to capture in the act of writing. Albertine and Agostinelli are loved, but the consciousness of the lover can never achieve happiness, if we define happiness as the achievement of harmonious tranquillity in the immanence of reality. The narrator contends that his passion for Albertine was "true," since he organized his life around seeing her, seducing her, imprisoning her, and since her absence was always felt as visceral pain. But at the same time he admits that Albertine and all women "avaient plutôt la propriété d'éveiller cet amour, de le porter à son paroxysme, qu'elles n'en étaient l'image. Quand je les voyais, quand je les entendais, je ne trouvais rien en elles qui ressemblât à mon amour et pût l'expliquer" (1126). Here, Proust traces quite clearly the parallel between the semiological structure of the allegorical sign and the "archaic" features of obsessional neurosis. The noncorrespondence between *signifiant* and *signifié* characteristic of allegory and expressed as the incompatibility of Albertine's superficially virtuous appearance and her hidden vice derives from Marcel's superstitious belief in a world beyond appearance to which Albertine relates arbitrarily and which she incorporates imperfectly. To believe in the existence of such a world while simultaneously reducing the beloved woman to a purely illustrative role is to invert the traditional priorities of the real and the imaginary, granting to the latter a precedence which, according to Freudian psychoanalysis, is typical both of the mental lives of savages and of obsessional neurotics. Proust performs this inversion at the beginning of the first of the final three paragraphs when he writes:

> Deux ou trois fois, pendant un instant, j'eus l'idée que le monde
> où étaient cette chambre et ces bibliothèques, et dans lequel

Albertine était si peu de chose, était peut-être un monde intellectuel, qui était la seule réalité, et mon chagrin, quelque chose comme
celui que donne la lecture d'un roman et dont un fou seul pourrait faire un chagrin durable et permanent et se prolongeant dans sa
vie; qu'il suffirait peut-être d'un petit mouvement de ma volonté
pour atteindre ce monde réel, y rentrer en dépassant ma douleur
comme un cerceau de papier qu'on crève, et ne plus me soucier
davantage de ce qu'avait fait Albertine que nous ne nous soucions
des actions de l'héroïne imaginaire d'un roman après que nous en
avons fini la lecture. (1126)

In order to render this passage rhetorically convincing, Proust does violence to the accepted sense of the word *reality* by transforming it into the
synonym of "intellectual world"; he then associates his own lived experience—"mon chagrin"—with the imaginary act of reading and with the
"madness" that would consist of extending the logic of imaginary activity
into the real world. But the desire to reach the realm of higher reality in
which intellectual significance abides implies the neutralization or abolition of concrete reality by an arbitrary act of the imagination that
metamorphoses "chagrin" or "douleur" into "un cerceau de papier qu'on
crève." The artificial replacement of real pain by an image that eliminates pain through fictionalization allows the passage to function per-
suasively. The actual (unconscious) purpose of the paragraph is that of
self-persuasion, where the author attempts to conjure away the madness that haunts him. What he fears most is precisely what his writing
accomplishes under the disguise of denegation: namely, the mad extension of the imaginary into the real, the absolute fictionalization of
life by a "reading" that has transgressed all boundaries. Proust's closeness to the savages described in *Totem and Taboo* (in whose minds the
world is merely the stage setting for the emergence of mana) is evident
throughout the paragraph and is quite striking if one juxtaposes the
novelist's statements about love to Freud's account of taboo as "magical
power":

FREUD:
The source of taboo is attributed to a peculiar magical power
which is inherent in persons and spirits and can be conveyed by
them through the medium of inanimate objects. *"Persons or things
which are regarded as taboo may be compared to objects charged
with electricity; they are the seat of a tremendous power which is
transmissible by contact,* and may be liberated with destructive
effect if the organisms which provoke its discharge are too weak to
resist it. . . . ." (20; my emphasis)[21]

PROUST:

On aurait dit qu'une vertu n'ayant aucun rapport avec elles [les femmes que l'on aime] leur avait été accessoirement adjointe par la nature, et que cette vertu, *ce pouvoir simili-électrique* avait pour effet sur moi d'exciter mon amour, c'est-à-dire de diriger toutes mes actions et de causer toutes mes souffrances. Mais de cela la beauté, ou l'intelligence, ou la bonté de ces femmes étaient entièrement distinctes. *Comme par un courant électrique qui vous meut, j'ai été secoué par mes amours,* je les ai vécus, je les ai sentis: jamais je n'ai pu arriver à les voir ou à les penser. J'incline même à croire que dans ces amours . . . sous l'apparence de la femme, c'est à ces forces invisibles dont elle est accessoirement accompagnée que nous nous adressons comme à d'obscures divinités. . . . Avec ces déesses, la femme, durant le rendez-vous, nous met en rapport et ne fait guère plus. (1127; my emphasis)

The reason for the intensity of Marcel's suffering in the context we are analyzing is that, like the savage who has come into contact with the tabooed object or has touched the king, the protagonist, in hearing the words "Cette amie, c'est Mlle Vinteuil," has liberated the dormant power of homosexual *otherness* that works through Albertine. Proust describes the transmissibility of Albertine's mana by an allusion to the deceptiveness of physical perception. He explains that when we are made to suffer by the woman we love, it is as if she had changed places and had come to inhabit our body. We see her outside us, but this is only a mirage:

Comme la vue est un sens trompeur! Un corps humain, même aimé, comme était celui d'Albertine, nous semble, à quelques mètres, à quelques centimètres, distant de nous. Et l'âme qui est à lui de même. Seulement, que quelque chose change violemment la place de cette âme par rapport à nous, nous montre qu'elle aime d'autres êtres et pas nous, alors, aux battements de notre coeur disloqué, nous sentons que c'est, non pas à quelques pas de nous, mais en nous, qu'était la créature chérie. En nous, dans des régions plus ou moins superficielles. Mais les mots: "Cette amie, c'est Mlle Vinteuil" avaient été le Sésame, que j'eusse été incapable de trouver moi-même, qui avait fait entrer Albertine dans la profondeur de mon coeur déchiré. Et la porte qui s'était refermée sur elle, j'aurais pu chercher pendant cent ans sans savoir comment on pourrait la rouvrir. (1127-28)[22]

Marcel's discovery of Albertine's homosexuality marks the beginning of a new period in his life. Henceforth, he will be enslaved to the alternations of ambivalence. When Albertine is present, within his grasp, he will control her, as he did his mother and grandmother, by forcing her to protect him and participate in his withdrawn existence. But when she is absent, he will succumb to depression and self-pity. In the final paragraph of *Sodome et Gomorrhe,* Albertine has departed and Marcel is left alone to examine the consequences of his decision to marry the woman who causes him torment. He concludes that each day awaiting him in the future will be the harbinger of suffering. Proust expresses the inner pain of the protagonist in a short passage that describes the latter's subjective reaction to the rising of the sun:

> Je n'avais jamais vu commencer une matinée si belle ni si douloureuse. En pensant à tous les paysages indifférents qui allaient s'illuminer et qui, la veille encore, ne m'auraient rempli que du désir de les visiter, je ne pus retenir un sanglot quand, dans un geste d'offertoire mécaniquement accompli et qui parut symboliser le sanglant sacrifice que j'allais avoir à faire de toute joie, chaque matin, jusqu'à la fin de ma vie, renouvellement solennellement célébré à chaque aurore de mon chagrin et du sang de ma plaie, l'oeuf d'or du soleil, comme propulsé par la rupture d'équilibre qu'amènerait au moment de la coagulation un changement de densité, barbelé de flammes comme dans les tableaux, creva d'un bond le rideau derrière lequel on le sentait depuis un moment frémissant et prêt à entrer en scène et à s'élancer, et dont il effaça sous des flots de lumière la pourpre mystérieuse et figée. (1128)

The peculiar power of this evocation resides in the relationship of the self to nature. It is evident that Marcel is projecting his own feelings onto the scene, and in this sense, the passage is an example of what Ruskin called the pathetic fallacy. The "mechanical" movement of "l'oeuf d'or du soleil" that bursts forth from behind a curtain contrasts with the gradual, sequentially even emergence of the sun in nature. The scene is doubly stylized: it is like a reproduction of medieval paintings that depict the crucifixion with the sun in the background, "barbelé de flammes," and it is theatrical, in that the lifting of the curtain reveals the protagonist's own "passion." The religious vocabulary ("offertoire," "sacrifice," "sang de ma plaie") merges with the drama of the self in such a way as to make of the protagonist the Lamb of God who has assumed the guilt of the world. But underneath the coherent sacremental/sacrificial symbolism is a more hidden level of allusiveness that reintroduces into the passage the logic of natural processes. The words "sanglant sacrifice," "renouvellement solennellement célébré," "sang de ma plaie," and especially "l'oeuf d'or du soleil ... propulsé par la rupture d'équilibre qu'amènerait au

moment de la coagulation un changement de densité" contain an unconscious reference to menstruation. In swallowing or interiorizing Albertine,
Marcel has become a woman and is condemned to the "curse" of renew-
able, repetitious bleeding. Analogous to the inversion of reality and
imagination that characterizes obsessional neurosis is the sexual inversion
of the self that takes place in a moment of extreme anguish. But the essential femininity of the protagonist is a threat to his emotional stability. The
"propulsion" of the sun/egg from behind the curtain is the poetic equivalent of the violence with which the unconscious tears the veil of repression.
What Proust does not wish to know or understand consciously is precisely
what his writing performs by fictional indirection: the "death-sentence"
of the *inverti*.

In the final pages of the episode, the force of hallucination and illusion
replaces the visible evidence of natural phenomena. When, after Marcel
has begun to cry in desperation, his mother enters the room to comfort
him, she appears not as herself, but as the ghostly apparition of the
grandmother. In becoming the grandmother, she assumes the latter's
physical and moral traits—her kindness, her permissive attitude toward
the protagonist's weaknesses, and her love for physical exercise and participatory immersion in the beautiful spectacle of concrete reality. Marcel
needs the intercession of the mother/grandmother in order to carry out
his plan of marrying Albertine: maternal permission alone will grant him
the strength necessary to make his final decision and move from the social
setting of Balbec to the isolation he will experience in Paris in *La Prisonnière* and *La Fugitive*. But Marcel, in wishing to gain his mother's favor
and convince her that his marriage plans are logical and inevitable, realizes,
with deep disappointment, that she will never understand the agonies of
his consciousness: in truth, her approval or disapproval will change nothing
in the patterns of thought that compel him to "love" Albertine.

The impossibility of communication between the mother/grandmother
and the protagonist is expressed most cogently in their differing reactions
to the sunrise, which Proust describes once again, but in greater detail. For
the mother now, as for the grandmother in the early pages of "Combray,"
the rising of the sun is a natural event that one should observe with an almost prayerful admiration. To contemplate the unfolding of such a spectacle is to become integrated into the cosmic order of things, to find one's
identity within the flux of temporal change. Marcel, on the other hand,
cannot perceive the reality of the sunrise as such. Instead, he sees "derrière la plage de Balbec, la mer, le lever du jour, que maman me montrait
. . . la chambre de Montjouvain où Albertine, rose, pelotonnée comme une
grosse chatte, le nez mutin, avait pris la place de l'amie de Mlle Vinteuil et
disait avec des éclats de son rire voluptueux: 'Hé bien! si on nous voit, ce

n'en sera que meilleur. Moi! je n'oserais pas cracher sur ce vieux singe?' C'est cette scène que je voyais derrière celle qui s'étendait dans la fenêtre et qui n'était sur l'autre qu'un voile morne, superposé comme un reflet" (1129). In this passage and in the description that follows, Proust's text is a perfect illustration of what Freud calls the "omnipotence of thoughts," where the "reflection of the internal world is bound to blot out the other picture of the world—the world which *we* [i.e., "normal" people] seem to perceive" (*Totem and Taboo*, 85, Freud's emphasis):

> Dans le désordre des brouillard de la nuit qui traînaient encore en loques roses et bleues sur les eaux encombrées des débris de nacre de l'aurore, des bateaux passaient en souriant à la lumière oblique qui jaunissait leur voile et la pointe de leur beaupré comme quand ils rentrent le soir: scène imaginaire, grelottante et déserte, pure évocation du couchant, qui ne reposait pas, comme le soir, sur la suite des heures du jour que j'avais l'habitude de voir le précéder, déliée, interpolée, plus inconsistante encore que l'image horrible de Montjouvain qu'elle ne parvenait pas à annuler, à couvrir, à cacher —poétique et vaine image du souvenir et du songe. (1130)

Proust's description adds an element of complexity to Freud's conception of the omnipotence of thoughts. It is true that what Marcel sees is a projection of his mind's conflicts and that this projection involves an inversion of natural reality: what appears to him is not the moment of transition between the end of night and the rising of the sun, but the opposite—a "pure évocation du couchant" totally unrelated to the predictable movement of solar circularity. This completely artificial spectacle, associated by the protagonist with coldness and isolation, is said to be even more "inconsistent" than the image of Montjouvain that it is unable to hide or negate. In fact, there are not two but three levels of descriptive appearance here: the purely natural, which has been effectively eliminated by the projective power of Marcel's anguish; the artificial ("scène imaginaire, grelottante et déserte"); and the moral (Montjouvain). The two latter categories are both inversions, but each has its own particular function in the novel. The artificial corresponds with what we have called allegory and is based upon a discrepancy between sign and meaning as perceived by the deciphering consciousness of the protagonist. Marcel sees a chaotic mixture of mutually antagonistic elements—"le désordre des brouillard de la nuit qui traînaient encore en loques roses et bleues sur les eaux encombrées des débris de nacre de l'aurore"—and concludes, falsely, that day is night. His misreading results from the nonorganic, nontransparent relationship of *signifiant* to *signifié*. His error is productive, however, in that it generates a hypothetical scene possessing its own independent beauty. In this sense, the psychological aberrance of the omnipotence of thoughts has a textual dimension with its own laws and deserving of critical attention.

The deconstruction of the symbolic-organic by the abstract-allegorical is metapsychological: it must be analyzed as an intrinsically literary phenomenon, and not reduced to the nonproblematic extension or expression of a mental state. The image of Montjouvain, however, is purely psychological and concrete: it represents the moral dilemma that allegorical abstraction purifies but never entirely cancels or removes. Thus, Albertine is the allegorical figure of Vice, but her various qualities and personality traits, like the scene at Balbec, exhibit a *désordre* that points, alternately, to vice or virtue and invites misreading. The hypothetical narration of this misreading yields *La Prisonnière* and *La Fugitive* as abstract fictions. But textual allegory can never constitute itself in the purity of esthetic distance because at certain unpredictable moments Albertine transmits to the narrator-hero the vice she incorporates: she becomes the evidence of homosexuality rather than its enigmatic sign. At this juncture, the indirection and stylization of fiction give way to the direct confession of autobiography, and the text is no longer properly speaking the narration of anguish, but anguish itself.

The fourth chapter of *Sodome et Gomorrhe* establishes the central importance of Albertine for the remainder of the novel. Henceforth, it is her dialogic relationship with the protagonist that will dominate the plot. What needs to be analyzed is the structure and meaning of this dialogue and its relevance to the question of fictional/allegorical *vs.* autobiographical/confessional writing. It is only by clarifying the textual function of Albertine that we can gain access to the problem of Proustian selfhood and come closer to uncovering the identity of the voice that says *je*.

## LA PRISONNIÈRE

The transition from *Sodome et Gomorrhe* to *La Prisonnière* involves both a change of scene, from Balbec to Paris, and a transformation of perceptual mode: from now on, the protagonist relates to the outside world not as an observer of visible phenomena but as a decipherer of "musical" codes. The esthetic unity of *La Prisonnière* derives less from the symmetries of episodic structure than from the poetically coherent system of analogical correspondences that link all kinds of experience under the aegis of music. From the first paragraph of the volume, in which the narrator describes how he can foretell the vagaries of a day's weather from the quality of the noises that enter his room (III, 9), to the elaborate development on Vinteuil's Septet (III, 248–65), *La Prisonnière* consists of a fictionalized reflection on the limits of human language and artistic communicability. The narrator's wish is to combine the comfort and protected enclosure of his room with the rigorous pursuit of knowledge, which he hopes to attain indirectly. To remain in the isolated, abstract space of the Paris apartment is tantamount to a loss of sight and a compensatory gain in hearing. Like a blind man who once knew the visible world, Marcel is able to convert what he hears into the intellectual equivalent of seen events: he is able to "live" *as if* he were still living.

It is a critical commonplace that Marcel's retreat from the world is a necessary preparatory step in his gradual assumption of the writer's vocation. Jean Rousset characterizes the long central volumes of the novel (*Le Côté de Guermantes, Sodome et Gomorrhe*) as "la traversée d'un désert" and finds in *La Prisonnière* the successful abolition of "le monde et ses fantoches" out of which Art's triumph can rise, as in the flight of the reborn Phoenix.[23] This interpretation sees in the progression of the *Recherche* a clear turn away from the norms of sociability and conversation, toward the innerness and solitude that Proust had recommended, in "Journées de lecture" and *Contre Sainte-Beuve,* as the only true conditions for reading and the reflective life. The problem with such an apparently logical view is that it does not account for the regressive nature of the turn inward: it does not examine the psychological consequences of the decision to abandon the social world. Most importantly, the exclusive focus on the triumphs of Art tends to overlook the fundamental fact that the esthetic revelations of music do not occur in ethereal abstraction, but struggle against the dark background of Homosexuality. Indeed, it would be more truthful to say that *La Prisonnière* is the testing ground on which Art attempts to transcend its rootedness in human limitations—notably the guilt and anguish with which Proust associates love.

On the most immediate thematic level, Art and Homosexuality oppose each other as contrary forces contending for dominance, but Proust adds some complexity to this scheme by demonstrating, in various contexts, that the two are interrelated, or, to borrow from the metaphor of textuality, "interwoven." The most evident example is that of the fictional character Albertine, who is *double,* in that she represents for Marcel, alternately, the threats of homosexual *otherness* (when she moves beyond the confines of the imprisoning room) and the beauty of a perfect, self-contained esthetic object. Albertine's function in the system of homosexual signs is more obvious than her possible meaning in the domain of Art, where she does not transmit explicit significance, but conveys metaphoric and associative connotations. At the very beginning of *La Prisonnière,* when the narrator evokes his sense of contentment at perceiving exterior reality through the indirect mediation of sound, he also describes the nature of his relationship with Albertine. It is clear that the tranquil but life-giving force of Albertine's love is itself analogous to the tonic effects of music. After describing the tongue of Albertine as a "pain quotidien . . . un élément nourrissant et ayant le caractère presque sacré de toute chair à qui les souffrances que nous avons endurées à cause d'elle ont fini par conférer une sorte de douceur morale" (III, 10), the narrator compares this erotic gift of the body to the sense of appeasement he felt as a young boy when his mother granted him her good-night kiss and spent the night with him. Proust invites the reader of his novel to juxtapose the protagonist's present love for Albertine with the earlier possessive affection for the mother, though he recognizes that such a comparison, in revealing the "identity" of the two emotional complexes, lays bare the primitive sexual urge that subtends "la scène du baiser" ("il y a presque un sacrilège apparent à constater l'identité de la grâce octroyée" [10]). Just as Albertine's sexual embrace is a variation on the theme of the mother's kiss, in the same way the protagonist's room in Paris is a repetition of his childhood rooms in Combray and Balbec. When we are told, "Les cloisons qui séparaient nos deux cabinets de toilette . . . étaient si minces que nous pouvions parler tout en nous lavant chacun dans le nôtre" (III, 11) we are reminded, inevitably, of the narrow partition that separated Marcel from his grandmother in the Grand-Hôtel, and we can see that the all-encompassing musical atmosphere of *La Prisonnière* partakes of the sensually satisfying "diaphanéité musicale" (II, 1118) that defined maternal closeness and transparent communication in earlier days.

The enchanting beauty of *La Prisonnière* derives from the combination of poetically equivalent themes that appear, on the surface, to defy amalgamation. It would seem that the regressive character of the desire to recapture the euphoric atmosphere of the womb/room has little in common with the exalted and transcendentally meaningful message of Vinteuil's Septet: yet both are translations of the peculiar power of music to create or re-create life. Throughout *La Prisonnière* music is associated with natural organic processes, especially birth, and with the overwhelming joy that accompanies the imposition of formal unity on the shapelessness of inert matter. The passages that deal with this subject most explicitly are among the most celebrated in the *Recherche*. They attract critical interest because they seem to abolish the negativity of their surrounding contexts: it is as if music, when attached to the burgeoning of flowers, were capable of eliminating all pain and doubt. This is the case in the so-called "Ouverture pour un jour de fête" that celebrates the happiness of a spring day "interpolated" into winter (III, 116–20). Leo Spitzer wrote an admirable short essay on the episode, in which he demonstrated that the numerous allusions to rebirth and the new life of spring that Proust expresses in the cries of street vendors are in fact slightly corrupt, modernized examples of a medieval literary song form called the *renverdie*.

"Verses" such as "A la tendresse, à la verduresse/Artichauts tendres et beaux/Artichauts" (118) echo a centuries-old tradition and perform, in modern Paris, the function of the renverdie, defined by Spitzer as a "genre de romance ou ballade (chanson de danse) printanière, où sont mis en scène, dans un cadre de verdure et de fleurs, soit le rossignol, symbole de l'Amour, soit l'Amour lui-même."[24] The effect of the passage as a whole is to exteriorize or objectify Marcel's desire to possess the tangible realities of his environment while remaining enclosed in his apartment/prison. The cries of the merchants, in penetrating the open windows of his lodgings, grant him the illusion of participation in the bustle of everyday concrete existence while retaining, in their formalized and fixed refrains, the unmistakable armature of an esthetic identity once removed from life.

Marcel's joy at discovering the "liturgical" quality of the street songs, his provocative comparison of contemporary Paris to "la France ecclésiastique d'autrefois" (116) deserve independent critical attention, as Spitzer has shown; but it is essential to recognize that the joyful atmosphere of the passage as such depends upon the fluid interpenetration of outside "music" and the inside calm provided by the docile figure of Albertine. The narrator explains: "Jamais je n'y [à ces scènes de la rue] avais pris tant de plaisir que depuis qu'Albertine habitait avec moi; elles [ces scènes] me semblaient comme un signal joyeux de son éveil et, en m'intéressant à la vie du dehors, me faisaient mieux sentir l'apaisante vertue d'une chère présence, aussi constante que je la souhaitais" (116–17). The attitude of the protagonist is not that of disinterested contemplation but of subjective participation in the "reading" of the street episode. The medieval/musical declamation of the vendors is especially beautiful because it relates analogously to the "apaisante vertue" of the imprisoned/loved woman. In the sentence just cited, the music is subordinated to the dramatic moment of Albertine's waking, which it "signals." But the metaphorical borrowing and lending function in the opposite direction as well: Albertine partakes of the life-forming, natural, re-creative energy of music; she incorporates the thematic content of the renverdie by "becoming" a blossoming plant. In the scene immediately preceding the "Ouverture pour un jour de fête" Albertine is compared successively to a "climbing plant" and to a musical instrument that the narrator plays:

> Je pouvais prendre sa tête, la relever, la poser contre mes lèvres, entourer mon cou de ses bras, elle continuait à dormir comme une montre qui ne s'arrête pas, comme une plante grimpante, un volubilis qui continue à pousser ses branches quelque appui qu'on lui donne. Seul son souffle était modifié par chacun de mes attouchements, comme si elle eût été un instrument dont j'eusse joué

et à qui je faisais exécuter des modulations en tirant de l'une, puis de l'autre de ses cordes, des notes différentes. (113)

In this context, it is clear that the protagonist's sensual pleasure derives from his sense of mastery or control of his beloved's involuntary movements, and such mastery is possible only when Albertine sleeps—that is, when she has abdicated her humanity and regressed to the stage of primitive unconscious life where the mechanical repetitions of breathing alone separate her from the absolute stasis of death. It becomes increasingly evident that the condition of possibility of the analogical equivalence between Albertine as "plant" and the joyful revelations of music is the appeasement of all the protagonist's doubts relating to the presumed homosexual activity of his beloved. Without this necessary appeasement, there can be no music, no transparent communication, no metaphorical unification of inside and outside, room and world. Hence the deluded quality of the narrator's assertion that the street scenes are like a "joyful signal" of Albertine's waking: it would be more precise to say that the wakefulness of the imprisoned woman is already an escape into the enigmatic reaches of Homosexuality and, therefore, an undermining of the unmediated conditions in which musical language can function. *La Prisonnière* carries out the emotional ambivalence foreshadowed in the fourth chapter of *Sodome et Gomorrhe:* the novel becomes the locus of violently juxtaposed alternations. When Albertine is active beyond the confines of the Paris apartment, Marcel lives his love as anguish and jealous curiosity, and the text loses its poetic coloration; when she sleeps in the protected environment of the room, Marcel enjoys uninterrupted peace, and the text blossoms into a symphonic concatenation of parallel themes and images. In such moments there is a recovery of the innocent paradise lost of Combray, but in the paradoxical mode of a nonliving emptiness:

> Ma jalousie s'apaisait, car je sentais Albertine devenue un être qui respire, qui n'est pas autre chose, comme le signifiait le souffle régulier par où s'exprime cette pure fonction physiologique, qui, tout fluide, n'a l'épaisseur ni de la parole, ni du silence et, dans son ignorance de tout mal, haleine tirée plutôt d'un roseau creusé que d'un être humain, vraiment paradisiaque pour moi qui dans ces moments-là sentais Albertine soustraite à tout, non pas seulement matériellement, mais moralement, étant le pur chant des Anges. Et dans ce souffle pourtant, je me disais tout à coup que peut-être bien des noms humains apportés par la mémoire devaient se jouer. (113-14)

The last sentence of the passage adds a note of dissonance to an otherwise harmonious scheme: if, as the narrator surmises in a later development (114), the "noms humains apportés par la mémoire" are those of lesbian acquaintances, then it is not legitimate to presume that Albertine is a morally empty plant-form, a "roseau creusé." The persuasive beauty of the "pur chant des Anges" can flower only when the homosexual energy of Albertine is kept in abeyance, only when the narrator arbitrarily decides to change her from living woman to esthetically closed form. The possibility arises that *all* poetic moments of *La Prisonnière,* including the Septet episode, are based upon a fundamental delusion: that Art can create its own self-sufficient universe impermeable to moral duplicity. The narrator's goal is to convince the reader that this proposition is not only not deluded, but perfectly logical, and he succeeds admirably if we consider that most critics are content to take his conclusions on the supremacy of music at face value without examining the context in which the Septet is inserted.

Viewed in isolation, as an anthology piece, the passage on the recital of Vinteuil's posthumous work is a pure affirmation of the joy that accompanies the creation of great art and of the joy felt by the intelligent listener/reader who recognizes, underneath the apparent novelty of variously disguised forms, the essential permanence of one man's genius. But this communion of author and interpreter, this rare "epiphany," takes place only when the force of moral conflict lies dormant, only when Marcel's beloved and Vinteuil's daughter sleep:

> Et au moment où je me la [Albertine] représentais ainsi m'attendant à la maison, trouvant le temps long, s'étant peut-être endormie un instant dans sa chambre, je fus caressé au passage par une tendre phrase familiale et domestique du septuor. Peut-être—tant tout s'entre-croise et se superpose dans notre vie intérieure—avait-elle été inspirée à Vinteuil par le sommeil de sa fille—de sa fille, cause aujourd'hui de tous mes troubles—quand il enveloppait de sa douceur, dans les paisibles soirées, le travail de musicien, cette phrase qui me calma tant par le même moelleux arrière-plan de silence qui pacifie certaines rêveries de Schumann, durant lesquelles, même quand "le Poète parle," on devine que "l'enfant dort." (253)

In the development following this passage the narrator hypothesizes that Vinteuil's Septet seems to promise "quelque chose de plus mystérieux que l'amour d'Albertine" (253), which is nothing less than the supralogical language of music, "aussi débarrassée des formes analytiques du raisonnement que si elle s'était exercée dans le monde des anges" (256). But the narrator can meditate on transcendental communication only by imposing on himself a significant form of mental discipline: "J'essayai de chasser la pensée de mon amie pour ne plus songer qu'au musicien" (253). According to traditional interpretations of the Septet, the progression from Love to Art is to be understood as a victory for the future author of the *Recherche:* the structure of this progression is left unquestioned. [25] But if we read Proust more literally and with a greater attention to contextual construction, we conclude necessarily that the movement away from Love toward Art is, in fact, a forgetfulness and a regression. It is because the narrator refuses to decipher Albertine, to recognize her for what she is, that he can elaborate a coherent but morally ambivalent theory of esthetics. The real question, which the majority of critics, including Deleuze, refuse to ask, is, What is the nature of the *entrecroisement* of musical revelation and homosexuality? Unless this question is posed explicitly, the bald assertion of Art's superiority remains abstract and a mere matter of subjective critical preference.

Proust answers us directly and unambiguously. Art is not the negation or overcoming of Love: it is born in the mysteries of sexual inversion. At the conclusion of the Septet passage (264–65) the narrator evokes "ce contraste apparent, cette union profonde entre le génie (le talent aussi, et même la vertu) et la gaîne de vices" (264) in which genius is enclosed. For our purposes, this translates as a warning against the temptation of reading the Septet episode in the "pure" atmosphere of esthetic isolation. We should remember that the scene has a double homosexual causation. If Vinteuil is played at the home of the Verdurin, it is because Charlus has organized the evening with the desire of displaying Morel's musical talents; and the Septet itself owes its existence to the painstaking efforts of Mlle Vinteuil's sapphic friend, who deciphered the deceased composer's hieroglyphics:

> Le motif proche, immédiat, de cette présence [i.e., celle de tant de personnes distinguées chez Mme Verdurin] résidait dans les relations qui existaient entre M. de Charlus et Morel, relations qui faisaient désirer au baron de donner le plus de retentissement possible aux succès artistiques de sa jeune idole, et d'obtenir pour lui la croix de la Légion d'honneur; la cause plus lointaine qui avait rendu cette réunion possible était qu'une jeune fille entretenant avec Mlle Vinteuil des relations parallèles à celles de Charlie et du baron, avait mis au jour toute une série d'oeuvres géniales et qui avaient été une telle révélation qu'une souscription n'allait pas tarder à être ouverte, sous le patronage du ministre de l'Instruction publique, en vue de faire élever une statue à Vinteuil. (264)

For Proust, the relationship of virtue to vice, of Art to homosexual Love, is that of mutual implication: there can be no appeal to amoral esthetic transcendence without the contradictory postulation of moral immanence. The Septet scene as such is merely a part of a larger whole. The passage on Vinteuil's music is surrounded by a broader context against which it stands in violent juxtaposition: the social "exclusion" of Charlus by the Verdurin. Viewed in context, the Septet may be nothing more than a pleasant diversion or "divertissement" in the Pascalian sense— a moment of oblivion, a chasing of phantoms, the poetic equivalent of a daydream that deflects the mind of the reader from the concentrated interpretation of the drama of homosexuality. Proust leaves us with two worlds, two sets of values, each of which is coherent in itself, but neither of which can conquer the other. In Freudian terms, the text constructs itself on *ambivalent* significance, on the "antithetical meaning of primal words." Thus, in the Septet episode the narrator associates the idea of the "unknown" (*l'Inconnu*) with the joy of discovery and with the thematic unity of the musical composition, whereas in an earlier context the same word has a radically different sense:

> Elles [les phrases musicales du septuor] s'éloignèrent, sauf une que
> je vis repasser jusqu'à cinq et six fois, sans que je pusse apercevoir
> son visage, mais si caressante, si différente—comme sans doute
> la petite phrase de la Sonate pour Swann—de ce qu'aucune femme
> m'avait jamais fait désirer, que cette phrase-là, qui m'offrait d'une
> voix si douce un bonheur qu'il eût vraiment valu la peine d'ob-
> tenir, c'est peut-être—cette créature invisible dont je ne connaissais
> pas le langage et que je comprenais si bien—*la seule Inconnue qu'il
> m'ait jamais été donné de rencontrer.* (260; my emphasis)

> Le mensonge, le mensonge parfait, sur les gens que nous con-
> naissons, les relations que nous avons eues avec eux, notre mobile
> dans telle action formulé par nous d'une façon toute différente,
> le mensonge sur ce que nous sommes, sur ce que nous aimons, sur
> ce que nous éprouvons à l'égard de l'être qui nous aime et qui
> croit nous avoir façonnés semblables à lui parce qu'il nous embrasse
> toute la journée, *ce mensonge-là est une des seules choses qui
> puissent nous ouvrir des perspectives sur du nouveau, sur de l'in-
> connu,* puisse ouvrir en nous des sens endormis pour la contem-
> plation d'univers que nous n'aurions jamais connus. (216; my
> emphasis)

If the critical interpretation of a work of art is based upon distinction and discrimination, if the act of reading depends upon the possibility of selecting among various potential meanings, then Proust has rendered reading "impossible" by making judgmental choices undecidable. Which is the "true" *Inconnu(e)* for Proust—Vinteuil's musical phrase, or the perfect lie? Which of these opens up vaster perspectives, larger horizons of meaning? To affirm the superiority of music over homosexuality is to take the risk (give in to the temptation) of making the impossible choice, of reading a work that presents itself, *strictu senso,* as unreadable. And the allegorical sign of this unreadability is Albertine.

The entirety of *La Prisonnière* tells the story of a reader's vacillations: it is the figural narration of the interpretive process as such. Marcel's relationship to Albertine is that of a jealous decipherer to a dark code, and his judgments alternate between what de Man has called "blindness" and "insight"—the poles of delusion and critical penetration which, like vice and virtue in the *Recherche,* cannot exist independently of each other. Until now, I have emphasized Marcel's blindness—his false assumption that Albertine is an empty sign in which he can insert the arbitrary poetry of vegetal purity and organic plant life. Allegorically, this translates as the inevitable but deluded gesture of reducing a text to the "organic" unity of parts and whole. But Marcel's assurance concerning the identity of Albertine is precarious indeed, and at certain moments in the text he recognizes that she is not the vivifying presence of life but the absolute enigma of significant opacity: her resistance to all interpretive understanding is a threat to the stability of the protagonist and seems to symbolize "death":

> Ce fut une morte en effet que je vis quand j'entrai dans sa chambre [i.e., celle d'Albertine]. Elle s'était endormie aussitôt couchée; ses draps, roulés comme un suaire autour de son corps, avaient pris, avec leurs beaux plis, une rigidité de pierre. . . . Et en voyant ce corps insignifiant couché là, je me demandais quelle table de logarithmes il constituait pour que toutes les actions auxquelles il avait pu être mêlé, depuis un poussement de coude jusqu'à un frolement de robe, pussent me causer, étendues à l'infini de tous les points qu'il avait occupés dans l'espace et dans le temps, et de temps à autre brusquement revivifiées dans mon souvenir, des angoisses si douloureuses. (359-60)

Proust expresses the inaccessibility of Albertine to critical comprehension by comparing her, throughout *La Prisonnière,* to an enveloping structure that hides its contents. In some cases, as in the above passage, Marcel learns that the "insignificant body" of his beloved opens out to an infinity of points in space and time; the decipherer's difficulty is in following overlapping and divergent significant paths. In other instances, Albertine's body (*le signifiant*) closes in completely on its mysterious inner core (*le signifié*), so that the interpreter has no way of access to the woman's reality. Following are examples of each variation:

> N'avais-je pas deviné en Albertine une de ces filles sous l'envelope charnelle desquelles palpitent plus d'êtres cachés . . . que dans la foule immense et renouvelée? Non pas seulement tant d'êtres, mais le désir, le souvenir voluptueux, l'inquiète recherche de tant d'êtres. . . . Et maintenant qu'elle m'avait dit un jour "Mlle Vinteuil", j'aurais voulu non pas arracher sa robe pour voir son corps, mais, à travers son corps, voir tout ce bloc-notes de ses souvenirs et de ses prochains et ardents rendez-vous. (94)

> Avant qu'Albertine m'eût obéi et eût enlevé ses souliers, j'entr'ouvrais sa chemise. Ses deux petits seins haut remontés étaient si ronds qu'ils avaient moins l'air de faire partie intégrante de son corps que d'y avoir mûri comme deux fruits; et son ventre (dissimulant la place qui chez l'homme s'enlaidit comme du crampon resté fiché dans une statue descellée) se refermait, à la jonction des cuisses, par deux valves d'une courbe aussi assoupie, aussi reposante, aussi claustrale que celle de l'horizon quand le soleil a disparu. (79)

In both cases the protagonist's efforts to understand Albertine (to imprison or possess her) are doomed to failure, and the "insight" he gains into her indecipherable status as allegorical sign is purely negative. In his moments of lucidity, Marcel recognizes Albertine for what she is: the figure of logical incompatibility, the fictive representation of the insuperable cleft between cause and effect. Albertine cannot be read, for she represents the radical impossibility of (her own) reading: "Albertine . . . était entrée pour moi dans cette période lamentable où un être, disséminé dans l'espace et dans le temps, n'est plus pour nous une femme, mais une suite d'événements sur lesquels nous ne pouvons faire la lumière, une suite de problèmes insolubles, une mer que nous essayons ridiculement, comme Xerxès, de battre pour la punir de ce qu'elle a englouti" (104).

The narrator's comparison of Albertine to the ocean which has swallowed up the ships of Xerxes deserves independent attention. Xerxes appears "ridiculous" because his actions—beating the water's edge—will not bring his ships back up from the bottom of the sea. There is an incompatibility between what he does and what he attempts to achieve because he has not understood that water is a medium that engulfs all things indiscriminately, that opens itself to descending objects but closes itself immediately thereafter and returns to its appearance of surface calm. Similarly, Marcel emblematizes the "ridiculous" reader who attempts to "punish" the text by flailing at its surface, not realizing that the relationship of sign to meaning is arbitrary, that the text itself is an ocean that engulfs its signs and renders impossible their recuperation in the immediacy of effective action. Proust's use of the adjective "disséminé" in this context is a provocative foreshadowing of Derrida's theory of textual *dissémination,* in that it inscribes the act of reading in an interminable process of differential temporality and presents the sign as an exploded constellation of fragmentary, non-unifiable parts.[26] Within this scheme of things, the relationship of reader to text is far from simple, and the "dialogue" between Marcel and Albertine risks being a *dialogue de sourds.* It seems that the process of reading a text involves both a semiological disjunction (the gap between the ocean's surface and the irretrievably lost vessels, between Albertine as *signifiant* and Albertine as *signifié*) and a psychological frustration. *Battre la mer* in French sounds strangely like *battre la mère*—as if Marcel, in beating away at the text, were punishing his mother for her "sin" of denying him for eternity the balm of her kiss. The discovery of Albertine's identity as textual ocean plunges the protagonist into a despotic form of despair: what we must examine now is the way in which the deciphering of Albertine impinges on the protagonist's sense of self, how he manages to obtain, create, and conserve an *identity*.

## THE NAMED SELF

The passage of the *Recherche* that stages most clearly the constitutive dynamics of Proustian selfhood occurs in the early pages of *La Prisonnière:* it is the episode in which Albertine "names" the protagonist (III, 64–75). As I indicated toward the beginning of this chapter with reference to Genette and Lejeune, the sudden and unexpected emergence of the name "Marcel" is especially disconcerting in that it introduces into the text an element of modal uncertainty: it becomes difficult to determine whether we are reading a novel or an autobiography, a fiction or a confession. The appreciable merit of Genette and Lejeune consists of their careful respect for this ambivalence: both critics note that an autobiographical tonality merges here with the more pervasive "impersonal" narration of imagined events, thereby producing a hybrid textual form. Although neither Genette nor Lejeune does more than observe this fact in a general way, their contribution to Proust scholarship is nonetheless praiseworthy, for they are affirming that the existence of the word "Marcel" in the text is not the result of an authorial oversight or idiosyncrasy, but a problem that demands interpretation.[27] I propose, in the following development, to examine the paragraph on naming in its contextual setting and to establish a coherent problematics concerning the identity of the *je* whose articulated states of textual presence ultimately determine the applicability of the term *autobiography* to Proust's novel. I shall begin my analysis with a discussion of the Proustian "double self" as it functions technically and thematically, before reading the passage on naming as such.

The best early study of the *Recherche* as autobiography is that of Hans-Robert Jauss, *Zeit und Erinnerung*. At a time when many critics had no vision of the novel as a totality, Jauss elaborated an interpretive grid that both respected the larger thematic movements and also included close analysis of images and symbols later to be taken up by Genette in a post-Saussurian, new-rhetorical terminology. The modern reader may feel a sense of estrangement in reading Jauss for two reasons: first, the latter's view of the novel as transformed "epic" may seem excessively literal in certain contexts; and secondly, the pervasive Hegelian terminology may seem somewhat out-of-date to readers for whom the implicit "referent" of deconstructive analyses has usually been the Hegelian system. Yet if we push Jauss a step further than he went in his interpretation, we discover to what extent the *Recherche* as novelistic form can be construed as a brilliant restatement of certain theoretical and methodological problems whose "answer" or working-out was the *Phenomenology of Mind*.

Jauss begins his study with the fundamental distinction between narrator ("das erinnernde ich," or "the remembering I") and "Marcel" ("das erinnerte ich," or "the remembered I"). He shows that this double register allows Proust to avoid the reductive tendencies of classical autobiography, in which a solidly established subject justifies his past from the retrospective and teleological point of view. It is to Jauss's credit to have demonstrated rigorously that the novelistic technique of Proust is inseparable from his esthetic tenets. Most importantly, the time of remembrance (as revelation of involuntary memory) does not stand outside the textual development, but is integrated into remembered time: it becomes part of that temporal movement which Jauss has characterized as "futur dans le passé" (as opposed to the "passé du savoir" that defines *Les Confessions* of Rousseau or Goethe's *Dichtung und Wahrheit*). From Jauss's theoretical perspective, the "Overture" to the *Recherche* (I, 3–9) is not to be understood simply as a modern version of *in medias res,* but rather as the only logical way to begin a novel which, because of its double register, must begin in its middle, or, in other terms, must already have started. This we recognize as the problem of the Hegelian preface, though Jauss does not make the connection in an explicit way. In his "Vorrede" to the *Phenomenology of Mind,* Hegel explains that all attempts to situate his own work in an historical or intellectual context miss the mark or stray from the central work of philosophy, which is to represent the truth in its progressive unfolding, as the general which includes the particular:

Denn wie und was von Philosophie in einer Vorrede zu sagen
schicklich wäre, —etwa eine historische *Angabe* der Tendenz und
des Standpunkts, des allgemeinen Inhalts und der Resultate, eine
Verbindung von hin und her sprechenden Behauptungen und
Versicherungen über das Wahre—kann nicht für die Art und Weise
gelten, in der die philosophische Wahrheit darzustellen sei.

Auch weil die Philosophie wesentlich im Elemente der Allgemein-
heit ist, die das Besondere in sich schliesst, so findet bei ihr mehr
als bei andern Wissenschaften der Schein statt, als ob in dem
Zwecke oder den letzten Resultaten die Sache selbst und sogar in
ihrem vollkommenen Wesen ausgedrückt wäre, gegen welches
die Ausführung eigentlich das Unwesentliche sei.

(For whatever it might be suitable to state about philosophy in a
preface—say, an historical sketch of the main drift and point of
view, the general content and results, a string of desultory assertions and assurances about the truth—this cannot be accepted as the
form and manner in which to expound philosophical truth.

Moreover, because philosophy has its being essentially in the element of that universality which encloses the particular within it,
the end or final result seems, in the case of philosophy more than
in that of other sciences, to have absolutely expressed the complete fact in its very nature; contrasted with that the mere process
of bringing it to light would seem, properly speaking, to have no
essential significance.) [28]

The achievement of Proust's "Overture" is to have effectively performed
what Hegel explained in a discursive manner. The opening pages of the
*Recherche* show the coming-to-consciousness of a *je* who is already observed by another *je*. What is confusion to the first is already illuminated
for the second self. Subjective consciousness is already its own object;
the text doubles into itself to produce its own temporal progress. In this
interiorized scheme of knowledge, *je* becomes itself in a succession of
ecstatic moments as the book demonstrates its (future) coming-into-being.

For Jauss, the revelations of the Matinée Guermantes at the close of the
novel create the esthetic impression of a *temps incorporé* that Marcel discovers as he understands the deep identity between his past and present
selves. Remembrance implies the continuity of an inner time, thereby presupposing a *moi permanent* in which "die Diskontinuität der *moi succes-
sifs* aufgehoben und zugleich bewahrt ist" ("the discontinuity of the
successive selves is both negated and preserved" [*Zeit und Erinnerung*,
198]). The major assumption in Jauss's argumentation is that the successive selves of the protagonist, however discontinuous in their form of

presentation, at least share the same essence. In rhetorical terms, we would say that the protagonist as "part" (momentary apparition) relates as meta-phorical synecdoche to the narrator as "whole" (truth of the hero's false-ness). Only this assumption will allow the Proustian system to function as a fluid progression.

The question that I would like to pose at this point, and then develop in a short analysis, is the following: can we safely suppose that the narrator relates to the protagonist as *Le Temps retrouvé* seems to affirm, or is the dual register of the *je* of a kind that does not allow for a Hegelian synthe-sis? I will now juxtapose the passage on naming from *La Prisonnière* to the well-known "Overture" of "Combray," which it resembles in many respects. The superposition of the two texts (in the strict geometrical sense) reveals a structural design that should help clarify the function and limits of the autobiographical mode in Proust's writing. (See the Appendix for material drawn from these passages.)

The pages leading up to the paragraph on naming thematize the double nature of Albertine: they compress into a series of quick and violent alter-nations the polar oppositions of virtue and vice, organic plant-object and disseminated, irrecuperable energy, that run throughout *La Prisonnière*. At first, the narrator emphasizes Albertine's fugitive tendencies and re-flects on the difficulty of immobilizing a being whose desires remain for-ever unknowable. He even states that whatever identity one may wish to assign her implies a false stability "que nous lui prêtons [et qui] n'est que fictive et pour la commodité du langage" (III, 65). This observation gains in irony as the text progresses, but for the moment we see especially its function as generalization or law: how indeed can Albertine be granted identity if her inner self contains the contradictory double presence of beauty (esthetic harmony) and of satanic evil? Moving inexplicably from the status of "rose jeune fille" to that of "lubrique Furie," she escapes categorization as she defies possession. Yet without the shadow of a transition, the narrator describes her also as the opposite of the creature of duplicity just evoked. Suddenly, we are told in a straightforward declaration: "Nos rapports étaient d'une simplicité qui les rendaient reposants" (67). No longer a threatening force whose inner core eludes understanding, she is now an empty vessel in, through, and beyond which Marcel can supply his own peaceful dreams. He sees her as an ap-parition who reawakens in him the forgotten seascapes of Balbec: "Der-rière cette jeune fille, comme derrière la lumière pourprée qui tombait aux pieds de mes rideaux à Balbec pendant qu'éclatait le concert des mu-siciens, se nacraient les ondulations bleuâtres de la mer" (ibid.). Later on, Albertine becomes a "plant" whose every movement "belongs" to Marcel: as plant, as poetic object, "son moi ne s'échappait pas à tous moments, comme quand nous causions, par les issues de la pensée inavouée et du regard" (70). The short passage preceding the naming of the protagonist is thus a microcosm of volumes 5 and 6 of the *Recherche:* the almost delirious and uncanny alternation between imprisonment and escape. The efforts to imprison, as we later learn in *La Fugitive,* are doomed to failure, and true knowledge of Albertine's wayward activities comes in an ironical series of retrospective telegrams and messages. To the reader aware of the ultimate outcome of the couple's liaison, it seems impossible not to conclude that those moments of repose in which Marcel "possesses" Albertine are in fact the result of extreme delusion. The prisoner is forever a fugitive, and the poetic beauty of the passage describing her as primitive inanimate vegetal life arises from an active forgetfulness, or strong repression.

The progression of the text is toward a highly charged eroticism. The hero at first lies alongside the body of Albertine, listening to her breathing, then comes to sexual climax while she continues to sleep. This is satisfying to him above other forms of enjoyment because, in the narrator's words, "il me semblait à ces moments-là que je venais de la posséder plus complètement, comme une chose inconsciente et sans résistance de la muette nature" (73). For our purposes, it is important to note as well that Albertine pronounces words, perhaps names of other people, as Marcel makes love to her, or rather, to himself. Yet these incoherent sounds do not bother him, since it is his hand and his body she touches. Masturbation *on* another human being whose maternal presence as sea and breath offers unmediated communion without the threat of sexual difference: this is, in Lacanian terms, identification with the mother's "phallus," the hero's desire being not to have, but to *be* the phallus.[29] The entire passage leading up to the paragraph on naming can be interpreted in a Lacanian vein, as an elaborate *mise en scène* of the "imaginaire," where intersubjective relationships never get beyond the vicious circle of continuously vacillating symmetrical opposites. Some eighty pages later, when the name "Marcel" is mentioned for the second and last time in the novel, it is in the context of a discussion of the master-slave duality that characterizes Marcel's life with Albertine. In a moment of aphoristic lucidity, the narrator admits: "J'étais plus maître que je n'avais cru. Plus maître, c'est-à-dire plus esclave" (157).

A presumed mastery is the mask for slavery, but what is the significance of *masking* as such? We can best understand the generalized paradigm underlying an apparently sexual combat in the guise of "jealousy" if we remember that Albertine is, among other things, a text. She is a "blocnotes" whose lies must be deciphered "à rebours" (90, 94). The ironical thrust of the passage under scrutiny resides in the false affirmation, on the most evident thematic level, that Marcel is Albertine's "master" also in the sense of "teacher" or initiator into the secrets of the beaux-arts. The allegorical level of the text deconstructs this literal level, revealing the monstrosity of the narrator's claim to master a text that is, by definition, the very essence of Proustian "fuite." The allegory of the text *as* text demonstrates the peculiar *tourniquet* that characterizes the act of reading: a movement of simultaneous affirmation and denial in which the meanings of the sign can never preclude the violent moment of semantic appropriation.

The erotic pleasure experienced by Marcel in the earlier part of the passage merges eventually into a general feeling of possessive power as Albertine makes her transition from sleep to wakefulness. For the protagonist-jailer (reader) it is gratifying to know that the imprisoned woman (text) comes to life within the confining walls of his own domain. The movement from unconsciousness or *vertige* to *certitude* will be recognized as a structural repetition of the novel's "Overture," in which the protagonist's acts of remembering emerge from the chaos of remembered time. In *La Prisonnière*, the duality narrator-protagonist ("das errinernde ich" and "das erinnerte ich") is replaced by the couple of Marcel and Albertine, but the very same question of the text's ultimate readability is at stake in both cases. If we superimpose the later version of Albertine's coming-to-consciousness upon the first pages of the *Recherche* (see the Appendix for this juxtaposition), we note an important and disquieting fact: for the (Hegelian) synthesis to take place, the narrator must "imprison" the protagonist as Marcel imprisons Albertine, by limiting the proliferation of his potential significance. Granted the structural equivalence:

$$\frac{\text{das erinnernde ich}}{\text{das erinnerte ich}} : \frac{\text{Marcel}}{\text{Albertine}}$$

the text then opens into deep irony. The apparent relationship of metaphorical synecdoche between narrator and protagonist collapses into pure metonymy or chance juxtaposition. According to this equivalence, the narrator "touches" the protagonist as Marcel lies *on* Albertine—for narcissistic gratification, without penetration or sharing of "essence." A simultaneous rereading of both passage shows that the "Eve" born of Marcel's thigh in the "Overture" is a model for Albertine as sex object: "Quelquefois, comme Ève naquit d'une côte d'Adam, une femme naissait pendant mon sommeil d'une fausse position de ma cuisse. Formée du plaisir que j'étais sur le point de goûter, je m'imaginais que c'était elle qui me l'offrait" (I, 4). The two passages undermine each other. On the one hand, the relationship between Marcel and Albertine is revealed as the false dialogue of a self-loving subject; and on the other hand, the posited unity of the two "I"'s becomes the vicious cycle of an eternal dialogue in which the point of contact between narrator and protagonist is nothing more than the imaginary space of a coincidence.

The final, most destructive irony of the text, emerges in Albertine's words at the moment of her awakening: "Elle retrouvait la parole, elle disait: 'Mon' ou 'Mon chéri', suivis l'un ou l'autre de mon nom de baptême, ce qui, en donnant au narrateur le même prénom qu'à l'auteur de ce livre, eût fait: 'Mon Marcel', 'Mon chéri Marcel'" (III, 75). In allegorical terms, the subject who thought to possess the *other* as object, is dispossessed in the very instant of his naming. Indeed, the narrator possesses nothing, since his name, derived hypothetically from that of the author, is produced or proffered by a purely fictional character. And since Albertine stands for the elusive temporality of the sign, we find, through another structural substitution, that the reader, thinking to control meanings, is "read" by the text. The Freudian resonance of the passage as a unit is clear: the effort to deny the castration complex in a prolonged dream of narcissistic self-satisfaction collapses as the differences of the text explode to split the ego's claim to mastery.

The "autobiography" of Proust's *Recherche* is not to be understood in the literality of etymology as a "coming alive to oneself in writing," but rather, as the textual differential movement by which the "I" is separated from itself and thrust from the stability of discursive control into the alienating repetitions of the narrative's all-encompassing, *self*-obliterating rule. Narrative allegory, the temporal displacement of hypothetical fictions, emerges from the deconstruction of the empirical self's attempts to take possession of the text's body.

This *impossibility* of possession-taking has appeared under various guises and in differing forms of completion and complexity in the preceding pages. Swann's misreading of tropological nothingness was narrated as a subject's desire to embrace the personified "feminine" charms of the *petite phrase:* Swann wished to grasp that which is, by its very nature, a creature of *fuite* and elusiveness. The Ruskinian/Romantic pattern of possession-taking was taken over by Proust and used primarily as a semiological investigation: the "essence" of the outside world, whether incorporated in the esthetic mysteries of music, the appeal of magic names, or the enigmatic significance of *jeunes filles en fleurs,* is clothed in the form of the Romantic symbol and expressed as a dream of plenitude whose false premises are revealed at every step of the *Recherche*'s disillusioning path. Proust's novel is, among other things, a search for essences or truths, but the narrative deployment of the quest itself takes place within the constitutive splits of the sign. The travel motif, which had been associated only with the ecstacies of artistic revelation in Ruskin's

*Praeterita*, becomes, for Proust, the most adequate fictional vehicle to depict the inner movement of negative self-discovery. The turn inward, which corresponds to the adoption of an abstract allegorical narration, yields the anguished, "jealous" investigations of the lover/reader in search of an absent, invisible, or undecipherable beloved/sign.

Confessional autobiography is the constantly repeated erroneous moment of subjective delusion whose "unravelling" in allegory produces a uniform subcurrent of irony. The reassuring appearance of authorial identity in the word "Marcel" is a disguise for the face that the name, by its very insertion in fiction, loses all "necessary" or "essential" significant ties to the outside world. The congruence of the fictional "Marcel" with Marcel Proust is the deceptive effect of a purely contingent coincidence. Yet the *Recherche* thrives on such deception, and it is impossible for the reader not to participate in the text's referential illusion. Reading, for Proust, involved two mutually contradictory postulations: the movement of appropriation whereby the self, in its efforts to embrace the meaning of textual events, extends beyond the confines of its subjective prison in its search for referential verification (autobiography); and the cycle of dispossession whereby the self's stability is undermined by the disseminated multiplicity of unreadable signs (fictional allegory). The *Recherche* is the space in which these opposing constellations collide, the imaginary locus of the reader's impossible choices.

# Appendix:
# The Named Self

**"Combray": The Dreamed "Eve" as Prefiguration of Albertine**
Quelquefois, comme Eve naquit d'une côte d'Adam, une femme naissait pendant mon sommeil d'une fausse position de ma cuisse. Formée du plaisir que j'étais sur le point de goûter, je m'imaginais que c'était elle qui me l'offrait. Mon corps qui sentait dans le sien ma propre chaleur voulait s'y rejoindre, je m'éveillais. Le reste des humains m'apparaissait comme bien lointain auprès de cette femme que j'avais quittée, il y avait quelques moments à peine; ma joue était chaude encore de son baiser, mon corps courbaturé par le poids de sa taille. Si, comme il arrivait quelquefois, elle avait les traits d'une femme que j'avais connue dans la vie, j'allais me donner tout entier à ce but: la retrouver, comme ceux qui partent en voyage pour voir de leurs yeux une cité désirée et s'imaginent qu'on peut goûter dans une réalité le charme du songe. (I, 4–5)

*La Prisonnière:* **Albertine, "Marcel,"**
**and Autobiographical Identity**
Mais ce plaisir de la voir dormir, et qui était aussi doux que la sentir vivre, un autre y mettait fin, et qui était celui de la voir s'éveiller. Il était, à un degré plus profond et plus mystérieux, le plaisir même qu'elle habitât chez moi. Sans doute il m'était doux, l'après-midi, quand elle descendait de voiture, que ce fût dans mon appartement qu'elle rentrât. Il me l'était plus encore que, quand du fond du sommeil elle remontait les derniers degrés de l'escalier des songes, ce fût dans ma chambre qu'elle renaquît à la conscience et à la vie, qu'elle se demandât un instant "où suis-je?" et, voyant les objets dont elle était entourée, la lampe dont la lumière lui faisait à peine cligner les yeux, pût se répondre qu'elle était

chez elle en constatant qu'elle s'éveillait chez moi. Dans ce premier moment délicieux d'incertitude, il me semblait que je prenais à nouveau plus complètement possession d'elle, puisque, au lieu que, après être sortie, elle entrât dans sa chambre, c'était ma chambre, dès qu'elle serait reconnue par Albertine, qui allait l'enserrer, la contenir, sans que les yeux de mon amie manifestassent aucun trouble, restant aussi calmes que si elle n'avait pas dormi. L'hésitation du réveil, révélée par son silence, ne l'était pas par son regard.

Elle retrouvait la parole, elle disait: "Mon" ou "Mon chéri", suivis l'un ou l'autre de mon nom de baptême, ce qui, en donnant au narrateur le même prénom qu'à l'auteur de ce livre, eût fait: "Mon Marcel", "Mon chéri Marcel", Je ne permettais plus dès lors qu'en famille une parente, en m'appelant aussi "chéri", ôtât leur prix d'être uniques aux mots délicieux que me disait Albertine. Tout en me les disant elle faisait une petite moue qu'elle changeait d'elle-même en baiser. Aussi vite qu'elle s'était tout à l'heure endormie, aussi vite elle s'était réveillée. (III, 74–75)

# Notes

## CHAPTER ONE

1. It is now well established in the critical literature that the term *méta-phore* in Proust means either an explicit or an implicit comparison (simile or meta-phor), that it is an imprecise way to say "analogy." It is now clear, as well, that the Proustian novel is the convergence point of metaphorical and metonymical con-figurations (see Gérard Genette, "Métonymie chez Proust," *Figures III* [Paris: Seuil, 1972], 41-63, and Samuel M. Weber, "Le Madrépore," *Poétique,* 13 [1973], 28-54). In the present chapter, as I study the metamorphoses of Proustian "métaphore," I will try to demonstrate that the terminological vagueness of Proust's theory does not preclude a profound authorial understanding of the figure in action.

2. Marcel Proust, *A la recherche du temps perdu* (Paris: Pléiade, 1954), III, 889. All further quotations from the *Recherche* will be drawn from the three-volume 1954 Pléiade edition. In subsequent chapters of my book I will refer to the two other Pléiade volumes of Proust's major writings: *'Jean Santeuil,' précédé de 'Les Plaisirs et les jours'* (1971) and *'Contre Sainte-Beuve,' précédé de 'Pastiches et mélanges' et suivi de Essais et articles* (1971).

3. Serge Doubrovsky, "Faire catleya," *Poétique,* 37 (1979), 116.

4. Philippe Sollers, "Le Monde au téléscope," *Le Nouvel Observateur,* 11 July 1971, 41, cited by Jeffrey Mehlman, *A Structural Study of Autobiography* (Ithaca: Cornell University Press, 1974), 63.

5. Jean Ricardou, "La métaphore d'un bout à l'autre," *Nouveaux prob-lèmes du roman* (Paris: Seuil, 1978), 93.

6. Paul Ricoeur, *La Métaphore vive* (Paris: Seuil, 1975); Jacques Derrida, "La Mythologie blanche," *Marges de la philosophie* (Paris: Minuit, 1972), 247-324.

7. Ricoeur describes one of the fundamental postulates of classical tropology in these terms: "Expliquer (ou comprendre) un trope, c'est, guidé par la raison du trope, c'est-à-dire le paradigme de la substitution, trouver le mot propre absent; c'est donc restituer le terme propre auquel un terme impropre a été substitué; la paraphrase en quoi consiste cette restitution est en principe exhaustive, la somme algébrique de

la substitution et de la restitution étant nulle: postulat de la paraphrase exhaustive" (*La Métaphore vive*, 66).

8. On this subject see the passage from Nietzsche that Derrida cites in "La Mythologie blanche," 258; "Qu'est-ce donc que la vérité? Une multitude mouvante de métaphores, de métonymies, d'anthropomorphismes, bref, une somme de relations humaines qui ont été poétiquement et rhétoriquement haussées, transposées, ornées, et qui, après un long usage, semblent à un peuple fermes, canoniales et contraignantes: les vérités sont des illusions dont on a oublié qu'elles le sont, des métaphores qui ont été usées et qui ont perdu leur force sensible (*die abgenutzt und sinnlich kraftlos geworden sind*), des pièces de monnaie qui ont perdu leur empreinte (*Bild*) et qui entrent dès lors en considération, non plus comme pièces de monnaie mais comme métal" ("Introduction théorétique sur la vérité et le mensonge au sens extra-moral [Summer 1873]," in *Le Livre du philosophe*, trans. A. K. Mariette [Paris: Aubier-Flammarion], 181–82).

9. "Surtout le mouvement de la métaphorisation (origine puis effacement de la métaphore, passage du sens propre sensible au sens propre spirituel à travers le détour des figures) n'est autre qu'un mouvement d'idéalisation. Et il est compris sous la catégorie maîtresse de l'idéalisme dialectique, à savoir la *relève* (*Aufhebung*), c'est-à-dire la mémoire qui produit les signes, les intériorise (*Erinnerung*) en élevant, supprimant et conservant l'extériorité sensible" ("La Mythologie blanche," 269).

10. "La métaphore, dit-il [Aristote], 'fait image' . . . autrement dit, elle donne à la saisie du genre cette coloration concrète que les modernes appelleront style imagé, style figuré. Aristote, il est vrai, n'emploie aucunement le mot *eikôn*, au sens où depuis Charles Sanders Peirce nous parlons de l'aspect iconique de la métaphore. Mais l'idée que la métaphore dépeint l'abstrait sous les traits du concret est déjà là. Comment Aristote rattache-t-il ce pouvoir de 'placer sous les yeux' au trait d'esprit? Par l'intermédiare du caractère de toute métaphore qui est de montrer, de 'faire voir'" (*La Métaphore vive*, 49).

11. Since metaphor is not controllable, context is not "saturable" (*Marges*, 369). Following is Derrida's most explicit statement on the impossibility of contextual closure: "Un signe écrit comporte une force de rupture avec son contexte, c'est-à-dire l'ensemble des présences qui organisent le moment de son inscription. Cette force de rupture n'est pas un prédicat accidentel, mais la structure même de l'écrit. . . . en raison de son itérabilité essentielle, on peut toujours prélever un syntagme écrit hors de l'enchaînement dans lequel il est pris ou donné, sans lui faire perdre toute possibilité de 'communication', précisément. On peut éventuellement lui en reconnaître d'autres en l'inscrivant ou en le *greffant* dans d'autres chaînes. Aucun contexte ne peut se clore sur lui" (*Marges*, 377). These ideas provoked an interesting debate in Anglo-American intellectual circles. See especially the article of John Searle "Reiterating the Differences: A Reply to Derrida," *Glyph*, 1 (1977), 198–208, and the long refutation of this response by Derrida: "Limited Inc abc . . .," *Glyph*, 2 (1977), 162–254.

12. "Ce *rapport unique* entre *deux termes différents*, il s'agit de l'*enchaîner à jamais*. Le fantasme carcéral reparaît dans toute sa force: on 'emprisonne' les termes, comme on 'emprisonne' les femmes, pour assurer un permanent circuit nutritif. Le style n'est rien qu'une autre des prisons proustiennes. . . . Avec les mots, on peut aller plus loin qu'avec Albertine. La 'nature', évidemment, 'met sur la voie de l'art, est commencement d'art', mais dans l'art, on peut aller jusqu'au bout du fantasme que nous interdit la vie. A moins, bien sûr, de le mimer, tel Charlus, dans son bordel, maison close qu'il transforme en geôle imaginaire: 'enchaîné sur un lit comme Prométhée sur son rocher' (III, 815), au point qu'on le nomme 'par allusion à un journal qui paraissait

à cette époque: l'Homme enchaîné' (III, 821). L'écrivain est aussi, à sa manière, plus subtile et non moins perverse, l'homme de l'enchaînement" (Serge Doubrovsky, *La Place de la madeleine: Écriture et fantasme chez Proust* [Paris: Mercure de France, 1974], 72).

13. See the celebrated anecdote (told first by Ruskin in *The Eagle's Nest*) in which Turner justifies his method of artistic representation to an officer of the Royal Navy: "Turner, dans la première période de sa vie, était quelquefois de bonne humeur et montrait aux gens ce qu'il faisait. Il était un jour à dessiner le port de Plymouth et quelques vaisseaux, à un mille ou deux de distance, vus à contre-jour. Ayant montré ce dessin à un officier de marine, celui-ci observa avec surprise et objecta avec une très compréhensible indignation que les vaisseaux de ligne n'avaient pas de sabords. 'Non, dit Turner, certainement non. Si vous montez sur le mont Edge-cumbe et si vous regardez les vaisseaux à contre-jour, sur le soleil couchant, vous verrez que vous ne pouvez apercevoir les sabords. —Bien, dit l'officier toujours indigné, mais vous savez qu'il y a là des sabords? —Oui, dit Turner, je le sais de reste, mais mon affaire est de dessiner ce que je vois, non ce que je sais'" (Marcel Proust, "John Ruskin," *Pastiches et mélanges*, in *Contre Sainte-Beuve*, Pléiade ed., 121).

14. According to Doubrovsky, the complexity of the expression *faire catleya* derives from its significant immanence in the play of textual *différences:* 'Faire catleya' est, en somme, un pur signifiant, sans signifié assignable en dehors du contexte référentiel dont il tire son sens. Aucune définition lexicale ne saurait nous aider à déterminer ici le champ sémantique" ("Faire catleya," 112).

15. Cesare Gnudi, *Giotto*, trans. R. H. Boothroyd (Milan: Aldo Martello, 1959), 173. Jean Autret also describes the fresco of *Injustice* in some detail and attempts to demonstrate that Proust's use of aquatic imagery in the "Soirée" derives from certain elements of Giotto's allegorical landscape. Autret recognizes, but does not interpret, the double representation of *Injustice* as abstract quality and as concrete activity: "Dans la planche, l'Injustice a bien une tête massive dont les lèvres serrées en un rictus amer peuvent en effet suggérer une tête de carpe. Quelques arbres au second plan rappellent plutôt des rameaux, mais pourraient aussi faire penser à certaines algues marines poussant sous une couche de sable ou de rocaille placée au fond d'un aquarium et à laquelle pourrait faire penser le dessin de la bande horizontale dans la partie inférieure de la planche. Dans cette partie, Giotto a dessiné une scène séparée de la représentation symbolique de l'Injustice: au premier plan, et comme dissimulé dans un repli de terrain, on voit des voleurs qui détroussent, semble-t-il, quelque voyageur, peut-être une femme" (*L'Influence de Ruskin sur la vie, les idées et l'oeuvre de Marcel Proust* [Geneva: Droz, 1955], 129).

16. For a good semiological description of Proustian society, see Gilles Deleuze, *Proust et les signes*, 3rd ed. (Paris: Presses Universitaires de France, 1979). In Deleuze's hierarchical scheme, the social sign is closest to pure form and surface emptiness: "Vide, bêtise, oubli: c'est la trinité du groupe mondain. Mais la mondanité y gagne une vitesse, une mobilité dans l'émission des signes, une perfection dans le formalisme, une généralité dans le sens: toutes choses qui en font un milieu nécessaire de l'apprentissage. A mesure que l'essence s'incarne de plus en plus lâchement, les signes prennent une puissance comique. Ils provoquent en nous une sorte d'exaltation nerveuse de plus en plus extérieure; ils excitent l'intelligence, pour être interprétés" (101).

17. The conversation between Mme de Gallardon and the Duchesse de Guermantes constitutes a modern reenactment or "rewriting" of the verbal duel opposing Arsinoé and Célimène in *Le Misanthrope.*

18. The furniture motif in the *Recherche* is associated not only with lying, but also with desecration, violation, and prostituted sexuality. The mentioning of a real person (Montesquiou, the principal model for Charlus) in this context is not without consequence, and is certainly appropriate enough if one remembers that Marcel Proust is said to have helped Albert Le Cuziat furnish a male brothel in the infamous rue de l'Arcade "with the second-best chairs, sofas and carpets of . . . [his] dead parents. This was the furniture which he had stored in a warehouse ever since its removal from the family home in 1906, and now gave away, as he told Mme Catusse truly in October 1917, 'to make a crowd of unfortunates happy.' . . . For the financing of Jupien's brothel (III, 817), and for many of the incidents which the Narrator sees there, Proust preferred to transfer the responsibility from himself to the Baron de Charlus" (George D. Painter, *Marcel Proust: A Biography*, II [New York: Random House, 1959], 264.) This transferal is attenuated in an earlier section of the novel, when the narrator himself confesses a gift: "Je cessai du reste d'aller dans cette maison [i.e., bordel] parce que, désireux de témoigner mes bons sentiments à la femme qui la tenait et avait besoin de meubles, je lui en donnai quelques-un—notamment un grand canapé—que j'avais hérités de ma tante Léonie. Je ne les voyais jamais, car le manque de place avait empêché mes parents de les laisser entrer chez nous, et ils étaient entassés dans un hangar. Mais dès que je les retrouvai dans la maison où ces femmes se servaient d'eux, toutes les vertus qu'on respirait dans la chambre de ma tante à Combray, m'apparurent, suppliciées par le contact cruel auquel je les avais livrées sans défense! J'aurais fait violer une morte que je n'aurais pas souffert davantage" (I, 578). We learn later in the same passage that the young hero received his first lesson in the amorous arts on the large sofa ("grand canapé") mentioned above, during a rare, mysterious one-house absence of Tante Léonie. The "je" who tells the story here is very close to the person Marcel Proust: the mask of fictional disguise is never thinner than at this stage of acute moral consciousness.

19. See Jean-Pierre Richard, *Proust et le monde sensible* (Paris: Seuil, 1974), 139: "La petite phrase existe d'abord pour Swann comme un sens apparaissant: ou plutôt elle est l'événement même de ce paraître. Toute sa mythologie, et sa fantasmatique, la relient à l'énigme d'une venue: elle est ce qui vient, ce qui advient, avant de se donner fugitivement, puis de se perdre. Le plus important en elle relève donc d'une rêverie de l'émergence, entendons émergence à partir d'elle-même: puisque la production de sens qu'elle effectue ne se sépare pas du fait de sa propre genèse, ou de son auto-engendrement."

20. Ibid., 114.

## CHAPTER TWO

1. The notebooks (*cahiers* and *carnets*) of 1909–10 in the Bibliothèque Nationale tend to confirm the idea that Proust's novel originated in the critical reflections and fictional developments of *Contre Sainte-Beuve*. The *cahiers* contain, often on the same page, criticisms of Sainte-Beuve's method and sketches that later became episodes of the *Recherche*. But attempts to locate the novel's points of origin in specific passages of these manuscripts cannot solve the more important question, How did Proust become so interested in the critical act of reading that he made it the constantly resurfacing theme of his self-representational work? Only by answering this question can we arrive at an understanding of the semiological structure of the *Recherche*.

2. See Jean Autret, *L'Influence de Ruskin* (see chap. 1, n. 15, above), 41, and note 13 in Chapter One of the present study.

3. See Robert Vigneron, "Structure de *Swann:* Balzac, Wagner et Proust," *French Review,* 19, No. 6 (May 1946), 370-84; and Vigneron, "Structure de *Swann:* Combray ou le cercle parfait," *Modern Philology,* 45, No. 3 (February 1948), 185-207. For the organizational/structural function within "Combray" of the "encapsulation" effect, see the excellent analysis of J. P. Houston, "Temporal Patterns in *A la recherche du temps perdu,*" *French Studies,* 16, No. 1 (1962), 33-44.

4. See George Duncan Painter, "Salvation through Ruskin," in *Marcel Proust: A Biography,* I (New York: Random House, 1959), 282; and John D. Rosenberg, *The Darkening Glass: A Portrait of Ruskin's Genius* (New York: Columbia University Press, 1961), 221-22.

5. Maurice Bardèche, *Marcel Proust romancier,* I (Paris: Les Sept Couleurs, 1971), 129-30.

6. Roland Barthes, "Proust et les noms," in *To Honor Roman Jakobson,* I (The Hague: Mouton, 1967), 150-58.

7. For a detailed discussion of this passage, see David R. Ellison, "Proust's Theory of the Novel," Diss. Yale 1975, 22-36.

8. Harold Bloom, *The Anxiety of Influence* (New York: Oxford University Press, 1973), 65-66.

9. John Ruskin, *Modern Painters II,* Vol. IV of *The Works of John Ruskin,* ed. E. T. Cook and Alexander Wedderburn, Library Edition, 39 vols. (London: George Allen, 1903-12), 42, 47. All further references in the present study will be to the Library Edition of Ruskin's works.

10. For an historically precise discussion of Ruskinian typology and allegory, see George P. Landow, *The Aesthetic and Critical Theories of John Ruskin* (Princeton: Princeton University Press, 1971).

11. Rosenberg, *The Darkening Glass,* 42. Rosenberg is quoting from *Modern Painters V,* "The Law of Help."

12. See Rosenberg, *The Darkening Glass,* 221, and Painter, *Marcel Proust: A Biography,* I, 282.

13. *Praeterita,* Library Edition, XXXV, 30-31. Anne's *esprit de contradiction,* which Ruskin calls a "republican aversion" to doing what is asked of her, corresponds to a more highly elaborated *code* in the case of Françoise. What appears to be simple perversity in Françoise's refusal to carry out certain orders or run certain errands is in fact the consequence of a coherent set of standards that hearken back to an earlier age. Whereas Anne is a modern, democratically educated servant, Françoise has roots in the Middle Ages and in a blind respect for the rooted values of custom: "Elle [Françoise] possédait à l'égard des choses qui peuvent ou ne peuvent pas se faire un code impérieux, abondant, subtil et intransigeant sur des distinctions insaisissables ou oiseuses (ce qui lui donnait l'apparence de ces lois antiques qui, à côté de prescriptions féroces comme de massacrer les enfants à la mamelle, défendent avec une délicatesse exagérée de faire bouillir le chevreau dans le lait de sa mère, ou de manger dans un animal le nerf de la cuisse). Ce code, si l'on en jugeait par l'entêtement soudain qu'elle mettait à ne pas vouloir faire certaines commissions que nous lui donnions, semblait avoir prévu des complexités sociales et des raffinements mondains tels que rien dans l'entourage de Françoise et dans sa vie de domestique de village n'avait pu les lui suggérer; et l'on était obligé de se dire qu'il y avait en elle un passé français très ancien, noble et mal compris, comme dans ces cités manufacturières où de vieux hôtels témoignent qu'il y eut jadis une vie de cour, et où les ouvriers d'une usine de produits chimiques travaillent au milieu de délicates sculptures qui représentent le miracle de saint Théophile ou les quatre fils Aymon" (I, 28-29).

14. Ruskin's adolescent "love" for Clotilde Domecq reminds one of Marcel's infatuation with Gilberte. (It is probably not coincidental that both girls are associated with the same prestigious place: the Champs-Élysées.) The Domecq sisters taken as a group are described in metaphorical terms, as are the "jeunes filles" of Balbec. For Ruskin, Clotilde, Cécile, and Caroline are like a "galaxy, or southern cross, of unconceived stars" (*Praeterita*, 178): for Proust, the young girls metamorphose into many shapes, including sea gulls (I, 788), statues (791), roses (798), and *"une lumineuse comète"* (791). The metaphoricity of the Proustian text is, of course, much more developed than that of its Ruskinian model.

15. In the *Recherche* Swann gives Marcel photographic reproductions of Giotto's *Vices and Virtues* depicted in the Arena Chapel at Padua (I, 80-81). This fictional gift is an obvious homage to Ruskin, who wrote a short book analyzing the allegorical significance of the frescoes (*Giotto and His Works in Padua*, Library Edition, XXIV, 11-123). Like the plates of Rogers' *Italy*, the iconography of Giotto demands interpretation and has an initiatory value for the young hero. Yet whereas Ruskin's analysis of Turner involves the confrontation of pictorial representation with reality through travel, Marcel's reading of Giotto takes place immediately, without the intrusion of a referential testing. When Marcel finally visits the Arena Chapel (III, 648), Proust limits himself to a cursory repetition of the remarks he had made earlier concerning the frescoes' realism, and humorously compares the *voltiges* of Giotto's angels to airplanes performing feats of showmanship. This passage occurs as a lateral development of the short, enigmatic, and schematically composed Venice episode in *La Fugitive*. No doubt the two visits at Balbec rendered the Venice section thematically superfluous, which would explain its progressive disappearance in the *cahiers;* on this subject, see the detailed manuscript study of Jo Yoshida, "Proust contre Ruskin: La Genèse de deux voyages dans *La Recherche* d'après des brouillons inédits," Diss. Paris-Sorbonne 1978, I, 96-213.

16. See, for example, Rosenberg, *The Darkening Glass*, 216-17, and Kenneth Clark, ed., *Praeterita* (London: Rupert Hart-Davis, 1949), ix.

17. The letters quoted are Nos. 54 and 53 (1875), 33 (1873), and 42 (1874). See the Library Edition, XXXV, xcii, for particulars.

18. Harold Bloom, ed., *The Literary Criticism of John Ruskin* (Garden City, N.Y.: Doubleday, 1965), xvi.

19. This statement is attributed to Mazzini, and is quoted by Ruskin in *Praeterita*, 44.

20. Jeffrey Mehlman has proposed a coherent Lacanian reading of the passage in "Proust's Counterplot," *A Structural Study of Autobiography*, 20-64.

21. For an excellent analysis of the contextual significance of *François le Champi* in the "scène du baiser," see Hiroshi Iwasaki, "Le Côté de Madeleine: *François le Champi* dans *A la recherche du temps perdu*," *Littérature*, 37 (February 1980), 86-99.

22. René Wellek, "John Ruskin," in *The Age of Transition*, Vol. III of *A History of Modern Criticism, 1750-1950* (New Haven: Yale University Press, 1965), 139.

23. See, for example, Alain Robbe-Grillet's comments on "ce vieux bateau crevé—l'opposition scolaire de la forme et du fond" in "Sur quelques notions périmées," *Pour un nouveau roman* (Paris: Gallimard "Idées," 1963), 48.

24. See Landow, *The Aesthetic and Critical Theories of John Ruskin*, 382: Landow contends that Ruskin's discussion of fancy and imagination derives more probably from Leigh Hunt and Wordsworth than from Coleridge.

25. Here are the two passages analyzed by Ruskin (*Modern Painters II*, 249-50):

[MILTON describes Satan in the first book of *Paradise Lost*]
Forthwith upright he rears from off the pool
His mighty stature; on each hand the flames,
Driv'n backward slope their pointing spires, and rolled
In billows, leave i' th' midst a horrid vale . . .
                As when the force
Of subterranean wind transports a hill
Torn from Pelorus, or the shattered side
Of thundering Aetna, whose combustible
And fuell'd entrails thence conceiving fire,
Sublimed with mineral fury, aid the winds,
And leave a singèd bottom, all involved
With stench and smoke; such resting found the sole
Of unblest feet.
                (*Paradise Lost* I. 221-24, 230-38)

[From *The Divine Comedy* of DANTE]
Feriami il sole in su l'omero destro,
    Che già, raggiando, tutto l'occidente
    Mutava in bianco aspetto di cilestro
Ed io facea con l'ombra più rovente
    Parer la fiamma.
                (*Purgatorio* XXVI. 4-8)

26. Near the end of *Le Temps retrouvé* the narrator speaks of rewriting unconsciously the *Arabian Nights* and the *Mémoires* of Saint-Simon in a modern vein (III, 1044). It is significant that these two works are at opposite poles of literary representation, the one being imaginative, creative, and magical in the Ruskinian sense, the other being analytic, demystifying, a product of the fancy. In Chapters Four and Five of the present study we will examine in some detail the problematic coexistence within the *Recherche* of the magical and analytical modes. The association of Ruskin with the former is most visible in the Venice episode of *La Fugitive*, where constant reference is made to the opening of doors and improbable encounters with guiding "genies" (III, 627, 639-41, 650-51). Like Ruskin, Proust interiorizes the theme of possession-taking: when walking through the "oriental" streets of Venice, the narrator remarks: "J'avais l'impression, qu'augmentait encore mon désir, de ne pas être dehors, mais d'entrer de plus en plus au fond de quelque chose de secret" (III, 627). Later, the narrator compares his own mind to a "Venise intérieure" that opens into the past of his former life with Albertine (III, 639). When a letter Marcel receives reveals to him retrospectively Albertine's lesbian activities in Balbec, the apparently insignificant words used by a female companion—"C'est moi qui la soignai"—have this effect: "Et ces mots qui ne m'étaient jamais revenus à l'esprit firent jouer comme un Sésame les gonds du cachot" (III, 641: here, "cachot" is a metaphor for the protagonist's "imprisoning" mind). As we shall see in the next chapter, Proust admired Ruskin's method of playing with the multiple meanings and connotations of "Sesame"; in the *Recherche*, whenever the word is used, it is used in an interpretive context. To open doors is to descend levels of meaning and decipher some previously unimagined message.

27. "Je trouve très raisonnable la croyance celtique que les âmes de ceux que nous avons perdus sont captives dans quelque être inférieur, dans une bête, un végétal, une chose inanimée, perdus en effet pour nous jusqu'au jour, qui pour beaucoup ne vient jamais, où nous nous trouvons passer près de l'arbre, *entrer en possession de l'objet qui est leur prison.* Alors elles tressaillent, nous appellent, et sitôt que nous les avons reconnues, *l'enchantement est brisé.* Délivrées par nous, elles ont vaincu la mort et reviennent vivre avec nous" (I, 44; my emphasis).

28. Landow, *The Aesthetic and Critical Theories of John Ruskin,* 107–10.

29. See René Wellek's justification of this term in the preface to his *Discriminations: Further Concepts of Criticism* (New Haven: Yale University Press, 1970), v.

30. After discussing separately and analytically the categories not to be confused with beauty—the true, the useful, custom, association—Ruskin concludes thus: "The subject being now in some measure *cleared of embarrassment,* let us briefly distinguish those qualities or types on whose combination is dependent the power of mere material loveliness" ("Of Typical Beauty," chap. 5 of *Modern Painters II,* 76; my emphasis).

31. For a tightly argued development parallel to the one I discuss in *The Stones of Venice* (Library Edition, X), see also *The Seven Lamps of Architecture* (1849), in which Ruskin equates the "fall" from the truths of the Middle Ages into the falsehood of the Renaissance with a change in the use of cathedral tracery. Whereas in the early Gothic period architects respected the density and unyielding character of stone, later their experimentation with filament-like ornamentation destroyed the original functionalism of their building-materials: "The first sign of serious change was like a low breeze, passing through the emaciated tracery, and making it tremble. It began to undulate like the threads of a cobweb lifted by the wind. It lost its essence as a structure of stone. Reduced to the slenderness of threads, it began to be considered as possessing also their flexibility. The architect was pleased with this his new fancy, and set himself to carry it out; and in a little time, the bars of tracery were caused to appear to the eye as if they had been woven together like a net. This was a change which sacrificed a great principle of truth; it sacrificed the expression of the qualities of the material; and, however delightful its results in their first developments, it was ultimately ruinous" (*The Seven Lamps of Architecture,* Library Edition, VIII, 91–92).

32. See Ruskin's explanation of the term in Appendix 10 of *The Stones of Venice II,* "Proper Sense of the Word *Idolatry,*" 450–52.

33. In *The Stones of Venice III,* Ruskin compares the fate of Venice to that of the destroyed capitals of vice in the Bible: "Thenceforward, year after year, the nation drank with deeper thirst from the fountains of forbidden pleasure, and dug for springs, hitherto unknown, in the dark places of the earth. In the ingenuity of indulgence, in the varieties of vanity, Venice surpassed the cities of Christendom, as of old she had surpassed them in fortitude and devotion; and as once the powers of Europe stood before her judgment-seat, to receive the decisions of her justice, so now the youth of Europe assembled in the halls of her luxury, to learn from her the arts of delight. . . . It is as needless as it is painful to trace the steps of her final ruin. That ancient curse was upon her, the curse of the Cities of the Plain, 'Pride, fulness of bread, and abundance of idleness.' By the inner burning of her own passions, as fatal as the fiery rain of Gomorrah, she was consumed from her place among the nations; and her ashes are choking the channels of the dead, salt sea" (195). Ruskin's tone of condemnation and rhetoric of prophecy find an echo in the *Recherche,* but they are largely

submerged by Proust's highly personal "botanical" analysis of homosexuality. In this case, Proust did not need to be influenced.

## CHAPTER THREE

1. Harold Bloom, *The Anxiety of Influence*, 106.

2. Richard Terdiman, *The Dialectics of Isolation: Self and Society in the French Novel from the Realists to Proust* (New Haven: Yale University Press, 1976).

3. Gérard Genette, *Figures III*, 148: "Ce type de récit, où une seule émission narrative assume ensemble plusieurs occurrences du même événement—nous le nommerons itératif."

4. Following is a brief delineation of the composition history and publication dates of these articles:

"Journées de pèlerinage" was first published in the *Mercure de France*, April 1900. "John Ruskin" appeared in the supplement to the *Gazette des Beaux-Arts (La Chronique des Arts et de la Curiosité)* in the issues of April and August 1900. Both articles combined to form the bulk of the translator's preface to *La Bible d'Amiens* (Paris: Mercure de France, 1904). Proust later included the two essays in *Pastiches et mélanges* (1919). The 1971 Pléiade edition of *Contre Sainte-Beuve*, to which I refer when quoting from all of Proust's critical work on Ruskin, contains the 1919 "definitive" versions of "Journées de pèlerinage," "John Ruskin," and also "Journées de lecture."

"Journées de lecture" (the final title, adopted in *Pastiches et mélanges*) first appeared as "Sur la lecture" in *La Renaissance latine*, June 1905, and was later included as part of the translator's preface to *Sésame et les lys* (Paris: Mercure de France, 1906).

5. See pp. 96-97 of "Journées de pèlerinage," in *Contre Sainte-Beuve* (Pléiade ed.). The humor of Ruskin's interpretations is due to the "realistic" manner in which the statues are read. Proust was especially intrigued with the potential divergence between allegorical sign and meaning—a factor not merely comical, but also productive of the most far-reaching semiological consequences. In "Combray" the narrator, alluding openly to Ruskin, compares the kitchen-maid who assists Françoise to Giotto's Charity in the Arena Chapel at Padua. Just as the kitchen-maid seems incapable of "understanding" the added burden of her pregnancy, in the same way Charity is represented as a "puissante ménagère" who does not express directly the virtue she is supposed to incarnate ("sans qu'aucune pensée de charité semble avoir jamais pu être exprimée par son visage énergique et vulgaire" [I, 81]). For a rigorous and complex meditation on the "radical hostility" between literal and figurative meanings in this scene, see Paul de Man, "Proust et l'Allégorie de la lecture," in *Mouvements premiers: Etudes critiques offertes à Georges Poulet* (Paris: Corti, 1972), 231-50 (translated into English and included by de Man as the third chapter of his *Allegories of Reading* [New Haven: Yale University Press, 1979], 57-78). In the final two chapters of the present study I will borrow from de Man and other contemporary critics in order to discuss the implications of the allegorical mode for the narrative structure of the *Recherche*.

6. The best analytical account of the ironic relationship between the naïve etymologies of the curé and the later revelations of Brichot is to be found in Gérard Genette, "Proust et le langage indirect," *Figures II* (Paris: Seuil, 1969), 244-47.

7. See Jean Autret, "Les Travaux ruskiniens de Proust," chap. 2 of *L'Influence de Ruskin*, pp. 16-86.

8. These theoretical remarks are restated in "Journées de pèlerinage," *Contre*

*Sainte-Beuve,* 75-76. Georges Poulet has written, justifiably, that Proust's use of footnotes in involved lateral developments constitutes the modern origin of thematic literary critcism; see Poulet's preface to René de Chantal's *Marcel Proust: Critique Littéraire,* 2 vols. (Montreal: Les Presses Universitaires de l'Université de Montréal, 1967), I, xiii. Ironically, the most distinguished exponent of thematic analyses in France, Jean-Pierre Richard, when attempting to explain his own use of extensive notes in *Proust et le monde sensible,* seems unaware of his debt to Proust. In his preface, Richard writes: "Le lecteur remarquera bien vite dans cet essai, peut-être pour s'en irriter, le nombre et souvent la longueur des notes. Aucune poétique de la note n'en est encore venue éclairer ni justifier le fonctionnement" (7).

9. "Texte de plaisir: celui qui contente, emplit, donne de l'euphorie; celui qui vient de la culture, ne rompt pas avec elle, est lié à une pratique *confortable* de la lecture" (Roland Barthes, *Le Plaisir du texte* [Paris: Seuil, 1973], 25; Barthes's emphasis). As we shall see in the final two chapters of the present study, the *Recherche* is better understood as the opposite of the "texte de plaisir," as what Barthes calls "texte de jouissance": "[texte] qui met en état de perte, celui qui déconforte (peut-être jusqu'à un certain ennui), fait vaciller les assises historiques, culturelles, psychologiques, du lecteur, la consistance de ses goûts, de ses valeurs et de ses souvenirs, met en crise son rapport au langage" (ibid.).

10. This is the title of the sixth chapter of Terdiman's *The Dialectics of Isolation,* 112-47.

11. Proust alludes here to Baudelaire's "Les Petites Vieilles," one of the cruelly dispassionate poems in the "Tableaux parisiens" section of *Les Fleurs du mal.* Proust comments on this poem briefly in "Sainte-Beuve et Baudelaire," *Contre Sainte-Beuve,* 250-51.

12. In the Pléiade edition of *Pastiches et mélanges,* the break between III and IV occurs on page 129. At the end of the first paragraph, Proust praises the dead Ruskin: "Mort, il continue à nous éclairer, comme ces étoiles éteintes dont la lumière nous arrive encore, et on peut dire de lui ce qu'il disait à la mort de Turner: 'C'est par ces yeux, fermés à jamais au fond du tombeau, que des générations qui ne sont pas encore nées verront la nature.'" In the following paragraph Proust begins to criticize Ruskin, accusing him of "idolatry"—a stylistic and moral fallacy which, as we saw in the second chapter of this study, Ruskin had already condemned in other authors. For a succinct account of Proust's ambivalence toward his master of esthetics, see Walter Kasell, "Proust the Pilgrim: His Idolatrous Reading of Ruskin," *Revue de Littérature Comparée,* October–December 1975, 547-60. Kasell locates Proust's turn away from the teachings of Ruskin at 1904, the date of publication of the "postscript" (the main body of "John Ruskin" had been published four years earlier). My analysis of Proustian "idolatry" agrees in many respects with that of Kasell, but I believe Kasell overstates his case by calling part III "extravagant" in its admiration and IV "vehement" in its criticism (549). For a more balanced view of Proust's change of heart toward Ruskin, see the admirably documented and elegantly written article of Richard A. Macksey, "Proust on the Margins of Ruskin," in *The John Ruskin Polygon: Essays on the Imagination of John Ruskin,* ed. J. D. Hunt and F. M. Holland (Manchester: Manchester University Press, 1982), 172-97.

13. Robert de la Sizeranne is the author of two important works devoted to English esthetic theories of the late nineteenth century, *La Peinture anglaise contemporaine* (1895) and *Ruskin et la Religion de la beauté* (1897). Jean Autret has shown the extent of Proust's debt to La Sizeranne in "La Fortune de Ruskin en France avant Proust," chap. 1 of *L'Influence de Ruskin,* 9-15.

14. *La Bible d'Amiens,* 330–32.

15. I borrow here from the evocative imagery of Walter Benjamin, "Zum Bilde Prousts," *Illuminationen: Ausgewählte Schriften* (Frankfurt am Main, 1961), 355–56. Benjamin compares Proust's method of writing to the "Penelope-work of forgetting": "Denn hier spielt für den erinnernden Autor die Hauptrolle gar nicht, was er erlebt hat, sondern das Weben seiner Erinnerung, die Penelopearbeit des Eingedenkens. Oder sollte man nicht besser von einem Penelopewerk des Vergessens reden? Steht nicht das ungewollte Eingedenken, Prousts mémoire involontaire dem Vergessen viel näher als dem, was meist Erinnerung genannt wird? Und ist dies Werk spontanen Eingedenkens, in dem Erinnerung der Einschlag und Vergessen der Zettel ist, nicht vielmehr ein Gegenstück zum Werk der Penelope als sein Ebenbild? Denn hier löst der Tag auf, was die Nacht wirkte. An jedem Morgen halten wir, erwacht, meist schwach und lose, nur an ein paar Fransen den Teppich des gelebten Daseins, wie Vergessen ihn in uns gewoben hat, in Händen. Aber jeder Tag löst mit dem zweckgebundenen Handeln und, noch mehr, mit zweckverhaftetem Erinnern das Geflecht, die Ornamente des Vergessens auf. Darum hat Proust am Ende seine Tage zur Nacht gemacht, um im verdunkelten Zimmer bei künstlichem Lichte all seine Studen ungestört dem Werk zu widmen, von den verschlungenen Arabesken sich keine entgehen zu lassen."

("For here it is not the remembering author's experience that plays the major role, but the weaving of his memory, the Penelope-work of remembrance. Or would it be better to speak of a Penelope-work of forgetting? Does Proust's involuntary memory [*mémoire involontaire*] not stand much closer to forgetting than to that which we usually call memory? And is this work of spontaneous remembrance—in which memory is the woof and forgetting the warp—not more appropriately seen as the antithesis of Penelope's work than its likeness? For here the day unravels what the night wove. Each morning, when we awake, we hold in our hands, weakly and loosely, only a few fringes of the carpet of lived existence, as forgetfulness has woven it in us. But each day, with its goal-oriented striving and, even more so, with its utilitarian form of memory, unravels the mesh, the ornaments of forgetfulness. Therefore Proust, in the end, made his days into night, in order to dedicate, undisturbed, all his hours in the darkened, artificially illuminated room, to his work, and let none of the entwined arabesques escape him.")

16. John Ruskin, *Sesame and Lilies,* Library Edition, XVIII, 75.

17. As John Rosenberg has pointed out (*The Darkening Glass,* 164), "Lilies" was written with a very personal goal in mind: Ruskin wished to dissuade Rose La Touche from what he considered an excessive religious fervor. The suggestions of books to read and proper feminine comportment to be maintained were expressed as a father's admonition to his disobedient daughter.

18. *Sésame et les lys,* 61–63.

19. The seven meanings of "Sesame" remind one necessarily of Vinteuil's Septet and of the seven volumes of the *Recherche.* Of course, this retrospective thematic resonance may be purely coincidental, but the coincidence is very Proustian.

20. The most memorable and most-quoted of Proust's theoretical statements in "Journées de lecture" associates reading with desire and exalts the individual's act of self-discovery in writing: "Et c'est là, en effet, un des grands et merveilleux caractères des beaux livres (et qui nous fera comprendre le rôle à la fois essentiel et limité que la lecture peut jouer dans notre vie spirituelle) que pour l'auteur ils pourraient s'appeler 'Conclusions' et pour le lecteur 'Incitations'. Nous sentons très bien que notre sagesse commence où celle de l'auteur finit, et nous voudrions qu'il nous donnât des réponses, quand tout ce qu'il peut faire est de nous donner des désirs. Et ces

désirs, il ne peut les éveiller en nous qu'en nous faisant contempler la beauté suprême à laquelle le dernier effort de son art lui a permis d'atteindre. Mais par une loi singulière et d'ailleurs providentielle de l'optique des esprits (loi qui signifie peut-être que nous ne pouvons recevoir la vérité de personne, et que nous devons la créer nous-même), ce qui est le terme de leur sagesse ne nous apparaît que comme le commencement de la nôtre, de sorte que c'est au moment où ils nous ont dit tout ce qu'ils pouvaient nous dire qu'ils font naître en nous le sentiment qu'ils ne nous ont encore rien dit" (176-77).

## CHAPTER FOUR

1. See Paul de Man, "Reading (Proust)," in *Allegories of Reading*. In his chapter on Proust, de Man begins with a close analysis of interpreting the *Recherche* as a whole in terms of an allegorical narration of this deconstruction. The question that then arises is whether such a narrative can "include" or "contain" the contradictions of reading and not be itself subject to the deconstructive power it attempts to unravel discursively (see esp. pp. 72 and 78). I will deal with this question in the second half of the present chapter when I interpret the metamorphoses of the *contenant-contenu* rhetorical manipulation in two of Proust's texts that hinge on the problem of possession-taking.

2. Quoted in Angus Fletcher, *Allegory: The Theory of a Symbolic Mode* (Ithaca: Cornell University Press, 1964), 16-17.

3. For a theoretically and historically precise account of this derivation, see René Wellek, "Coleridge," in *A History of Modern Criticism: 1750-1950*, II, esp. 151-57.

4. The theoretical and philosophical implications of the symbol-allegory polarity within the historical context of German Romanticism have been reexamined recently by Tzvetan Todorov, "La Crise romantique," in *Théories du symbole* (Paris: Seuil, 1977), 179-260. Paul de Man has studied the interplay of symbolic and allegorical modes in a detailed analysis of specific Romantic texts: see his "The Rhetoric of Temporality," in *Interpretation: Theory and Practice,* ed. Charles S. Singleton (Baltimore: The Johns Hopkins University Press, 1969), 173-209.

5. This tableau concentrates in the skeletal form of a résumé what Todorov develops with contextual clarity in "La Crise romantique." The phrases in quotes are my translations of the German authors' actual formulations. I have added Hegel to the list, even though Todorov claims that "symbole et allégorie ne s'opposent pas directement chez lui" (256). But Hegel condemns allegory for its coldness and its emptiness, for not being a representation of concrete subjectivity: "Man sagt es daher mit Recht der Allegorie nach, dass sie frostig und kahl und bei der Verstandesabstraktion ihrer Bedeutungen auch in Rücksicht auf Erfindung mehr eine Sache des Verstandes als der Konkreten Anschauung und Gemütstiefe der Phantasie sei." (*Ästhetik* [Berlin: Aufbau-Verlag, 1955], 393). ("It has thus been correctly said that allegory is chilly and barren and, because of the intellectual abstraction of its meanings, that it is also, with respect to inventiveness, more a matter of the intellect than of concrete intuition and emotional depth of imagination." We recognize here, in the contrast between rational understanding and the "Gemütstiefe der Phantasie," the familiar differentiation between symbol and allegory in the Romantic sense.

6. Johann Wolfgang von Goethe, *Maximen und Reflexionen*, in *Sämtliche Werke* (Berlin: Jubiläums-Ausgabe, 1907), vol. XXXVIII: *Schriften zur Literatur 3*, p. 261; quoted in Walter Benjamin, *Ursprung des deutschen Trauerspiels* (Frankfurt

am Main, 1961), 176: "One must make the following important distinction: whether the poet seeks the particular for the general or perceives the general in the particular. From the former manner originates allegory, where the particular is considered only as an example or illustration of the general; the latter, however, is in fact the nature of poetry: the symbol expresses the particular without thinking of or referring to the general. Whoever grasps this particular in its life force obtains at once the general with it, without catching sight of it, or only later" (my translation).

7. See Philippe Lejeune, "Ecriture et sexualité," *Europe*, February–March 1971, 104–22; also the previously quoted Doubrovsky, *La Place de la madeleine* (see chap. 1, n. 12, above), and Iwasaki, "Le Côté de Madeleine" (chap. 2, n. 21).

8. Genette, "Métonymie chez Proust," 62–63.

9. The two most comprehensive prestructuralist accounts of Proust's narrative devices are Marcel Müller, *Les Voix narratives dans 'A la recherche du temps perdu'* (Geneva: Droz, 1965), and B. G. Rogers, *Proust's Narrative Techniques* (Geneva: Droz, 1965).

10. Christian Metz, *Essais sur la signification au cinéma* (Paris: Klincksieck, 1968), 27; quoted by Genette in *Figures III*, 77: "Le récit est une séquence deux fois temporelle . . . il y a le temps de la chose-racontée et le temps du récit (temps du signifié et temps du signifiant). Cette dualité n'est pas seulement ce qui rend possibles toutes les distortions temporelles qu'il est banal de relever dans les récits (trois ans de la vie du héros résumé en deux phrases d'un roman, ou en quelques plans d'un montage 'fréquentatif' de cinéma, etc.); plus fondamentalement, elle nous invite à constater que l'une des fonctions du récit est de monnayer un temps dans un autre temps."

11. Leo Spitzer, "Zum Stil Marcel Proust's," in *Stilsprachen*, vol. II of *Stilstudien*, 2nd ed. [unchanged from the original 1928 ed.] (Munich: Max Hueber Verlag, 1961), 365–497. (Fr. transl.: "Le Style de Marcel Proust," in *Etudes de style* [Paris: Gallimard, 1970], 397–473.)

12. Proust begins his essay against Sainte-Beuve with the sentences: "Chaque jour j'attache moins de prix à l'intelligence. Chaque jour je me rends mieux compte que ce n'est qu'en dehors d'elle que l'écrivain peut ressaisir quelque chose de nos impressions passées, c'est-à-dire atteindre quelque chose de lui-même et la seule matière de l'art. Ce que l'intelligence nous rend sous le nom du passé n'est pas lui" (*Contre Sainte-Beuve*, Pléiade ed., 211). The "madeleine" episode and the revelations of the matinée Guermantes in *Le Temps retrouvé* are to be found, in their earliest form, in this preface. But Rogers argues, convincingly, that the presentation of the poetic-ecstatic moments in *Contre Sainte-Beuve* is rational and theoretical. He reasons thus: "The basis of the preface is an intellectual argument—against intelligence. The examples Proust furnishes to this end depend entirely for their effect, however, not upon reasoning but upon the recreation of *sensation*. Their development therefore obeys laws foreign to those of intellectual reasoning, and consequently threatens to destroy the framework which supports them and which their very presence contradicts. . . . the problem which continually faces Proust in *A la Recherche*, the fundamental disparity between the essence of the experience conveyed and the structure conceived to convey it, is present at an early stage" (*Proust's Narrative Techniques*, 65).

13. Rogers never explicitly uses this wording, but I believe that the phrase "modal incompatibility" most adequately describes the conflictive copresence of symbol and allegory in the *Recherche*.

14. See especially the Montjouvain episode (I, 159–63), the "conjonction" of Charlus and Jupien at the beginning of *Sodome et Gomorrhe* (II, 601–9), and the description of Charlus's masochistic rituals in *Le Temps retrouvé* (III, 815–20). In

each case, the dramatic power of the narrative presentation of events depends on Marcel's surreptitious presence as unobserved observer.

15. This passage is to be found in the thematic grouping "De l'amour," *Jean Santeuil*, Pléiade ed., 837–42.

16. The unnatural desire of self-fecundation alluded to here in a subtle way is condemned by the narrator in his "botanical" discussion of homosexuality at the beginning of *Sodome et Gomorrhe:* "Si la visite d'un insecte, c'est-à-dire l'apport de la semence d'une autre fleur, est habituellement nécessaire pour féconder une fleur, c'est que l'auto-fécondation, la fécondation de la fleur par elle- même, comme les mariages répétés dans une même famille, amènerait la dégénérescence et la stérilité, tandis que le croisement opéré par les insectes donne aux générations suivantes de la même espèce une vigueur inconnue aux aînés" (II, 613). The unconscious textual level of "De l'Amitié au désir" is the dream of self-sufficient homosexual plenitude that evades, by its metaphorical indirection, the censorship of conscious narrative control.

17. See tableau on symbol and allegory in the first section of this chapter.

18. In Lacanian terms, the Proustian quest for self-possession involves the imprisonment of the subject within the *stade du miroir* and the impossibility of his making the transition from the *imaginaire* to the systematic "lawfulness" of the *symbolique*. See Jacques Lacan, "Le stade du miroir comme formation de la fonction du Je" and "L'aggressivité en psychanalyse," in *Ecrits* (Paris: Seuil, 1966), 93–100 and 101–24. For concise elucidation of Lacan's terminology, consult J. Laplanche and J. -B. Pontalis, *Vocabulaire de la psychanalyse* (Paris: P.U.F., 1967), the articles "Imaginaire" (pp. 195–96), "Stade du miroir" (pp. 452–53), and "Symbolique" (pp. 474–76).

## CHAPTER FIVE

1. Some recent "genetic" analyses of the Proustian text are Claudine Quémar, "Rêverie(s) onomastique(s) proustienne(s) à la lumière des avants-textes," *Littérature*, 28 (December 1977), 77–99; Kazuyoshi Yoshikawa, "Historique du roman proustien avant 1915, à travers l'analyse détaillée des brouillons de *la Prisonnière*," *Bulletin d'Informations proustiennes*, 7 (Spring 1978), 7–27; Jo Yoshida, "Proust contre Ruskin: La Genèse de deux voyages dans *La Recherche* d'après des brouillons inédits," Diss. Paris-Sorbonne 1978.

2. "C'est parce que je l'avais vue comme un oiseau mystérieux, puis comme une grande actrice de la plage, désirée, obtenue peut-être, que je l'avais trouvée merveilleuse. Une fois captif chez moi l'oiseau que j'avais vu un soir marcher à pas comptés sur la digue, entourée de la congrégation des autres jeunes filles pareilles à des mouettes venues on ne sait d'où, Albertine avait perdu toutes ses couleurs. . . . je pouvais très bien diviser son séjour chez moi en deux périodes: la première où elle était encore, quoique moins chaque jour, la chatoyante actrice de la plage; la seconde où, devenue la grise prisonnière, réduite à son terne elle-même, il lui fallait ces éclairs où je me ressouvenais du passé pour lui rendre des couleurs" (III, 173).

3. In Ruskinian terms, as we have seen earlier, a clear distinction between *signifié* and referent is necessary if the reader wishes to avoid the error of idolatry. The amalgamation of fictive Combray and real Illiers has produced, in the reality of modern French geography, the town now referred to as Illiers-Combray—for pastry shops and the mayor's office, a most lucrative idolatrous confusion.

4. Germaine Brée writes: "Le récit à la première personne est le fruit d'un choix esthétique conscient, et non le signe de la confidence directe, de la confession,

de l'autobiographie" (*Du Temps perdu au temps retrouvé* [Paris: Les Belles Lettres, 1969], 37; quoted by Genette in *Figures III*, 255).

5. The *nom propre* functions as a unifying leitmotiv in Lejeune's theoretical essay. Some examples:

I. "C'est . . . par rapport au *nom propre* que l'on doit situer les problèmes de l'auto-biographie. Dans les textes imprimés, toute l'énonciation est prise en charge par une personne qui a coutume de placer son *nom* sur la couverture du livre, et sur la page de garde, au-dessus ou au-dessous du titre du volume. C'est dans ce nom que se résume toute l'existence de ce qu'on appelle *l'auteur:* seule marque dans le texte d'un indubi-table hors-texte, renvoyant à une personne réelle, qui demande ainsi qu'on lui attribue, en dernier ressort, la responsabilité de l'énonciation de tout le texte écrit. Dans beau-coup de cas, la présence de l'auteur dans le texte se réduit à ce seul nom. Mais la place assignée à ce nom est capitale: elle est liée, par une convention sociale, à l'engagement de responsabilité d'une *personne réelle.* J'entends par ces mots, qui figurent plus haut dans ma définition de l'autobiographie, une personne dont l'existence est attestée par l'état civil et vérifiable" (*Le Pacte autobiographique*, 22–23; Lejeune's emphasis).

II. "Ce qui définit l'autobiographie pour celui qui la lit, c'est avant tout un contrat d'identité qui est scellé par le nom propre. Et cela est vrai aussi pour celui qui écrit le texte. Si j'écris l'histoire de ma vie sans y dire mon nom, comment mon lecteur saura-t-il que c'était *moi?* Il est impossible que la vocation autobiographique et la passion de l'anonymat coexistent dans le même être" (23; Lejeune's emphasis).

III. "Le sujet profond de l'autobiographie, c'est le nom propre" (33).

6. By the term "instance de discours" Benveniste means "les actes discrets et chaque fois uniques par lesquels la langue est actualisée en parole par un locuteur" ("La Nature des pronoms," in *Problèmes de linguistique générale*, 251).

7. Lewis notes that the writer who "admits us so intimately into the age of allegory and silent reading is St. Augustine: Sometimes he does so by accident, as when he comments on the fact—to him, apparently, remarkable—that Ambrose, when reading to himself, read silently. You could see his eyes moving, but you could hear nothing. In such a passage one has the solemn privilege of being present at the birth of a new world. Behind us is that almost unimaginable period, so relentlessly objective that in it even 'reading' (in our sense) did not yet exist. The book was still a *lógos,* a speech; thinking was still *dialégesthai,* talking. Before us is our world, the world of the printed page, and of the solitary reader who is accustomed to pass hours in the silent society of mental images evoked by written characters. This is a new light, and a better one than we have yet had, on that turning inward which I have tried to describe. It is the very moment of a transition more important, I would suggest, than any that is commonly recorded in our works of 'history'" (C. S. Lewis, *The Allegory of Love: A Study in Medieval Tradition* [London: Oxford University Press, 1951], 64–65).

8. "Et, en elles-mêmes, qu'étaient Albertine et Andrée? Pour le savoir, il fau-drait vous immobiliser, ne plus vivre dans cette attente perpétuelle de vous où vous passez toujours autres; il faudrait ne plus vous aimer pour vous fixer, ne plus con-naître votre interminable et toujours déconcertante arrivée, ô jeunes filles, ô rayon successif dans le tourbillon où nous palpitons de vous voir reparaître en ne vous recon-naissant qu'à peine, dans la vitesse vertigineuse de la lumière. . . . A chaque fois, une jeune fille ressemble si peu à ce qu'elle était la fois précédente (mettant en pièces dès

que nous l'apercevons le souvenir que nous avions gardé et le désir que nous nous proposions) que la stabilité de nature que nous lui prêtons n'est que fictive et pour la commodité du langage" (III, 64–65).

"Et je comprenais l'impossibilité où se heurte l'amour. Nous nous imaginons qu'il a pour objet un être qui peut être couché devant nous, enfermé dans un corps. Hélas! il est l'extension de cet être à tous les point de l'espace et du temps que cet être a occupés et occupera. Si nous ne possédons pas son contact avec tel lieu, avec telle heure, nous ne le possédons pas" (III, 100).

9. For a good discussion of psychomachia as well as analyses of Prudentius's work by that title, see C. S. Lewis, *The Allegory of Love*, 66–73, and Angus Fletcher, "Symbolic Action: Progress and Battle," chap. 3 of *Allegory: The Theory of a Symbolic Mode*. In the *Recherche*, Proust's conception of the human mind as arena of combat for virtues and vices emerges consistently in the narrator's description of his own anguish, and more comically in his assessment of Charlus: "L'amour cause . . . de véritables soulèvements géologiques de la pensée. Dans celui [l'esprit] de M. de Charlus qui, il y a quelques jours, ressemblait à une plaine si uniforme qu'au plus loin il n'aurait pu apercevoir une idée au ras du sol, s'étaient brusquement dressées, dures comme la pierre, un massif de montagnes, mais de montagnes aussi sculptées que si quelque statuaire, au lieu d'emporter le marbre, l'avait ciselé sur place et où se tordaient, en groupes géants et titaniques, la Fureur, la Jalousie, la Curiosité, l'Envie, la Haine, la Souffrance, l'Orgueil, l'Epouvante et l'Amour" (II, 1078).

10. In *La Prisonnière*, when Marcel compares his early adolescent feelings for the young girl-flowers of Balbec to the state of indifference and/or disillusionment of his more recent thoughts, he alludes to the rose image explicitly: "D'ailleurs, entre les deux tableaux de Balbec, au premier séjour et au second, composés des mêmes villas d'où sortaient les mêmes jeunes filles devant la même mer, quelle différence! Dans les amies d'Albertine du second séjour, si bien connues de moi, aux qualités et aux défauts si nettement gravés dans leur visage, pouvais-je retrouver ces fraîches et mystérieuses inconnues qui jadis ne pouvaient, sans que battît mon coeur, faire crier sur le sable la porte de leur chalet et en froisser au passage les tamaris frémissants? . . . Elles étaient devenues pour moi, obéissantes à mes caprices, de simples jeunes filles en fleurs, desquelles je n'étais pas médiocrement fier d'avoir cueilli, dérobé à tous, la plus belle rose" (III, 68).

11. See his *Literaturgeschichte als Provokation* (Frankfurt am Main: Suhrkamp, 1970). This volume contains the seminal essay "Literaturgeschichte als Provokation der Literaturwissenschaft," translated by Elizabeth Benzinger as "Literary History as a Challenge to Literary Theory," *New Literary History*, 2, No. 1 (Autumn 1970), 7–37. Jauss's work is now increasingly available to the English-speaking public. For a good selection of the critic's writing, see Hans Robert Jauss, *Toward an Aesthetic of Reception*, trans. Timothy Bahti, intro. Paul de Man (Minneapolis: University of Minnesota Press, 1982).

12. Paul de Man's interpretation of the passage on Giotto's noncharitable Charity ("Proust et l'Allégorie de la lecture") differs from that of Jauss in that it emphasizes the *absolute* noncommunication of appearance and reality, *signifiant* and *signifié*. De Man puts into question the very possibility of Marcel's retrospective knowledge (Jauss: "Der Knabe . . . wird *erst später verstehen lernen*") by demonstrating that the nature of the allegorical sign involves a blocking of all understanding.

13. The relevant passage quoted by Jauss (*Zeit und Erinnerung*, 158) comes from the end of *Sodome et Gomorrhe*: "J'incline même à croire que dans ces amours (je mets de côté le plaisir physique, qui les accompagne d'ailleurs habituellement, mais

ne suffit pas à les constituer), sous l'apparence de la femme, c'est à ces forces invisibles dont elle est accessoirement accompagnée que nous nous adressons comme à d'obscures divinités" (II, 1127). I will analyze this passage in context later in the present chapter.

14. My own references to these works will be drawn from the following editions: Sigmund Freud, *Totem and Taboo* (New York: Norton, 1950), and Otto Fenichel, *The Psychoanalytic Theory of the Neuroses* (New York: Norton, 1945).

15. J. G. Frazer, *The Magic Art*, in *The Golden Bough*, 3rd ed., pt. I (London, 1911), 420; quoted in *Totem and Taboo*, 83.

16. At the beginning of the chapter "Taboo and Emotional Ambivalence" Freud indicates the diversity of tabooed objects: powerful persons (chiefs, priests, etc.), the weak (women and children), corpses, certain foods, animals, etc. (*Totem and Taboo*, 19–20).

17. This fascination does not just emerge in the interests of the man Marcel Proust, but also appears in various guises in the *Recherche*. See, for example, the young protagonist's evocation of "le beau train généreux d'une heure vingt-deux dont je ne pouvais jamais sans que mon coeur palpitât lire, dans les réclames des Compagnies de chemin de fer, dans les annonces de voyages circulaires, l'heure de départ" (I, 385), and his later feeling of disillusionment when the magic of names of places in Normandy has faded: "Les mêmes noms de lieux, si troublants pour moi jadis que le simple *Annuaire des Châteaux*, feuilleté au chapitre du département de la Manche, me causait autant d'émotion que l'Indicateur des chemins de fer, m'étaient devenus si familiers que cet indicateur même, j'aurais pu le consulter, à la page Balbec-Douville par Doncières, avec la même heureuse tranquillité qu'un dictionnaire d'adresses" (II, 1112).

18. The name is, of course, "Guermantes." Along with the other aristocratic names of its type, it loses its magical charm as the narrator-hero becomes better acquainted with the real people it designates: "Les noms cités avaient pour effet de désincarner les invités de la duchesse que leur masque de chair de d'inintelligence ou d'intelligence commune avait changés en hommes quelconques, si bien qu'en somme j'avais atterri au paillasson du vestibule, non pas comme au seuil, ainsi que je l'avais cru, mais au terme du monde enchanté des noms" (II, 542).

19. Habit accompanies the narrator's loss of love for Albertine and serves to empty the names of towns of their original mystery: "Mais ce retour [de la Raspelière], de même que l'aller, si, en me donnant quelque impression de poésie, il réveillait en moi le désir de faire des voyages, de mener une vie nouvelle, et me faisait par là souhaiter d'abandonner tout projet de mariage avec Albertine, et même de rompre définitivement nos relations, me rendait aussi, et à cause même de leur nature contradictoire, cette rupture plus facile. Car, au retour aussi bien qu'à l'aller à chaque station montaient avec nous ou disaient bonjour du quai des gens de connaissance; sur les plaisirs furtifs de l'imagination dominaient ceux, continuels, de la sociabilité, qui sont si apaisants, si endormeurs. Déjà, avant les stations elles-mêmes, leurs noms (qui m'avaient tant fait rêver depuis le jour où je les avais entendus, le premier soir où j'avais voyagé avec ma grand'mère) s'étaient humanisés, avaient perdu leur singularité depuis le soir où Brichot, à la prière d'Albertine, nous en avait plus complètement expliqué les étymologies" (II, 1098).

20. Albertine's reaction to the narrator's fictional account of an unhappy love resembles the mother's decision in "Combray" to spend the night with her son: "Mon pauvre petit [dit Albertine], si j'avais su, j'aurais passé la nuit auprès de vous" (II, 1118). Later in the same episode, Marcel emphasizes explicitly the parallel roles of the mother and Albertine: "Je l'embrassai [Albertine] aussi purement que si j'avais

embrassé ma mère pour calmer un chagrin d'enfant que je croyais alors ne pouvoir jamais arracher de mon coeur" (II, 1124).

21. The passage quoted by Freud here is taken from the article "Taboo" in the _Encyclopaedia Britannica_ (1910-11), the author of which was the anthropologist Northcote W. Thomas. See _Totem and Taboo_, 19-20, for the complete citation.

22. The image of the closed door associated with the discovery of Albertine's enigmatic homosexuality is the inversion/negation of the sentence that introduces the joyful revelations of involuntary memory during the Matinée Guermantes at the conclusion of the novel: "Mais c'est quelquefois au moment où tout nous semble perdu que l'avertissement arrive qui peut nous sauver; on a frappé à toutes les portes qui ne donnent sur rien, et la seule par où on peut entrer et qu'on aurait cherchée en vain pendant cent ans, on y heurte sans le savoir, et elle s'ouvre" (III, 866).

23. Following is Rousset's general assessment of the novel's dramatic progression: "Cette partie médiane de l'oeuvre [_Le Côte de Guermantes, Sodome et Gomorrhe_], qui fait foisonner les groupes humains et les personnages de toutes sortes, est destinée à mettre sous nos yeux une vérité dont le héros ne prendra conscience que plus tard: toute activité sociale est un leurre et engendre un état de mort spirituelle pour qui a vocation de créateur; plus on donne au monde extérieur, plus on s'éloigne des 'graces' sans lesquelles il n'y a pas d'artiste. . . . De fait, les signes et les réminiscences se rarifient à l'extrême durant cette période, c'est la traversée d'un désert. . . . Les sources taries vont rejaillir dès _la Prisonnière_. La soudaine explosion de l'amour-jalousie abolit d'un coup le monde et ses fantoches, ramène le héros sinon à lui-même, du moins à sa chambre fermée où lui sont accordées parfois des heures de solitude. Aussitôt reparaissent les réminiscences, bientôt suives de la rencontre d'une grande oeuvre, le septuor de Vinteuil: longuement, dans ce champ clos, l'amour et l'art lutteront l'un contre l'autre. La victoire de l'art fera le sujet du _Temps retrouvé_" (_Forme et signification_ [Paris: Corti, 1962], 165-66).

24. Leo Spitzer, "L'Étymologie d'un 'Cri de Paris,'" in _Etudes de style_, 476.

25. This is the case not only for Rousset but also for Deleuze, who assigns a lower position to Love in the hierarchy of signs than to Art. And Art dominates all other signs as the "deepest" goal of the narrator's intellectual pursuits. See _Proust et les signes_, 51-53.

26. For a complete development of Derrida's theoretical position see _La Dissémination_ (Paris: Seuil, 1972), especially the "Hors Livre" (pp. 9-67) and "La Double Séance" (pp. 201-318).

27. One cannot say the same for Michihiko Suzuki, who attempts to dilute the meaning of the first "Marcel" occurrence (II, 75) by arguing that a deletion of the narrator's name in a subsequent passage of _La Prisonnière_ can lead us to assume that Proust, if given the time in his race against imminent death, would have eliminated all other such references ("Le 'Je' proustien," _Bulletin de la Société des Amis de Marcel Proust et des Amis de Combray_, 9 [1959], 74). Suzuki's thesis—that Proust was tending toward an "anonymous" fictional form in his later years—is highly debatable in itself and masks the modal dichotomy novel/autobiography whose significance cannot be dismissed out of hand, but must be interpreted.

28. Georg Wilhelm Friedrich Hegel, _Phänomenologie des Geistes_ (Hamburg: Felix Meiner Verlag, 1952), 9; English translation by J. B. Baillie, _The Phenomenology of Mind_ (New York: Harper Torchbooks, 1967), 67.

29. Jacques Lacan, "D'une question préliminaire à tout traitement possible de la psychose," *Ecrits,* 559. For a clear discussion of "phallocentism" in the context of autobiographical texts, see Jeffrey Mehlman, *A Structural Study of Autobiography,* 176-79.

# Index

References to works are indexed under their authors.

*David R. Ellison is Dean of Students and Associate Professor of French at Mount Holyoke College.*

## THE JOHNS HOPKINS UNIVERSITY PRESS

The Reading of Proust

*This book was composed in Baskerville text and display type by Horne Associates, Inc., from a design by Cynthia Hotvedt. It was printed on Glatfelter's 50-lb. Offset paper and bound in Kivar 5 by Thomson-Shore, Inc.*